PROVEN

PROVEN

THE "STEP-BY-STEP" MARKETING FORMULA OF A WEALTHY ORTHODONTIST . . .

The Key to Attracting High-Quality Patients, Working Less & Earning More ... Guaranteed!

TERAN R. DALE

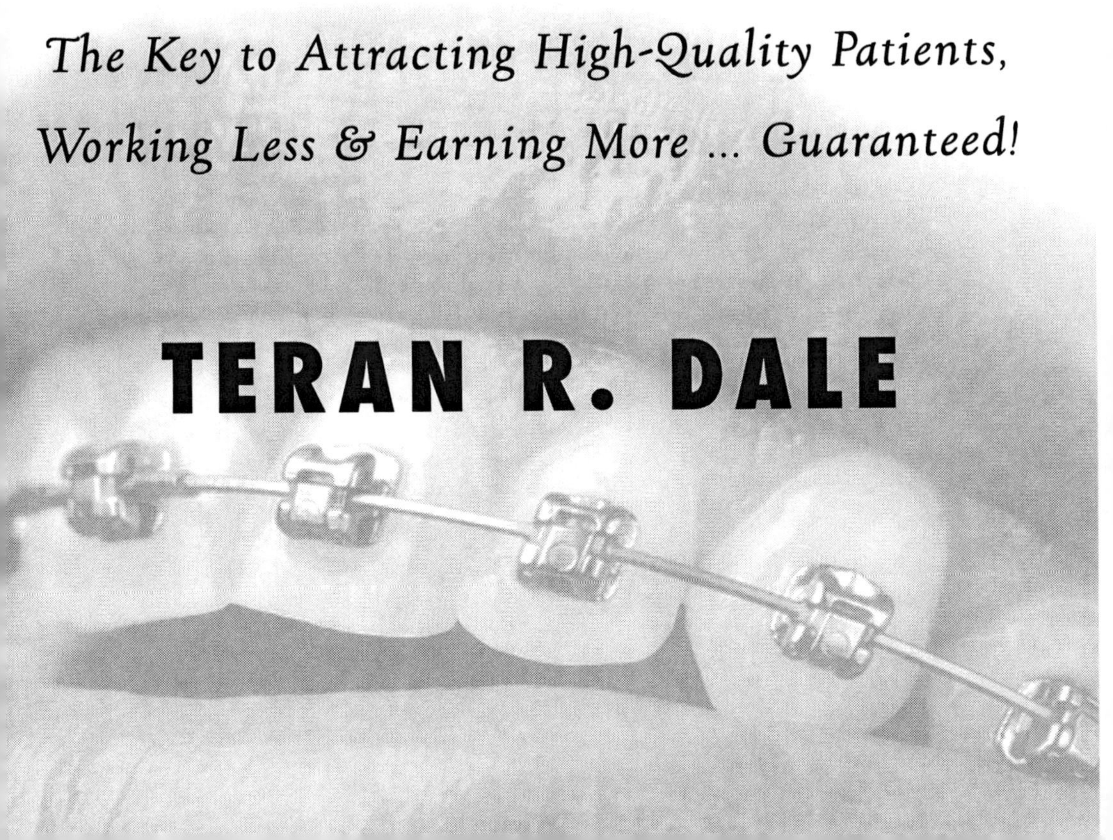

PROVEN
The Step-by-Step Marketing System of a Wealthy Orthodontist ...
The Key to Attracting High-Quality Patients, Working Less & Earning More ...
Guaranteed!

Teran R. Dale
Foreword by Dr. James Noble
Published by Thomas Mann Publishing

ISBN 978-0-9921437-0-1
First Edition, 2014
Printed in the United States of America

This book is dedicated to

My beautiful wife Barbara and loving children Kayla, Noah, Jacob, and Gabriel

And to my dear, loving parents Brenton and Megan

Contents

FOREWORD 1

PREFACE 3

Chapter 1 *Client Profile: The Secret Formula for Success* 7

Chapter 2 *Trust* 26

Chapter 3 *Old-World Marketing vs. New-World Marketing* ... 37

Chapter 4 *Copywriting: How Your Words Can Turn into Instant Cash* 50

Chapter 5 *Developing Your Cash Cow Website* 63

Chapter 6 *Shock and Awe* 81

Chapter 7 *Google Local+ for Your Business: Get Your Bank Account to Shout for Joy* 91

Chapter 8 *PPC: The Secret on Using Google AdWords Pay-Per-Click* 105

Chapter 9 *Facebook Advertising* 124

Chapter 10 *YouTube Marketing* 140

Chapter 11 *Email Marketing* 157

Chapter 12 *Mobile Marketing* 172

Chapter 13 *Pinterest* 188

Chapter 14 *Blogging* 203

Chapter 15 *SEO* 214

Chapter 16 *Webinars: How to Add an Easy $100K to Your Bank Account* 228

Chapter 17 *Launching Your Practice* 241

Chapter 18 *Conclusion* 253

GET TERAN TO WORK WITH YOU! 255

SOMETHING SPECIAL FOR YOU 256

Foreword

IT HAS NEVER BEEN MORE CHALLENGING than it is today for an orthodontist to have a financially successful practice. General dentists are providing more orthodontic care as technology, courses, and consultants are encouraging them to keep orthodontic cases in house. More and more orthodontists are graduating and competition is fierce. It is not uncommon for patients to seek multiple free consultations, generating price wars. Because of the uncertain economy, parents are questioning the necessity of orthodontics and being forced to use their disposable income for more basic needs. These are just a few reasons why an orthodontist cannot focus solely on providing excellent care for his or her patients.

In order to practice the trade they love, orthodontists are forced to become businesspersons and salespeople to be able to sustain their practice, pay back their debt, and lead a good lifestyle. And so the herculean task of practicing excellent clinical orthodontics, attending continuing education courses, and keeping abreast with the literature must be coupled with marketing strategies such as maintaining a good website and an Internet presence (including on social media sites), and the list goes on. Orthodontists, though, do not have a marketing degree, and here lies the importance of this book for orthodontists.

This book contains a plethora of principles and guidelines that will make it possible for the orthodontist to be able to navigate through the roiling and confusing waters of marketing and building their practice so that they need not worry about how to get quality, paying patients through the door and starting treatment. What Teran Dale has done is to create one very easy-to-read and understand book that will save the orthodontist from having to attend countless courses and seminars. This book will lead you to a path of success, working less, and earning more. The choice is yours.

Dr. James Noble, BS, DDS, MSC, FRCD (C)

Preface

IT WAS 2:30 P.M. and I had been on the phone for an hour and a half with Dr. Thomas (not his real name). When our time was up, he insisted on paying for another half hour of consultation time. He was furious and unhappy. Over the past sixteen months, his practice's revenues had fallen 35 percent, and his referrals from local Dentists had completely dried up.

I could hear the fear and concern in his voice. Then he admitted it, "Teran, if I don't fix this now, I am going to have to close my practice in the next fourteen months. What the hell am I going to do then?"

It was actually worse than that. I knew he would be under within six months unless he did something right then.

As I sat there and listened to all the dramatic changes taking place in his practice, I could not help but wonder if this trend was taking place across the Orthodontic Industry.

I had decided to find the answer out for myself when all of sudden I started to receive calls from Orthodontists across North America. The same issues were constantly coming up: Business was down. Dentists were either no longer referring clients to their practices or they were hiring out Orthodontists to come in once a week.

They were all calling for help, and then I started to notice Orthodontists in other countries voicing the same concerns. This was a massive epidemic. The doctors had tried so many other ways to grow their business: They had hired practice management companies, practice building firms, and/or marketing organizations without any success or with only minuscule improvement.

You see, the industry as a whole was relying heavily on the general Dentist to build their practice. I just found that unwise. Why leave the future and success of my business—the ability to make as much money as possible—in someone else's hands? Why put my practice at their mercy? It made no sense.

I continued to conduct my research and developed a marketing system that brought Dr. Thomas's practice back to life, and I discovered the problem: A startling majority of Orthodontists were not marketing their practice. Dentists were taking weekend courses in Orthodontic treatment and solutions and then offering their services to existing and new clients. The Dentists were undercutting the Orthodontists in price and marketing their services across the board.

The Dentists were now performing the work of an Orthodontist. They were now the so-called specialist. The Orthodontic Industry was not doing anything about this, and on top of that, they had no solution to compete with this new rival—a rival that had once been on their side.

Consumers do not understand the difference between a specialized Orthodontist and a general practice Dentist working on their mouth. They just follow the Dentist's advice, which is usually based on the lowest price; however, the advice is often not the lowest-priced service because the Dentist sometimes adds services that the client does not need at all.

If you are competing with a Dentist, today you are more than in luck.

What you hold in your hand right now will enable you to take back your practice and become a wealthy, successful Orthodontist. You will work less and make more money—guaranteed.

The Wealthy Orthodontist holds the solution to cornering your market and making price and your competitors irrelevant wherever your practice resides. You will become the superstar amongst your peers and in your area of practice.

This PROVEN marketing plan contains powerful systems which solve the problems you are facing right now. There is no fluff or fillers, just facts, strategies, and techniques that ***will work***.

The time is at hand to take control and make those with whom you compete obsolete. The decision is all up to you. It is time to choose.

P.S. There is an Important *OPPORTUNITY* from me on the last page of this book. This Opportunity can change your life and business. It can contribute to dramatic growth in profit, prestige, success, and freedom. It is also the chance to continue our relationship after reading this book. I encourage you to act on it.

CONGRATULATIONS! YOU HAVE MADE THE RIGHT CHOICE. THIS IS THE WISEST INVESTMENT YOU COULD MAKE FOR YOUR PRACTICE AND YOUR FUTURE. LET'S GET STARTED.

CHAPTER 1

Client Profile: The Secret Formula for Success

DISCERNING WHO YOUR IDEAL client is will be the foundation, strength, and growth of your practice. What I am about to share with you is a secret formula no one else in the Orthodontic or Dental Practice Industry is using to their advantage. Please pay close attention to what you are about to discover; this chapter alone is worth 10,000 times more than what you paid for the whole book.

Knowing who you are selling to and what they want is crucial to the success of growing your practice and to making a lot more money than you are making right now. After all, that is the reason you bought this book, correct? To make more money? I am going to provide the solutions for you to do just that.

Your first step is to find out who your client really is. You need to get into the mindset of your prospects and clients. Once you do this, you will discover what it really takes for you to go over the hump and make you the only choice for a trusted advisor to your clients and ideal prospects.

If you do not know who you are selling to and if you have no idea what they want, you cannot be successful in your endeavors. Your goal is to build a relationship with your prospects, to let them know that you care, and then to collect the money that belongs to you.

When you discover what they truly want, you can provide the value they want. Price will not be an issue; the only thing they will look forward to is for you to deliver what you promised.

Success, happiness, and money are what we strive for in life. In business, we measure success by dollars. If you think otherwise, I have some news for you: If you don't get the money you deserve, you won't be in business, and you will have to find another profession. It is harsh, I know, but it is true.

Profiling your client gives you, the business owner, all three things—success, happiness, and money—when done correctly. I have shared this profiling technique with my clients and their businesses more than doubled in less than a year.

Think about this for a second: What could you do, and what would you want to do when your practice brings in twice or more than the amount you are currently making? Could you spend more time with your friends and family or hobbies you enjoy? Could you travel around the world? Give back to your community? It is basically up to you.

The other beauty of profiling your ideal client is that your client will love you for it. Why? Because now you are connecting with them on a different level. Your client is tired of going from one Dentist to the other Orthodontist, only to be confused and frustrated with choices.

Now you're in luck—you are going to make the choice clear as day for them, and they will reward you for doing so.

Profiling your ideal client will bring you the success, money, and happiness you deserve. Soon we will dive into the formula that will put you on top.

The ideal client understands the value that you bring to them, and they understand price is not a main issue or concern. You and I know if everyone bought on price, there would be few products and services created in this world.

It matters to your ideal client that you care about them. They are looking for someone they can trust, someone who can become their trusted advisor. In your practice, it is your goal to become a trusted advisor to all your prospects and clients. You don't want them to make a move without your input and advice. This is how you are going to grow your practice and take it to new heights.

Unfortunately, many Orthodontists don't care about their clients; they care only about the money and how to quickly get the next client in the chair. Clients know this. They can pick up on the person that cares only about the money and not about their well-being and what they want to achieve.

Listening is a skill rarely taught, but it is important to the success of your practice. Reading someone's body language, recognizing what frustrates them, and responding in a way that builds credibility, trust, and honesty is a must.

Think about how you feel when you are purchasing a big-ticket item. What do you want the salesperson to do? You are looking for the salesperson who is interested in your needs and not just the sale. This should be your approach as well.

Attracting your ideal client is much easier when you use the profiling system. This technique will help make your competitors a nonfactor once you complete it.

Warning—when you finish using this system, you will be so surprised as to how much easier your marketing and your sales-closing techniques become when you finally realize what your ideal client is after. You and your bank account will be jumping for joy.

It is crucial that you let your staff know as well of the type of clients you want coming into your practice. They will weed out the tire kickers and give you more time to build upon your practice. Would it be nice to work less and make more money? The formula you are about to discover will give you such an opportunity. Please use it to your advantage.

Profiling your ideal client starts with knowing your ideal client. This is where the lost skills of listening, asking questions, and writing responses come into play. Each day, you interact with clients, your staff, and your colleagues at your practice. The information you need is available to you right now.

Here is the formula below. After you review it, we will break down the segments of the formula to make sure you understand completely how this will add as much cash as you want to your practice.

SBC = Starving Buying Prospects

+

PVG = Provide Value & Kindness x EP = Expert Positioning

+

HVS = High-Value Resolution

+

KBO = Kick-Butt Offer Sequence

=

CASH

Let's look at the Starving Buying Prospect. The starving buying prospect is the potential client that comes into your practice and is ready to get new braces or any additional products or services you offer. You should have a list of the top-performing services that you do each month and each week. If you don't have this kind of information handy, you better start keeping track of the top-performing services that bring in the most cash as well as the other services that are lagging.

The second equation for success is providing value and kindness. You are going to hear me preach value throughout this entire book because the more value that you provide your ideal prospect, the more money you will make. If you combine this with kindness—showing you care for their well-being and you're not only after the cash—you will have a willing client who wants to buy now and for life.

The third equation is what makes you stand out from your competitors and leaves them in the dust scratching their heads. Positioning yourself as the expert and telling your story is how you become the expert of choice.

The fourth formula in the system is to give a high-value resolution. Your prospect came to you for one reason and one reason only—to solve their problem with their teeth and/or their jaw. As the Orthodontist, you must provide the right high-value resolution to solve their problem.

The fifth equation is a kick-butt offer. The offer you present to your clients and ideal prospects should be so irresistible they have no other choice but to choose you. The offer you present must match their ultimate desires and needs. Later in this book, we talk about how to find the true desire of every single prospect and client that step into your practice.

The following form should be used to obtain your ideal client. Once you have completed the form, you will need to create a secondary profile of your ideal client.

Questions you must ask yourself:

1. What is the age of your ideal client?
2. What do they physically look like (height, hair color, body weight)?
3. What is their income?
4. What is their level of education?
5. Do they have children? If so, how many kids do they have?
6. Where do they live?
7. What is their occupation?
8. Are they married? If so, how long have they been married?
9. What are their favorite TV shows?
10. What is their favorite radio station?
11. What newspapers and magazines do they read?
12. What are their hobbies?

13. At what restaurants do they eat?
14. What type of car do they drive and how many vehicles do they own?
15. Get a physical picture of your ideal client and keep it in a file along with the form you just filled out. You can get an image from Google images.

Who Is My Ideal Client?
THESE ARE THE PEOPLE WHO ARE STARVING FOR MY SERVICES:
WHAT DO THEY DREAM OF?
WHAT ARE THEIR FEARS?
WHAT DO THEY NEED?
WHAT DO THEY SEARCH FOR ON INTERNET SEARCH ENGINES?
WHOM DO THEY FOLLOW ONLINE AND OFFLINE?
WHOM DO THEY NOT LIKE?
FOR WHAT WOULD THEY PAY TOP DOLLAR?

Providing Kindness and Value
WHAT WOULD MY CLIENTS LOVE ME FOR?
WHAT RESULTS ARE THEY TRYING TO ACHIEVE?
WHAT PROBLEMS ARE THEY FACING?
WHAT STEPS DO THEY NEED TO TAKE TO ACHIEVE THE RESULTS THEY WANT?
HOW WILL THE SERVICES I PROVIDE DIFFER FROM MY COMPETITORS?
I AM GOING TO PROVIDE . . .

Expert Positioning
BUILDING CREDIBILITY, RAPPORT, AND TRUST
YOUR STORY OF EXPERTISE:
YOUR STORY OF SEARCHING FOR THE SOLUTION:
YOUR SURPRISING RESULTS:

YOUR SECRET DISCLOSED:
YOUR STORY STRUCTURE:
HIGH-VALUE RESOLUTION
FOR WHAT WILL MY IDEAL CLIENTS GIVE ME BIG MONEY?
WHAT MUST THE CLIENT DO TO GET THE RESULTS THEY WANT?
WHAT BENEFITS WILL THE CLIENT RECEIVE?
WHAT IS THE REASON THAT IT WILL WORK?
HOW WILL THE IDEAL CLIENT ACHIEVE THEIR DESIRES?
TO PAY MY PRICE POINT, THE IDEAL CLIENT MUST BELIEVE ...

Kick-Butt Offer Sequence

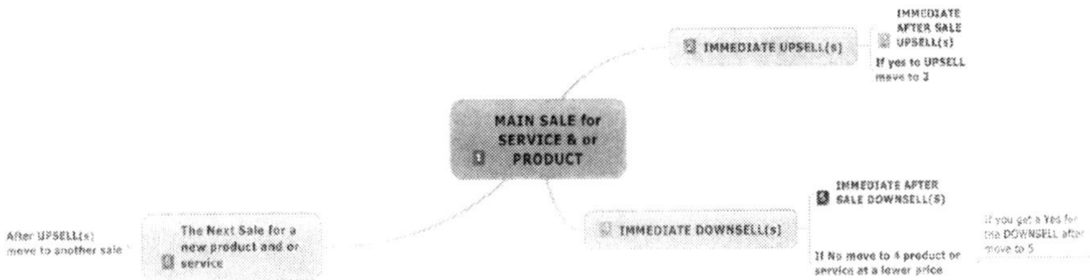

Get-the-Cash Formula

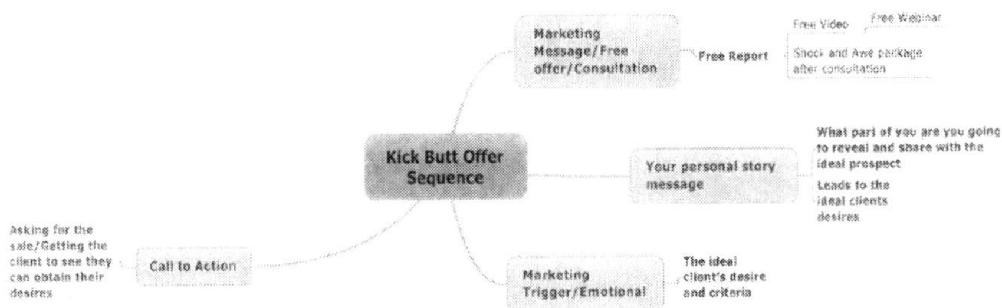

To get a free video report of a complete breakdown of the Kick-Butt Offer Sequence and the Get-the-Cash Formula, visit www.WealthyOrthodontist.com/OrthoBook-Chapter-One-Formula.

After you have completed the questions outlined above, follow up by asking your prospects and clients questions. Listening to their answers will give you a complete and clear picture of what exactly your client is looking for.

Not many Orthodontists take the necessary time to do such a task. However, it should always be your practice to ask your ideal prospects and clients what they are looking for, and what they do like and do not like regarding the service and/or practice. That is the only way you will continue to improve—and put your competitors out of business.

Building on your skills to connect with your prospects will put you far ahead of everyone else. Have you ever met someone that you connected with right away, someone it seems you have known for years yet you met them only five minutes ago? You should approach each client you come into contact with the same way. If you do, these clients and prospects will put you on a pedestal and will not make any decision without your blessing. This will lead to more profits for your practice and better communication with your clients, staff, and any other referrals you may get from general practice Dentists (which I hope you know you will no longer need once you put this system into use).

Businesses are built on systems that are put in place and implemented. The right system builds a multi-million dollar practice of which you, your family, and your bank account can be proud.

Along these lines, marketing to attract a flow of leads every single day is the lifeblood of any business. When you have compiled the information that we just described, the next step is to create a file that you are going to use for all your marketing material; you will test this on a regular basis to improve the leads coming into the practice.

The first thing you need to do is review all the information you obtained. Analyze the responses and the profile of the ideal client. You must create your marketing materials around what your ideal client is looking for, the way they speak, their desired end results, their fears, and the solutions they are seeking to improve their life.

You see, the prospect is coming to you for a solution that will improve the outlook they have about themselves. If you show them the end result they will get by working with you and only you, they will more than love you for what you have done.

Think about Apple: They have such a huge devoted following that people line up for days just to get their new products. You want the same kind of dedicated clients. I know an Orthodontist that accepts only the clients he wants. He works only two times a week and has a practice worth well over $5 million just by implementing the system. He is in control of what he wants out of his life and what he provides to his prospects.

HERE ARE THE STEPS TO GET YOU TO THAT POINT:

1. You are going to use the information to craft your marketing message for your website.
2. Use this marketing message for all local advertising, referrals, and lead generation.
3. You are going to track the results.
4. You are going to test and tweak the results.
5. "Rinse and repeat" and continue to grow the practice.

Trust is the name of the game in business. Without trust, no one will buy from you, and you will be out of business very quickly. When you provide value and show you care about your prospects' end results and the situation they are going through, you will have not only a client but also a friend who will sing praises about you to his other friends who will gladly help to continue to build your practice.

Building the profile helps you bring more money into your practice because you are now finally connecting to the prospects and clients you want in your practice. What is better than knowing you have clients you want, clients who want your services and with whom you love to work?

Achieving this will more than grow your practice. Remember, you should not get complacent; you need to do something each day to continue to grow your practice. The more revenue you bring in, the better. There will be rainy days, and your goal is to make sure you are protected and that you are continuing to grow your lead flow. You should also make it a priority to ensure your clients are also participating in your lead flow with referrals. The funny thing is they will be more than happy to assist you in doing so.

The first step any of your ideal prospects will take is to research their options. With the Internet, they are first going to search online for a local Orthodontist they can visit for a consultation. Or they will go to a friend or a family member for a referral to book an appointment.

Next, they will follow up by talking with others who have had a similar experience with you or with the recommendation they received. They will go online and look at reviews to see what others are saying. Were they happy with the results? Was the doctor friendly and caring? Did he or she provide valuable information and the right information to help them make a decision?

At this stage, they are weighing the pros and cons. They are looking for a reason (or reasons) they should not choose you. Your objective is to handle and respond to any objections and negative thoughts going through their mind.

Think back when you were making a purchase for a big-ticket item. What was your thought process? What did you do first? Second? Third? Did you look for reasons why you should not go with the purchase? You ideal client is doing the same thing.

Once they have made their decision to go with you, they look for justification to assure themselves they have made the right decision. This is the reason that, once your ideal client has decided on you, you need to assure them they have made the right decision by sending a letter that outlines why the investment is the right choice. Remind them that they are on their way to getting their ultimate desire. You should also provide additional valuable information about your practice—testimonials from your happy clients and a gift welcoming them to your practice.

This is how you will continue to outshine your competition and build upon your practice.

Reading your ideal client's body language is extremely important when you are presenting your sales pitch. The questions they ask you and the questions you ask them will give you a very clear picture of who the true decision maker is so that you can get the "YES! I would like for you to be my doctor for the procedure."

To quickly identify your decision maker, you simply ask the following question: Is there anyone else that you need to speak to in order to make your decision? If they say yes, you need to focus on this person too. (Don't worry! We have an amazing solution for you in Chapter 6 where we talk about Shock and Awe. This will leave your ideal prospect and the decision maker speechless.)

The majority of the time in a family situation, the mother is the decision maker; however, sometimes she needs to confirm the decision with her husband. Studies have shown women are the decision makers in the household in the majority of big-ticket purchases.

Connecting with your prospect is a must. This is why we strive for you to complete the questionnaire and follow the system we have outlined for you. Once in action, presenting your offer will be a lot easier and you will quickly get the YES.

Once you have identified the decision maker, building a rapport with trust and honesty is a must. Don't just stop there—make sure you provide value all the way. The following system I developed will enable you to increase your weekly sales. When you ask the client the following questions, you should have the questions on a clipboard or a pad when you conduct the consultation with your client or ideal prospect.

Questions to ask:

First, you need to let the ideal prospect know you will be asking a few questions to help solve their problem. In reality, you probably already have the solution; these questions are so that the prospect and you can find out what the prospect's true desires are. (Remember, we all make purchases based on our emotions.)

1. **(Client name), what's most important to you about (their situation)?**
2. **Excellent! (Client's name), what's most important about (their answer to #1 = criteria = what they want)?**
   (You are looking to get their criteria—in other words, their desire. This will let the client know you are listening and interested in getting them the results they want.)

3. **What will (criteria = what they want) do for you?**
(You are digging deeper to get their true desire, their ultimate want.)
4. **Tell me a little about your current situation (the client's problem).**
(You are starting to build a rapport; you want to know what problems and/or pain they are facing.)
5. **Have you seen other doctors for your (situation)?**
(You want to know if they are price shopping or if they are serious. You want to know what the other doctor is saying about their problem.)
6. **Is there anything which helped or provided some sort of relief?**
(You are continuing to build upon their situation. You are getting into their thought process. You are looking to see how actively they are seeking a solution.)
7. **How did you feel when things did not work out?**
(You are now bringing up the pain; you want the client to feel the pain. All buying decisions are made emotionally. Pain is one thing we, as humans, want to avoid.)
8. **Do you have any stress?**
(You are getting the client to think about the situation they are going through by not fixing the problem.)
9. **Is there any impact on family or friends?**
(Sometimes the situation the prospect is going through—especially their mood—will impact those around them. You want them to think about how this is impacting not just them but those they come into contact with on a daily basis.)
10. **Does your partner know you are talking to me now?**
(You are trying to find out who the true decision maker is, who will decide to go for the treatment you prescribe.)
11. If not, I am curious as to why.

(You want to know why they have decided to leave their partner out of the decision process. This will help you channel and deliver your message to the right person.)

12. **What's the worst thing about (situation)?**
(You are still building on the pain; we want them to feel and see it. Some clients might begin to cry.)
13. **What would you have to overcome to solve the problem?**
(You are asking what they believe is necessary to solve the problem. This is again to build a rapport with trust and credibility. You are showing that you care. Take note because this will be addressed when you ask for the sale.)
14. **How is (current situation) going to be affected if you don't solve the problem(s)?**
(You are letting them see and feel their situation deeply; if they don't fix the situation, it's just going to get worse.)
15. **What are you missing out on a result of this?**
(You ask this question to get them to see all the good things they are missing or not doing because the problem they have is not being taken care of.)
16. **Quality of life**
17. **What effect will this have on (criteria = what they want)?**
(You want to show the effect it will continue to have on obtaining their desire.)
18. **How will you feel if you don't solve this problem?**
(You are building upon their emotional state to bring them to a YES decision.)
19. **What do you think you would need to make this situation successful?**
(You are looking for their input; you have put them in a deep thought process. This is putting them into the emotional state that will help them say YES.)
20. **What would your life be like if you solved this problem?**
(You are showing them what they will get once they

decide to make the decision. Their ultimate desire will be obtained.)

21. **On a scale from zero to ten, how much do you want to solve this problem? How motivated are you to take action?** *(You are actually getting them to commit to a YES; anything from eight on up means it is time to close the deal. If they give you a number below an eight, you did not solicit their true desire; however, you will provide them with a shock and awe package as discussed in Chapter 6.)*
22. **Pattern Interrupt: You are going to interrupt your session of asking questions and make a positive statement to the client.** *(You decide on the statement.)* **This will put your ideal client into a positive emotional state and get them ready for the close of the sale.**
23. **Now you are going to explain to the client your prescribed solution to get what they want and solve their problem. Let them know the date and time when the treatment can start and what the cost will be, etc.** *(They just gave you a score of eight or more, so they are committed.)*

The TDCS (Teran Dale Closing System) will quickly and easily eliminate the tire kickers from your practice when you implement the ideal client questioning form outlined above. Please use this form if you want to increase your sales by 50 percent or more. Yes, it is that good. You will quickly build upon your client profile if you follow this system. It has been tested and proven. You see, this system quickly shows the ideal client you're not only interested in the money but their well-being too. You want them to achieve what they want as outlined in the ideal client profile system.

When you start asking these questions, they are going to think twice about the kind of doctor you are. They are going to notice that you are different from everyone else and you will have positioned yourself in their minds as the expert who is looking out for their well-being.

All you have to do is prove it to them and get paid. It is simple when done correctly. Many times Orthodontists say to me, "Teran, I can't ask those questions. The client might think I am weird." My friend, the very opposite will happen. The client will bond with you and see you as a trusted source and friend.

Once you establish your expertise, make the connection with your ideal client, and become likeable, price will no longer be an issue. Your ideal client will gladly pay more for the service. Remember, all of us buy on value; if we see value in the product and/or service we are looking to purchase; we will gladly pay more for it because we are getting what we want.

In addition, most people want to do business with other people that they like, with other individuals that make a connection, that not only listen to what they have to say but actually hear what they have to say. There is a big difference between the two, and the majority of Orthodontist totally miss this distinction. They miss the opportunity to hear what the client has to say in order to make the necessary changes in their marketing.

This is a golden nugget: Let the potential client do the majority of the talking; just sit back and take notes on what they have to say. This will actually help you craft your marketing message by hitting the points that continue to come up for them.

Paying higher prices is not an issue; in fact, you should raise your prices. When you start building the connection with your ideal prospects, you will be extremely surprised at the lack of resistance to price once you provide the value and the formula I outline below.

Don't forget to have an open mind, and do not dismiss what I am telling you. In fact, after you use the system, I want you to give me a call and tell me how everything has increased in your business by just following what we covered in this chapter.

Results + value = cash, and I mean big CASH in your practice. When you provide value and give results to all your clients and prospects, they will be obligated to share their experience with others. They will actually become your marketing sales force and you will not have to pay them a single dime.

As you know, word-of-mouth marketing is also important in the Orthodontist Industry. For every bad comment or unsatisfied client, ten more individuals will be told about the unhappiness or poor service they received. On the other hand, if you provide the value and the results, the opposite will occur: For every single person that is happy with you as their doctor, they will tell ten more people and those ten will tell another ten and so and so on. This is how word-of-mouth marketing becomes extremely effective.

You should also get your staff to participate in the changes you will be making to your practice. Perception is extremely important. The way the staff greets potential clients and/or existing clients, and the way they answer the phone, take messages, and schedule appointments are all important to the success and the growth of your practice.

You must get a team that is on the same page as you when it comes to growing the practice. I am a strong believer that a happy, satisfied employee contributes to the success of any organization. Most employees just want to be recognized and acknowledged for the good work they do and the majority of the time it is not money they are looking for.

Results, happiness, and confidence are what you are selling to everyone that sits in your chair. Once you have gone through the TDCS and the ideal client system, it will become clear as day that all your clients want to benefit from achieving and getting what you deliver to them.

If you remember, in the TDCS system we continue to dig to find the real reason that a client comes to you and what they are actually looking to achieve after you have provided your services.

You are not selling braces—you're selling the end results that the braces and/or any other product that you offer will provide to client. This will put you far head of the Dentists that you are competing against and any other Orthodontists that have not read this book.

The funny thing is that the majority of your competitors who do pick up this book will not do the necessary work to get the results. If you do the work, you will achieve happiness, success and a growing bank account.

Selling will become so much easier. You won't feel like you're pressing someone to go with you because you are going to provide so much value and they are going to see it for themselves. You won't have any competition—especially when you implement the shock and awe technique you are going to learn in Chapter 6.

Your ideal clients and prospects are going to be totally blown away. They will have no other choice but to say YES.

CHAPTER 2

Trust

BUILDING A RAPPORT with your ideal prospect and being seen as likeable, honest, and caring builds trust. Without trust, it is impossible to operate a successful business or relationship for a long period time. Trust is a main ingredient your prospects and clients require in order to do business with you.

When did you first truly understand the meaning of trust? Can you remember feeling comfortable working with someone or buying a product or service and feeling completely at ease, knowing you made the right decision?

This is how your prospects and clients want to feel when they do business with you. They want to see you as the doctor who cares about them and not only about the money. They can tell if your main concentration is charging as much as possible without adding value. Showing you are trustworthy with your recommendations and solutions to their problem is something they can see and feel.

You will see and feel this too; it will come forth in your speech, your writing of marketing material, your consultations, and your relationships with your staff and family. You can't hide your character; it is only a matter of time until someone finds out the real you.

This chapter is a bit different from other chapters in this book, but it is a very important chapter. Do not skip this chapter and say to yourself, "I know about trust—I don't need any explanation." Don't be fooled! You can always learn something, and in this chapter you are going to learn how to take trust to the next level and build an empire that you will be proud of and that will have you and your bank account grinning from ear to ear.

Success in any business begins with trust; without trust, your business cannot grow and you cannot become the trusted source for your clients and ideal prospects. With trust, you can get the answer you want—YES.

You are in business for yourself to grow your practice, provide value, and get the YES from your clients and referrals. Consider this question: Would you do business with someone you do not trust? Let's look at an example: You're going to buy a new car—let's say a new 6 Series BMW—and you approach the car salesman at the dealership. During your entire conversation, he never asks any questions to find out what exactly you're looking for. He shows no interest in what you want in the car. He focuses only on getting the sale and nothing else. Then he provides you with incorrect information about the vehicle. Would you do business with this individual? Wouldn't you just cut the conversation short, get up, walk away, and buy your car somewhere else?

I'm sure you would say that this is one of the problems in the Orthodontist Industry. Many doctors are not showing their clients and potential clients that they are trust worthy and that they care about the results the client is looking for.

Establishing trust from the very beginning with your staff, family members, clients, and prospects leads to a fulfilling and caring relationship. Your character will shine right through, and you will witness a dramatic increase in your business profits and you will have better relationships throughout your life.

Authenticity is a cornerstone of a successful business and of successful relationships. It builds the right connection to contribute to the growth of your practice. It also leads your prospects to the decision to do business with you and to buy your products and services more than once. It also turns your clients into true believers—evangelists who spread the good news about your practice.

This all leads to you gaining a bigger piece of the pie of your market share. Once you are known as the doctor who cares, who is willing to provide solutions for all patients and prospects, you will not have competition. You will be above and beyond your competitors because you have established the true meaning of trust.

All this trust talk might be bothering you right now, but think for a minute. When you decide to make a bigger purchase or to allow your son or daughter to take your car to go out or to go to a concert without any adult supervision, your decision is built on trust. So why not show your clients, "Yes, I am a trustworthy doctor who is not just looking for your money. I want you to become a client who stays with me for life, a client who will share their opinions with others to grow my practice."

Listening is like breathing—we do it every day. Hearing, on the other hand, is a lost art form that many of us do not do very well. In order to gain the trust of our ideal prospect, we must use the following tools to our advantage. This costs you nothing. We just have to turn it on and use it.

1. **Listening** – paying attention when the client is talking and providing their answers; remember the TCSL System.
2. **Hearing** – Taking in exactly what the client is saying and reiterating their answers to them; you then use this information to build the right marketing material to dramatically boost the growth of your practice.
3. **Caring** – By listening, hearing, and asking additional questions, you elicit more information from your ideal prospect and clients, showing you care about them and their well-being.
4. **Authenticity** – one of the main ingredients you cannot fake. Clients are not dumb; they can tell instantly when you are

> not being authentic and not providing the full story and/or solution that is in their best interest. They will have a puzzled look on their face or a reaction that says, "I don't believe you."

Put all four of these elements together and you have the ability to gain the trust and respect of your prospects and clients.

Lying to or misleading your prospects or clients will earn their automatic distrust and an obvious look of "I want to get out of here and I am pissed." Clients and prospects can tell when you are misleading them or providing inaccurate information to them. On top of that, being rude to the client (which I have seen many times on client visits to Orthodontists' practices) leaves the client with a bad taste in their mouth.

Here's the thing: The client will not tell you they are displeased. Of those who are not happy with a product or service, 95 percent do not relay their thoughts to a manager or even to a staff member. Instead, they just cut ties with the business completely and look for another competitor to get what they want.

Unfortunately, it gets worse from there. They may not tell *you*, but they *will* tell ten to fifteen of their friends what took place, and those ten to fifteen friends will tell ten other friends and so on. This negative press will spread about you and your practice like wildfire.

I am a strong believer of giving my client my full attention and providing exactly what they want. When you do this, you have a client for life who looks at you as their trusted and caring advisor.

Another "must" when working with new patients and prospects is upfront value proposition. You have to show them that you are willing to listen and to hear what they have to say to gain their trust. Remember, they do not know who you are, they have no idea if your service is good or not, and they have no clue if you're trustworthy. This means that you as the doctor have to gain their trust first—the same would apply if you were ready to spend $7,000 or more on an item or service.

New patients are also looking to see if their doctor is likeable. If you think about it, we do not buy on price; we make our purchase decisions based on value and the individual who is selling the item to us. We want to do business with people we like. Now, not everyone is going to like you—this is a fact. Some people just do not "click" for one reason or another. However, we established our ideal client profile, and this will greatly reduce the chance of picking up prospects that might be a pain to deal with. (You do not need patients in your practice who do not like you no matter how much money you get because eventually you are going to get sick and tired of the situations that may arise with the patient.)

Gaining clients' trust is priority number one when you are selling your services. Here's a little secret you probably have not heard before: We are always selling. The customer is buying you first and your service second.

Throughout our lives, we are selling ourselves to individuals with whom we come into contact on a daily basis. (If you're married, did you not have to go through the process of gaining your spouse's trust first before he or she said, "Yes, I will marry you"? Just think back to the steps you had to take to gain their trust. Your clients and prospects are looking for the same thing.)

One of the first steps to becoming a trusted source to your clients and prospects is to show that you truly care about them. According to the old saying, actions speak louder than words, and it is absolutely true. Your clients, staff, prospects, and any other meaningful relationship in your life all want to see that both parties care about whatever conversation, problem, or solution arises.

Becoming trusted is an extremely powerful position to be in; being trusted by others means they have put their faith, hope, and belief in you and that you are someone who is required to be in their life. Gaining trust is a process you should not take lightly; you should look upon it as an honor.

Now, you may have become an Orthodontist because you

want to help people, or maybe you were looking at it as a way to make as much money as possible from your profession—and there is nothing wrong with that. However, taking your profession to the next level of showing you care about your patients, your career, and those around you cannot be hidden if it is the truth. If you provide your client with the right high-value solution to solve their problem, they will trust you, which will bring more cash into your practice because they will let everyone know how wonderful and caring you are. Price will not be an issue.

Algebra was a subject I did not understand at first in school; it took a bit of time for me to grasp the concept. Then one day, it finally clicked and I got it. Consider this equation: Given that X = trust. Earlier in the book, I did hint as to what X is. We are going to dig deeper into why X truly builds upon your success, why X = Value, Authenticity, and Honesty.

When you provide value up front to your prospects or clients without any strings attached, they will see you as an individual who cares and who is honest and authentic. Wouldn't you want to do business with someone who has these characteristics? It makes your decision so much easier and it puts you at ease.

You and I know that if we want something badly, price is not a factor. However, a small number of prospects that you will run into make price a factor. When this happens, you will know up front the prospect's positioning and that the prospect you are trying to close is not the one you want for your practice. In other words, it is a way to verify your work—just like in math class when we had to show our work and check to see if it is right—to see if you are positioned correctly with the client you want who will pay handsomely for what they want.

Getting money is easy. All you have to do is get the YES and the money will flow into your practice. You can get the YES through referrals, building your list, and direct contact from prospects that pick up the phone and call you for a consultation.

Getting the NO is also easy: If you do not provide the right information and value up front to your clients and prospects, you will get the NO. But remember, the majority of the time your prospects and clients won't verbalize the answer NO; their actions will say it. There lies the difference.

If we put this all together, trust is the main ingredient which will get you the YES. This is what you're after and this is what is going to build your practice and make it extremely successful.

Let's look at the roadblocks which will stop you from getting a YES from the client.

1. Not using the ideal client prospect system
2. Not positioning your practice differently from your competitors
3. Not providing value up front
4. Employees who are rude toward clients and new prospects
5. Not caring about your prospects and clients
6. Not being Authentic
7. Not being Honest
8. Not providing a USP (unique selling point) that is memorable
9. Not educating your client on the difference between you and the general practice Dentist

Use the checklist and have it visible on your next consultation so that it reminds you that you are seeking the YES and so that you can quickly remove the roadblocks that will get you the NO.

Humans seek relationships that will make them feel good and make the other individuals feel good as well. We look for the value that a person brings into our life. Now, each individual will value something different; it just depends on what they consider to be of value to them.

When we provide value up front and when our results back up the value we provide, we become a trusted source, an individual who is indispensable to the person whom we have helped out or to whom we provided a solution to their problems.

All successful business is based on this principle: Trust is the foundation to the success and growth of any business. Do you remember a couple of years ago when Mattel toys got in a huge public mess with their toys? It came out that their suppliers were using lead in their paint and lead in their toys and selling it to the masses, putting children at risk across the world. It came out that Mattel knew of the problem and knew their suppliers were using lead in their paint. They allowed this practice to save money, but at the end it cost them hundreds of millions of dollars in business.

Once your clients' and ideal prospects' trust is broken, you will lose business and it will be difficult for you to get up from the mess. It is possible, though, for you to gain back the trust of those you let down if you focus on making things right and acknowledging what went wrong.

Because trust is so important, I have a great little exercise I want you to do right now. This exercise will give you a complete breakdown on how you currently gain trust and how well others trust you. This will reinforce with your subconscious the importance of making sure you are following through on building trust with all your relationships, not only the personal ones.

Throughout our lives we have come to trust certain individuals in society; it could be our parents, teachers, those in authority, and so forth.

1. Write down a list of individuals that you trust in your life.
2. Once you're done compiling the list in #1, write down why you trust each individual.
3. Finally, write down how they gained your trust.

After you have finished the first exercise, I want you to write down all the individuals you believe trust you. These would be the individuals to whom you have contributed value and provided solutions in their life, both big and small.

1. Write a list of all the individuals whom you believe trust you.
2. Write down all the reasons that you believe they trust you.
3. Describe how you gained their trust.

4. After completing this, ask each individual why they trust you and see if their answers match up with what you thought.

You are doing this to see if there are any qualities you can add to your arsenal when working with your clients, prospects, and staff. This is a powerful exercise that contributes to your exponential growth as a person and in your practice. Remember, your goal is to become a trusted advisor to all your patients, and a trusted advisor means more cash and success in your business.

A trustworthy person's formula for success starts with the following fifteen keys. Providing your services to your ideal prospects and clients becomes a lot easier—and so does your quest for the ultimate response of "YES! I want to do business with you"—if you take these to heart.

1. To obtain trust, you must first give trust.
2. Being genuine when helping someone leads to trust.
3. Providing value first leads to trust.
4. Being the expert and showcasing your skills leads to trust.
5. Asking the right questions (that are different than your competitors) leads to trust (The TDCPL System).
6. Being truthful without sugar-coating leads to trust.
7. Being caring leads to trust.
8. Providing accurate advice without expecting something in return leads to trust.
9. Providing excellent service leads to trust.
10. Being respectful and being responsible lead to trust.
11. The zeal to do the best job possible leads to trust.
12. Providing exceptional results with desire leads to trust.
13. Eagerness to help leads to trust.
14. Truth and honesty leads to trust.
15. Trusting yourself first leads to trust.

"The truth shall set you free" is a famous saying we all have heard before. To fix distrust or recover from broken trust with your patients or any relationship that you have, you must first acknowledge the fact you have broken the trust in the relationship. Apologize for what took place and fix it.

However, I do not think you should ever say, "I am sorry." I believe the word "sorry" is empty; it has no backbone and it does not help the individual you are saying sorry to. When you apologize and state that you apologize for breaking the trust, the response and acceptance of the apology is much more sincere.

Telling the truth and apologizing will gain you much more respect. Clients and those with whom you have personal relationships will look at you as an honest person who is making things right by admitting to the fault. After you own up to the problem, it is important for you to fix the situation completely until you and the other party involved are satisfied.

In addition, likeability plays an important role in becoming a trusted advisor, along with providing value and results. Likeability makes a significant contribution toward gaining the ultimate position as the go-to guy in your area.

The following elements are the ingredients to becoming a trusted advisor.

1. A trusted advisor is seen and known as a true friend by their clients.
2. Trusted advisors provide exceptional value.
3. Trusted advisors focus on building a business by building on the benefit of their clients.
4. Trusted advisors are believed, respected, liked, and trusted by their clients, staff, and peers.
5. Trusted advisors present at all times valuable information to their clients.
6. Trusted advisors are exceptionally talented in uniting valuable information and expectation.
7. Trusted advisors are great listeners and are brilliant at understanding all situations their clients are in. Their focus is doing right and what is best for their clients.

8. Trusted advisors give the client what they want; the end result of using their services makes their clients' lives better.
9. Trusted advisors initiate their verdict based on the relationship they have with their clients and prospects, not the money alone.
10. Trusted advisors get a YES!

There is a lot more you can do to become a trusted advisor. The following keys are the foundation to gaining the status of being trusted. Remember, a trusted advisor is a person that is professional, friendly, caring, and understanding. A trusted advisor showcases their expertise and is also a person who is proficient at communicating and providing the end results their client's desire.

CHAPTER 3

Old-World Marketing vs. New-World Marketing

SMART ORTHODONTISTS in this economy research and commit to marketing strategies which are proven and which provide a high return on investment. Time and time again, I see Orthodontists invest in marketing strategies that no longer work which are not measurable in any format other than money out of their pockets.

This chapter will put a stop to this nonsense once and for all—if you decide to listen and implement the proven money-making strategies for you and practice.

Old-world marketing refers to different media techniques and strategies which were once effective and may still be effective in today's quickly changing world. Examples of these would be the use of newspapers advertising, the Yellow Pages, direct mail, radio, Valpak, flyers, and TV.

New-world advertising refers to online marketing strategies for implementing tactics and campaigns to attract new clients as well as the use of e-mail, videos, and pay-per-click marketing. It also includes search engine optimization, media buys, and using social media to get your ideal prospects and clients to become evangelists for your products and services, turning your prospects and your campaigns viral, spreading the good news about you and your services.

Now, you may be wondering, "Teran, what marketing strategy should I use?" Great question, and later on in this chapter I am going to tell you exactly what you should do if you want to make money NOW. In fact, the strategies throughout this chapter and the entire book will help you build a $2 million-dollar practice—or more. If you are at $2 million now, I am going to show you how to double your practice's profit in sixteen months or less, all by working less—guaranteed.

Traditional marketing is considered old-school marketing; some may say it is outdated and has lost its effectiveness over the years. Because of this, there has been a monumental shift from traditional marketing (e.g., TV, newspaper, Yellow Pages, magazines, radio) to online marketing. However, there are areas that are still highly effective through the use of each of these mediums.

The reason that business owners both big and small state that traditional marketing/advertising has lost its effectiveness is that they have moved from the number one technique to make their advertising dollars pay—the use of direct-response marketing.

Direct-response marketing builds trust because it makes the business owner accountable for the marketing they produce to bring new patients into the practice. The problem many Orthodontists face with their marketing is they believe it is about them. I'm here to tell you it is not about you at all. It is all about the ideal prospect you want to attract, the prospect you want to pick up the phone and do business with you.

The old-school mediums still work to some degree, but they need to be used with direct-response strategies to achieve a high return on investment. Remember, if it does not produce a return which is measurable, do not implement the strategy because you have no idea if it is working or not.

Social media, Internet marketing, e-mail marketing, and mobile marketing are new mediums that are considered new-world marketing. You should use these mediums to attract new patients to your practice and to keep in touch with your existing clients.

When used properly, new-world marketing is cost effective, measurable, and provides a high ROI on your advertising dollars. The biggest problem many Orthodontists are facing using new-world marketing (or marketing in general) is they have no idea how to use this new, exciting medium to their advantage.

Using the Internet to attract and keep in touch with your new prospects and clients is a must if your practice is to survive and thrive in this economy and the economy to come.

Here's the thing: The medium might change, but effective marketing will never change. Direct-response marketing will add a significant amount of cash and new clients to your practice.

Social media has been pushed to the front of this marketing era, so your goal is to use it to your advantage and let your prospects and clients partake in building your practice. To do this, you must use the various online entities like Facebook, Pinterest, Google+, and others to build your brand.

One thing you must realize is that Google and the other search engines (such as Yahoo! and Bing) are on a mission to provide relevant information and to clean all the spam from the Internet that is out there. They are doing this by making sure any business out there builds their brand across the various different platforms. Lucky for you, we will go through each platform and explain exactly how to make as much money as you want in the new-world marketing era.

Results is the name of the game and direct-response marketing measures results. Over the years, the Yellow Pages have been effective; however, with the monumental shift that has occurred, the effectiveness it once had is no longer there. The main reason the Yellow Pages have lost their luster is because consumers have moved away from using them. Now, not everyone has stopped using the Yellow Pages for finding an Orthodontist; yet, a big chunk has.

The other problem is the ads that run in the Yellow Pages are not direct-response ads at all. They are boring, dry, and do not provide any benefits or reasons for a customer to do business with you.

However, if you craft the right direct-response ad copy, you can own the Yellow Pages for your area. Writing great copy that gets the client to pick up the phone and call you is the first step in the process.

Look at the ads in the Yellow Pages. Do any of the ads provide a reason that you should do business with them? Do they provide a benefit and a call to action? I can guarantee that maybe one is close to providing what the ideal prospect is looking for.

The right time to use the Yellow Pages to attract new clients to your business is when you have the right message crafted. In the copywriting chapter, we will discuss this and show you how to craft the right message so that your phone will ring off the hook and flood your office with new patients. I would not direct a big chunk of your advertising dollars toward the Yellow Pages; however, the worthiness of the investment does depend on the city you're in.

Achieving great results puts more cash in your bank account and it starts with effective marketing and advertising. That being said, the best time to use old-world marketing is when you are implementing direct-response marketing.

Direct-response marketing is the only time when old-school marketing should be implemented. The only formula you need, the only formula you should implement to grow your practice is when you can see the actual results and measure the dollar amount from your efforts.

Old-school marketing is not dead. It is alive and well; however, few marketing consultants and Orthodontists know how to use it to their advantage.

When we are reading a magazine, newspaper, or an advertisement, whether online or offline, the first thing that grabs our attention is the headline. If the headline does not grab our attention, we will not read the rest of the article. The headline must provide what we want—in other words, what piques our interest. If it does not give us what we want, we will move to the next article or just throw away the entire newspaper.

This is direct-response marketing in action: If it holds our interest, we will continue to read on and find out more about what the article is talking about. This is old-school marketing using direct-response marketing the right way. You can implement the same strategy in your Yellow Pages ads and all your marketing material you create for your ideal clients and prospects.

To gain a significant amount of the market share in the city or town where you practice, you should always use new-world marketing strategies to grow your presence online.

If you decide not to use online marketing for your practice because you have a well-established practice with clients who spread the good news of your service to others offline, you will lose market share because your ideal prospects and clients use the Internet to conduct searches for the best Orthodontist who can help them.

I have come across a few well-established practices that do not even have a website and where the doctor has told me flatly he has no reason to market online. The reasoning behind his decision is that word-of-mouth has built his establishment and it will continue.

I'm here to tell you that yes, word-of-mouth advertising is GREAT; however, you cannot depend on one avenue to continue to hold up and build your practice. This is just insane.

When implemented correctly, online marketing measures, tracks, and builds leads for you cost effectively just like direct-response marketing. In fact, here's the shocking truth: Direct-response marketing should not be your only marketing avenue; you should also use online marketing.

Nothing else should be implemented if you are looking to seriously build a practice that you can sell for a profit or where you can work when you want to work, making as much money as you want.

The strategies here will give you the opportunity to work less, charge more, and put more cash in your pocket. It is all up to you. There is a lesson my lovely grandmother used to say to me when I was a little boy: "Those who don't hear will feel."

However, I have a very strong feeling that you are on your way to implementing the important information I am sharing with you today.

You want to combine both strategies, old and new, while testing and tweaking your direct-response marketing and measuring the results. Doing so will definitely make you the king of the hill—I guarantee it.

Here's the thing: You should be using old-school marketing with new-school marketing every opportunity you get. You should map out a plan for exactly what areas you want to advertise in (which would be all the major mediums, by the way).

You should be testing and measuring the results for every dollar that you invest. To integrate both old- and new-school marketing, you are going to start to track the results. You want to see what is working and what is not working. I am amazed that so many Orthodontists do not track their advertising; instead, they leave it up to chance.

That's like performing an operation on the client and saying, "Well, I know I am supposed to wash my hands before the operation; however, I know I washed them this morning, so I should be fine."

This approach surely will get bad results for you and the patient. You have to approach your marketing as results only.

We will discuss further in the chapter the different avenues of implementing direct marketing offline (TV, radio, and newspaper) to capture the best results for your practice. In other chapters we will discuss social media, search engine optimization, and paid search.

Measuring the success of your online and offline marketing efforts starts with tracking the results. By tracking the results, you can make the necessary changes to improve the entire process and the profitability of your marketing efforts.

Let's start with tracking results with online marketing first.

With online marketing, we have various software and platforms that will do the job for you. You will learn a little bit more about using the Google AdWords conversion tracking code, which will show you how many people are signing up for additional information from your website.

Google Analytics, which is free and which must be added to every single page of your website, provides in great detail the type of individual visiting your site. It tracks their movements and drop-off points so that you can make the necessary changes to improve the entire process for your client and prospects. This all leads to putting more money into your bank account and a practice of which you can surely be proud.

There are many other tools you can use, but these two will do a great job when you start to track the results for your online marketing.

For offline marketing, we can track results by using codes in our marketing material. With your sales letters, post cards, and follow-up calls that you send or make to clients, you can see your prospects' and clients' responses by simply adding letters to your letters to track the response. For example, let's say you asked the prospect or client to call in and ask for Susan, your office manager, to book their appointment. Here you can see the number of prospects who called in versus the number of sales letters and/or postcards that you sent out. This will tell you if your marketing material is effective; from there you can see the dollar amount in sales from the response.

You can also combine old-school tracking with new-school tracking, such as having a direct landing page for each prospect to whom you sent a letter. For example, you would send out a sales letter and tell your prospect to go to the following website to watch the webinar or to sign up for a video presentation. You would implement a PURL, which is personal URL, with the client's name and you can actually see from your logs and the sign-up process if they actually visited the page (e.g., www.GreatestOrthodontist.com/Ms-Joe_Johnson). This also builds trust and credibility right off the bat. So start tracking all your marketing efforts.

Marketing your practice in all different avenues is a must if you are looking to make it extremely profitable. The majority of Orthodontists try only one particular marketing strategy, and they try it only once and then give up on it and say it does not work.

The first thing is—you must know your target market. Your ideal client profile builds out exactly the type of client and prospects you want for your practice. You do not want to go after everyone. You want the client who will help you grow your practice and bring in more customers and make you more money.

Your selection process is crucial for success, which is the secret in developing any business. Selecting only clients you want to work with is the way you bring more cash into your practice than you can handle.

The next step of the process is to make sure your marketing material matches all the desires of your ideal prospects and clients, which you should know because you are constantly keeping in contact with your prospects. You must create a marketing system—and *system* is the keyword here—that continues to pump more leads and cash into your practice.

The third step of the process is to make sure you track every aspect of your marketing efforts. Without tracking, you will have no clue what is working and how well it is working. You want to cut the fat immediately and direct the cash to what is growing your practice. Do not waste your time on marketing your practice to areas where you can't track the dollars you are investing to grow your practice.

Integrating your ideal client profile and the research you conducted in Chapter One is going to make your marketing much more powerful than your competition's. To get the best results, write all your advertisements with your ideal client profile right by your side—if you want to put more cash in your pockets. Do not write any of your advertisements or any marketing material without your ideal client profile right beside you. If you do, your results will not be what you are looking for—I can guarantee.

The ideal prospect's file should have all the answers to counterattack any objections your ideal clients and prospects may have. Your goal is to answer all the objections in your marketing material and provide the right solution to your prospects.

You must record the results from your efforts for everything you develop. Track your marketing to see how much money each particular advertisement generated for you.

Success can be obtained by using Valpak for marketing your practice. I am amazed when I look at Valpak's marketing: The majority of the competition is Dentists and all their marketing is the same. They do not have a USP, and they are not talking about the benefits and the desires of the target market at all. On top of that, I have never seen an Orthodontist market their service at all using Valpak.

Fact: There is a 90 percent open rate with Valpaks. The decision maker in the home reads through the ads.

Well, luckily for you today, I am going to share with you how you can wipe out the Dentist and any other Orthodontist who uses Valpak.

The first thing is you are going to do is create your marketing piece catering to "What's in it for me?" (WIFM) and the desires of your target market through the research you conducted in your ideal client profile.

Next, you are going to take the marketing piece and message and direct your prospects to a specific landing page where they are going to obtain a free report regarding the benefits and advantages of using you and your services. Remember, it is going to be centered on WIFM (what's in it for your ideal client and prospects).

You are then going to build your list of contacts and follow up with them via the telephone, e-mail, and snail mail. Your office manager should offer them a special to come in for their first appointment.

Another successful technique you can use to your advantage is you can target your Valpak to be delivered to specific zip codes. You should target your Valpak in areas where the majority of your clients reside and from where you want to get additional clients from your ideal client profile. No one in the industry is using this information to their advantage; it is time for you to get all the money that belongs to you now.

Geographical targeting is a must if you want your newspaper advertising to pay off for you and your practice. There are two options you can choose when developing your marketing campaign for newspapers.

The first campaign is to target the daily newspapers; the second is the community newspapers that are sent out once or twice a week.

Newspaper readership has continued to decline over the past several years; however, it can still be profitable for your practice when used correctly. It is especially profitable with the target market of those who are 50-68 years of age because they still read the newspaper.

When contacting your daily paper to place an advertisement, you want at least a half a page to advertise your practice. Remember, the marketing material should be all about the desires of your ideal prospect. The second thing you want is a really strong offer and maybe a coupon that your prospects must cut out and bring with them to your practice.

The next thing you want to test is directing the prospect to a specific page you set up strictly for the newspaper advertising so that you can track your results.

You want your ad to have the look and feel of an advertorial advertisement. Making your ad look like an article is a massive advantage to getting users to read your ad. You also want to target your ads to be shown in cities and/or zip codes of your target market so that you are not wasting your advertising dollars and so that you are setting yourself to get the highest return on your investment.

These techniques should also apply to your local newspapers. Always ask for the rate of advertisement to compare. To get a ninja technique you can use for your newspaper advertising, sign up at www.WealthyOrthodontist.com/Ortho-Newspaper-Ads. You will not be disappointed.

I developed the GCP system for getting the best results for radio advertising which definitely adds cash to your pockets. GCP stands for Geographical, Copy, and Testing.

When setting up your radio advertising campaign, you want to do a couple of things first:

1. You want to find out what radio station your current clients listen to. You can simply ask them at each visit, or you can have the office manager give them a call.
2. You don't want to advertise on the #1 radio station just because it is #1. The #1 radio station may control only 10-20 percent of the entire market, which means you can advertise on the remaining 80-90 percent and gain access to wider coverage of the ideal prospect you are going after.
3. You definitely what to find the rate for advertising. You should look at the CPM, which stands for cost per thousand. You want to find out from each station the cost to reach 1,000 listeners. Whatever rate they give you, you want to negotiate a minimum discount of 10 percent.
4. You want your ad spot to run a minimum of five times per day but the more the better. Your ad should repeat your practice's number at least three times, and your location or website two times as well.
5. You want to get a radio spot for sixty seconds.
6. Target your ads to be heard in the locations where your prospects and ideal clients reside.
7. Test all your radio scripts. They should sound exciting, and the ad should be all about WIFM for your prospects and clients.

To get a super ninja tactic to get a huge discount when starting your radio advertising campaign, go to www.WealthyOrthodontist.com/Radio-Secrets.

I also developed the LMLT system, which is a very powerful money-making system that generates new leads and more cash by using TV advertising. LMLT stands for Local, Message, Lead, and Test. Let's break down this powerful formula so that you can use it for your advantage.

Local stands for targeting your advertising to the local stations your ideal clients and prospects watch. If you are targeting baby boomers (ages 50-68), local community TV is very powerful to advertise on.

Next, look at your message. What are you going to say in your script, your advertisement, to your target market? What is the goal or the outcome you are looking to achieve?

In your commercial, you are looking to get the lead. A really powerful way to do so is to direct your prospects to a specific landing page where you can track the results. You want to have a kick-butt offer that they can't refuse; in exchange, you collect their personal information (e.g., e-mail, telephone number, and name). This will enable you to add them to your database to market to via mail.

You also want to test all your scripts to find out which one provides the best return on your investment.

The following are a few things you should do before you launch your TV campaign:

1. You need to find out the SQUAD rate. SQUAD will give you the real cost for local and radio advertising cost. You want to compare it to the CPP, which is the cost per unit for the target market you are going after.
2. Look into purchasing spots in a specific zone for your ideal clients and prospects. You may pay a bit more; however, you are targeting exactly where your ideal clients and prospects reside.

3. Negotiate for a minimum of 25 percent off the rate you are quoted for your TV advertising campaign.

To get a kick-butt ninja technique on negotiating for TV advertising, go to www.WealthyOrthodontist.com/TV-Advertising-Negotiating.

Combining the three systems I shared in this chapter is a must in order to gain the biggest market share for your practice. Invest in only what is necessary to grow your practice. If you cannot measure the marketing, or if you have a limited budget, start off with direct mail, then move to newspapers, radio, and lastly TV. You want to test all your marketing material you create as well.

You want to be like McDonald's in terms of marketing: You want to be everywhere, and you want to be constantly in contact with your prospects and clients. As everybody knows, McDonald's has the largest share of the fast-food burger industry because they are constantly marketing to their target market.

Using this chapter and the other things you are going to learn will definitely put you on top. Your competitors will have no idea what hit them. You see, they will be scared to do this type of marketing as well because they will say it is too much work and it will take too long.

Meanwhile, you will be laughing all the way to the bank, taking their clients and prospects away because you decided to care about the client and give them exactly what they want. Don't waste time—get started now.

CHAPTER 4

Copywriting: How Your Words Can Turn into Instant Cash

ACCORDING TO ROSER REEVES, a famous ad man, copywriting is salesmanship in print. It is using print to persuade and influence your ideal prospects to spend their money on your services.

Your marketing material can become your sales force if you create an advertisement and marketing material with the right message and make sure it is seen by thousands if not millions of people. All you have to do is use the right words in the right market.

As an Orthodontist, you might say to yourself, "I find persuasion manipulative or evil." In actual fact, though, it is not. It is only evil if you are trying to obtain something that is not good and you are not providing anything of value in return.

Let me show you how we humans are constantly in the action of influencing and persuading others on a daily basis. It might not be for money, but it is for something that we want; in exchange, the other person will get whatever it is that they want.

For those who are married, did you not have to sell yourself to your spouse before you got married? You had to prove that you are the right individual for him or her with the actions and words you delivered on a daily basis. If you have children, you know they do the same thing by making the argument for what they want and by backing it up with their actions and with proof.

Copywriting is simply putting your thoughts in print to make the case for your prospect to do business with you. In this chapter, we are going discover the techniques to craft the right marketing message that will put as much cash in your bank account as it can hold by attracting the right client for your practice so that it will grow and be successful.

Copywriting not only helps get the right clients to grow your practice, it also allows your clients to express to others how happy they are about you and your services. They will become your unpaid sales force.

If you do not use great copywriting in your business, your practice will fail. (Heck, if you don't do any form of marketing, your business will fail.) You want to have the best message in front of your prospects so that they can make the right—and only—decision to go with you as their doctor.

Copywriting done correctly can not only save a practice from bankruptcy, it can make a practice the number one practice in an entire city. Potential clients will seek you out without you constantly prospecting for new business.

Yes, it is that powerful. Ignore it and it will cost your business. Embrace it and learn how to do it well, and I guarantee you will be able to write you own ticket. In the following pages, we are going to discuss proven techniques which will get others to take out their wallet and pay you for your services. Get ready for an exciting and profitable ride.

You are going to hear WIFM a lot throughout this book; it is the cornerstone to your practice's success. Remember, WIFM stands for "What's in it for me?" Your prospects and clients care about only one thing: What am I going to get out of doing business with you?

This is extremely important: None of your prospects and clients care about what you have done or accomplished. They are looking only at what are you going to give them and why they should listen to you. Why should they give you money?

Too many times I will see advertisements and marketing material talking about the doctor because the doctor believes his clients want to know how long he has been married and how many kids he has, even their grades in school, etc. Believe me, the client does not care.

They care only about themselves and their goals. Craft your message around that simple fact and you will be well on your way to cornering the market in whatever city you practice.

You can even quickly overtake existing practices that are well established by focusing your marketing message around your prospects' desires and goals. Not many Orthodontists know this secret, and they focus on "me marketing"—it's all about me.

Eliminate "me marketing" from your arsenal and follow the information on this page. If you do, you will be on the right track to becoming king of the hill—I guarantee it.

Embarking on the creation of your marketing material starts off with unlocking the desires of your ideal clients and prospects. Tapping into these desires will give you the upper hand in every advertisement and marketing material you create for your practice.

I call these desires SOM—"Soul of Mankind."

Mankind is wired for the following elements in life. No matter what, every single human being desires the following:

1. To survive and enjoy life to its fullest
2. To enjoy eating and drinking
3. Liberty from fear, pain, and danger
4. Living contented and happy in a place of your choosing
5. Sexual relationship and friendship
6. To protect and care for those you love
7. To be the best and to have the things that you desire
8. Approval from others

Reading this list, I am sure you would agree that we humans want all of these things in our life. Here's the thing to remember—so does your client. Your objective is to craft your marketing materials and advertisements around SOM. This will put you far ahead of the competition because they have no clue this is what people want. Using the SOM technique lets you tap into the essence of how human beings operate.

Fear, ego, and vanity are some of the triggers you can use to tap into your clients' desires and wallets. If you feel uncomfortable with that statement, you should stop reading this book now. If you're uneasy persuading your clients and asking for money for your services, this book is not for you. You should take the book, put it back in its package, and send it to your competitor down the street. Within the space of six months or less, you will be out of business because you don't want to make money. If you do want to make money, please keep reading.

Fear is a very powerful trigger. When used correctly, it can produce outrageous results, bringing new clients and cash into your practice. The ability to use fear in your marketing and advertising is a huge plus, but it should be used only if the fear you put in front of the prospect can be solved legitimately.

Fear comes in at the point when your client cannot deal with the loss of obtaining what they want. All your marketing material should describe some loss the client will suffer if the client does not act now. For example, if you add a time limit and/or limit the product or service you are offering, the client knows he or she could lose out on it if they do not act. Remember, it has to be legitimate. Do not use fake or underhanded techniques because it will kill your business.

Appealing to one's vanity and ego is also extremely powerful. This is where your marketing matches your clients' inadequacies—what they feel they are lacking to become better and/or look better in their own eyes and in the eyes of society as whole.

Another example of appealing to one's vanity is to look at car and perfume commercials. They link the product to the audience's desire to look and feel the way the model looks in the commercial. It puts them in the position that they can get what they want.

Something your advertisements and marketing material must contain is believability. Your target market must believe everything you say and do. If they don't feel your message is real and truthful, you will not get the sale.

There is a huge list of triggers you can implement in crafting your advertising and marketing material which would take another book to cover. To get the additional tips and strategies, you can go to www.WealthyOrthodontist.com/Copy_Triggers.

Your ideal client profile will come in handy before you start writing your first advertisement or marketing material for your website. The first thing you want to do is research what your prospects and clients want. You want to make sure that you create a list of talking points that you want to mention in your material.

The second thing you want to do is make sure you ask your ideal prospect to take action in your advertisement. Too many times I will see marketing material from Orthodontists where they have not asked for the sale or at least some form of action to be taken after the prospect has read or watched the advertisement.

Your ideal client profile will guide you, along with additional research you have conducted, in crafting the right message at the right time. Make sure you also get your staff's input. Remember, they see everything in the office, including how the client feels and any other suggestions or complaints the client may make directly to them and not to you.

Let your staff know it is okay for them to share their opinions openly. This is a very smart way to grow your practice and have the staff participate in your business's vision.

Before you start putting together the formal advertisement or marketing message, write your ad out by hand first. Get a blank piece of paper and a pen or pencil to start; the first thing we are going to conquer is the headline for any advertisement you write.

Grabbing your prospects' attention so that they will continue to read your marketing message or advertisement all starts with a powerful headline that captures and connects with your prospects' and clients' desires. It makes them want to read more. The headline will do 75 percent of the job of getting the sale. Did you know this is how newspapers and magazine publishers make a majority of their money? They test hundreds if not thousands of different headlines to grab your attention so that you will buy their product.

Here's a fact that you must use to your advantage: You have fewer than seven seconds to grab your prospect's attention. If you do not get their attention in seven seconds or less, you have just lost the sale.

The headline should contain a benefit—in this case, the ultimate benefit your prospect or client will achieve. It should be front and center and it should not be misleading. It should be believable and real.

Let's take a look at a few examples of powerful headlines. This will give you a good idea as to what your headline should do.

1. Transform Your Smile, Gain Confidence and a Strong Self-Image with Invisalign. No One Will Know You Are Wearing Braces. It's Invisible. Save 20%! Call Now!
2. If You're over 40, This Is the Best Solution to Transform Your Smile & Your Life. Get Invisalign, the Invisible Braces.
3. My Wife Was "Stunned"! In Less than 5 Months My Life and Smile Were Transformed from Just Doing This One Simple Thing.
4. I Thought I Would Never Get a Beautiful Smile! Then I Finally Gave Up and Saw Dr. Johnson. In Less than a Day, My Life & Smile Were Transformed.
5. Get Invisalign! In only a day I guarantee that friends, colleagues, and family will gasp in astonishment at your new smile, confidence, and courage.
6. One Sentence Transformed This Man's Smile and Life!

Get into the habit of crafting a minimum of fifty headlines when you are getting ready to start to write your advertisement and marketing materials.

Creating an irresistible offer starts by providing something of extreme value, something that appeals to your ideal clients' and prospects' desires. Remember, to get the sale you must ask for the sale. If you don't ask, you will not get the sale. I am amazed by how many Orthodontists' marketing material completely forgets to ask for the money.

Although your offer should link to your client's ultimate desires, you must convert all the features of your service or product to a benefit. This must be stated up front in the offer. If it does not come up, your prospect will throw your marketing material away or just click away from your website.

If you remember the movie *The Godfather*, Marlon Brando, who played the head of the Corleone crime family, had a famous line, "I gonna make him an offer he can't refuse." This is what you want to do with all your marketing material and advertisements; you want to make sure your offer is such a no-brainer that your prospect and client will pick up the phone, book the appointment, and give you money in return for your services and/or products. Remember, though, you must put a value on your products and services so that your client can clearly see what they are getting in return for the ultimate benefit that will change their life.

Once you have provided the benefit, you must ask for the sale. Let them know exactly what they have to do next to get the benefits they desire.

Gaining your prospects' and ideal clients' attention is not the only process you need to achieve with your marketing material. The next step is to make sure your marketing is valuable and that you provide an advantage in your advertisement and marketing pieces. When you provide an advantage and make your marketing valuable, you separate yourself from your competition. This will automatically lead to your marketing material being read more often. It will not look like a sales pitch to your prospects and clients but valuable information they must read once they have gotten their hands on it.

This strategy differentiates you from your competitors. I bet you cannot tell me when you last saw an advertisement or marketing material that contained valuable information that you could use right away. Right? By using this strategy, you are going to gain a significant amount of the market share.

This all leads to one thing—more cash hitting your bank account and wallet simply by providing exactly what your clients want. You might remember having heard this saying once or twice through this book: People don't want to be pitched a sale; they want a connection. Once you get the connection, your offer will be accepted and bought once it matches their desires.

Consider the following formulas:

B (BELIEVABILITY) + C (CREDIBILITY) = P (PROOF)

P + D (DESIRES) = S (SALES)

You should remember these formulas and engrain them in your memory. Proof in your marketing material is obtained by making sure it is believable and factual; this leads to credibility. Then, adding proof (in the way of testimonials and third-party verification of what you are saying) to your prospects' desires will generate sales.

You cannot eliminate one element from this equation; if you do, you will lose the sale. You are marketing to generate sales; therefore, your material must get into the mindset and the conversations all your prospects and clients are having. If you make sure you answer all objections, you and your practice will be the obvious choice.

When clients hire me to do their marketing campaigns, I start to review their marketing material to see if they have any proof to substantiate the claims and/or statements that they make. Nine times out of ten, there is no proof to support what they claim to the prospect, which makes the marketing material or advertisement a big waste. Always check to make sure any claims you make are backed up and that you have proof to support that what you are offering is the solution to your prospects' or clients' problem.

Asking for the sale can be difficult sometimes because most Orthodontists do not see themselves as a salesperson. Asking for the sale in print is even harder if you have no clue as to how to do it in a way that is smooth and that actually leads to the prospect giving you money for your services. (Part of this is addressed in Chapter 2 regarding the profiling and in Chapter 7 with the script that leads to the prospect giving you money.)

You want your advertisements and marketing pieces to be natural, so write your advertisement and ask for the sale like you were speaking to a friend. That will ease the process and help you get it right.

The next thing is that you don't want to sell from your heels (as my mentor use to say to me). This means do not hesitate; you need to be completely up front and get to the point.

If you make an irresistible offer to your clients and prospects, asking for the sale will be a no-brainer. They will gladly pay you for your service and/or product. So you need to create a kick-butt offer they just can't refuse.

It is important to write several drafts of your marketing material and your advertisements before you let them go live to the public. What you want to do is have your staff read the draft and provide you with feedback. If they say they love it, ask them which parts they like and which parts they don't like. If they say they like everything, go back and tweak the copy because your staff may say what they think you want to hear and not give their true feelings. If they cringe or they feel uncomfortable with the copy, you are on the right track. Your copy should just push the boundaries to get your prospects and clients to take action.

You can also get family members to review your copy to gauge their reaction. This too can be helpful. If you are still not sure, you can send me one piece of your copy, and I will critique the first ten for free—a value of $2,500 each—send it to Critiquemycopy@WealthyOrthodontist.com.

Once you have received the reviews and suggestions for the copy, it is time to write the final copy to be released to your prospects and clients.

Increasing the response and conversions from all your marketing material is a must if you want to annihilate your competition and make a lot more money. The fastest way to do this is to split test all the marketing material you put out to your prospects and clients. You should create two separate pieces for each piece of marketing material and advertisement you write.

The headline is the first thing you want to test both pieces against each other. As stated before, the headline is responsible for 75 percent of the readership of your ad. Remember, you also have fewer than seven seconds to grab the attention of your clients and prospects.

Here's how to do it: If you are sending out a sales letter or postcard to your list of clients, send half of the postcards to Group A and send the other half of the postcards to Group B. Then see what type of response you get. The winning postcard will be the new control to use because it is the one that made you the most money. The following will give you a good example of how a 10 percent increase can dramatically put more cash in your bank account.

- Service X costs the client $8,500
- You send out 200 postcards in total
- 100 postcards to Group A
- 100 postcards to Group B
- Response for A postcard is 5% so that would be 5 clients at $8,500 = $42,500
- Response for B postcard is 10% so that would be 10 clients at $8,500 = $85,000

You doubled your money with a 10 percent increase in sales. Do you see how powerful it is to test all your marketing materials? I have tested and written many marketing pieces for my clients that have generated hundreds of thousands of dollars more by using this key principle.

Next, you want to test the offer. You want to create two separate offers and do exactly what I listed above. These are the two most important things you should test first before you distribute your marketing materials to your prospects and clients.

Write the way you speak and write to a single person in all your marketing material. This will automatically boost the response and the effectiveness of your advertisement and all your marketing material.

You also want to focus on writing at a grade 6 level of education so that the copy is easy for your clients and prospects to read and understand. This is essential if you want to grab and keep their attention.

Telling a story in your sales letter and advertisements that incorporates the desires of your prospects and clients will dramatically increase their engagement with the ad. In fact, it will persuade your prospects and clients to buy and to buy more frequently.

You should also test sending out an editorial marketing ad in newspapers and magazines. Editorial ads look and feel like an article; they provide valuable information that keeps the reader completely engaged. This technique has been shown to boost response rates as much as 50 percent.

You also want to remember to always use the client's or prospect's name in your e-mails and personal marketing material. Using their name builds a connection and they will continue to read what you have to say. It is also nice to handwrite envelopes that are sent out with your marketing material and to handwrite the salutation; this can increase sales as much as 50 percent because it makes your material look less commercial and more personal.

If you get a winner, never neglect the following technique: Resend that winner again to those on your list who did not respond. This may seem strange, but it is an effective strategy that has helped a client double their sales.

Always use captions in your advertisements and marketing material, especially under pictures. Remember to use images and pictures that draw your clients and prospects to what you are offering. Do not just add an image to the advertisement or ad to make it look better; it must serve a purpose to illustrate the clients' and prospects' desires.

The easiest and most effective technique to test your copy for readability and connection is to read your copy out loud to yourself before you send any copy or marketing material out to your prospects and clients either online or offline. This simple little technique will show you exactly where you are messing up in your copy. When reading your copy out loud, if you stumble over the words, pause, or take a long break; something is wrong and you need to rewrite it. Also, if you are reading the copy out loud and it does not make any sense or you feel that something is not right, it is better to rewrite the copy.

You should also give it to your staff to read out loud. The same rules apply: Listen to where they are having trouble reading your copy. It if is not smooth or they do not understand what you are trying to say, you have lost them.

You must take notes and go back and rewrite the copy. Do this several times until the copy is easy to read and it flows well. Remember, all your copy must include an effective story which goes after your prospects' desires. The following formula is what you should use for all your marketing material. This is what I use when doctors hire me to craft their online and offline marketing messages.

Checklist to Follow

- Your ideal prospects and clients care only about WIFM—nothing else. They care only about how you can solve their problem. Do you have a high-value solution?
- Does your copy get into their true desires, fears, needs and wants? Does your copy show them they can get the ultimate result(s) they are after?
- Remember, you are offering the ultimate solution; always present this to your ideal prospects and clients.
- Write to one person. Your copy should be written in a friendly tone like you are speaking with a friend. Your marketing material and advertisements should be easy to understand and read.
- Use short paragraphs, sentences, and words. It will increase sales.
- Remember, your headline is KING—it must grab their attention.
- For body copy, state the problem, agitation, and the solution.
- Your goal is to get them to read the entire advertisement or marketing material. Your intro must guide them into reading the next line and so on.
- Provide sub-headlines that guide them to the solution they are looking for.
- Always provide proof and back up your claims. It can be many testimonials and/or a demonstration of the product or service in action, showing that it works and linking back to the ideal client and/or prospect's desire.
- Load up on the benefits your ideal prospects and clients will receive. Don't forget rule #1: WIFM.
- Address any objections the prospect will be discussing in their heads.
- Have an irresistible offer and ask for the sale.

CHAPTER 5

Developing Your Cash Cow Website

USABILITY IS A CRUCIAL ELEMENT to a successful Orthodontist website. Without it, you will lose leads and kill your chance for success with the search engines. However, I am going to share with you three advantages that, if you implement them immediately, will leave your competitors in the dust and have your ideal clients booking appointments with you in as little as fifteen minutes.

Usability refers to the function and flow of your website. Have you ever gone to a particular site looking for an item only to be frustrated in your search for the item or service, unable to find the page or the button or the information that the site clearly states that they have? That is usability, the flow of categories, tabs, and information buttons, the flow of everything on your site. You want to make sure the important information is visible to your ideal client so that they can find it with ease, without getting frustrated.

Remember, you know you have fewer than seven seconds to grab your ideal client's attention when they hit the website. If you don't grab their attention, they will leave immediately and go to your competitor.

(If you want to see a site that is a good example of usability, you should look at Amazon.com. Amazon spends millions of dollars testing and tweaking their website.)

Once you know what categories and services you are going to offer your ideal client, the next step you should take is to get a couple of index cards and write on them the services you offer. Then put them in the right order, let one of your employees look at the cards, and have them put the cards in the order they think they should be. This will give you a clue as to what people are looking for when they hit your site.

The next step is to look at your competitors' sites. Take note on how their websites flow and the ease of finding information.

Use the following usability checklist to build a profitable Orthodontic website:

1. Your website should load fast.
2. Background color should make text readable.
3. Font size and spacing of text is readable to all ages.
4. Flash is used sparingly on your website.
5. Alt tags for all your images
6. 404 pages should be customized, guiding clients to an appropriate page.
7. Company logo is visible and placed appropriately throughout the site.
8. Practice tagline is clear, concise, and provides a benefit to clients and ideal prospects.
9. Landing page grabs clients' attention in seven seconds or less.
10. "About Us" information is easily and quickly found.
11. Navigation is smooth and identifiable.
12. Navigation label is clear.
13. Reasonable number of buttons
14. The practice's logo (when clicked on) goes back to the home page.
15. Links are identifiable and easy to find.
16. Site search is easy to access.

17. Headings throughout the website are descriptive, benefit driven, and clear.
18. Important content is above the fold.
19. The style and color of your website are constant.
20. Copy throughout the site is geared toward the client and ideal prospects (WIFM).
21. Title page tags (HTML) are descriptive and provide clear meaning of the subject matter of the page.
22. Test your site on all browsers to see how it looks and functions.

On the Internet, trust is a huge issue, especially for your ideal client. A great design builds trust; it shouts that you are a real business that cares for your clientele. Now, if your site looks like everyone else's, please tell me what advantage do you have against your competitors?

Time and time again when I am working with an Orthodontist, I find they have been taken by a huckster who gives them a cookie-cutter site which does nothing for them or their ideal client. I remember once, one of the big, practice-building Orthodontic companies copied a site word for word and sold it to another client. You do not ever want this to happen to you. Further on in the book, I am going to discuss and provide proven website designs, strategies, and tactics for you to look at that have grown practices to over a million dollars in revenues.

Secondly, Google hires quality assurance reps to actually go through your entire site to make sure your design and what you are offering is trustworthy, honest, and true. If it is not, they will penalize your site by either de-indexing it (which means your rankings will fall for the main keywords that bring you traffic) and if you use Pay Per Click (Google AdWords), you will see a lower-quality score, which will force you to pay more to advertise.

It is important to remember that a great design caters to your ideal client. Recall the ideal client system you developed in Chapter 1. This is going to be a huge help in developing your site.

Your design should also have pictures and content that speak to your ideal client. You must have pictures of your clients with their stories and videos of your clients giving testimonials for your services. You should use sharp, crisp images to show you are professional and your site is not cheesy or a cookie-cutter site, like your competitors.

The ultimate thing is that a well-designed website will dramatically contribute to building leads and profits for your practice. Value = money. Please remember this statement. Whatever you do in your practice, remember the more value you provide to your ideal client as you respond to their desires, the more money you will make. This is how you should approach the design of your website.

Let's start off talking about the content of your site. When I evaluate most Orthodontists' marketing material, I see no mention of value or benefit to get their ideal client to do business with them. This is where the majority of Orthodontists will compete with each other—on price. But let me tell you something: No one buys on price; they buy on value and with their emotions.

Okay, I know you might be saying, "Teran, I don't believe you. Prove it to me." Here's a quick example: If people bought only on price, there would not be multi-million-dollar homes, and there would not be any sports cars. Everyone would shop at Wal-Mart. However, if you show someone the value that they are going to achieve by obtaining the more expensive item, this will lead them to purchase your service and build a relationship with you. This is what you want in your practice—a relationship with your client where you become their trusted source and friend.

So your content or web copy should state what benefit they will achieve by working with you, why you have the expertise and why others do not. We will get deeper into that when we talk about positioning, which you will have to do in your practice or it will fail. The good news is if you listen to me, you will be far ahead of the competition.

LOOK AT THE FOLLOWING CHECKLIST:

1. Website copy provides benefits / the end result your ideal client will achieve.
2. The content is caring and provides additional data that your competitors do not provide.
3. You provide additional information to help a potential client make their decision (e.g., free report, white papers, and/or video).

Positioning is what 99 percent of Orthodontists are missing in their practice that would take them to the next level. Positioning will increase your bottom line and eliminate the competition when put into practice. The reason you bought this book is to take home more money at the end of the day. If you forget everything else in this book, don't forget what I am going to tell you right now.

Positioning is money. To position yourself well, you must come up with a USP (unique selling proposition)—something that makes you stand out from your competitors. If everyone else is saying the same thing and doing the same thing, it is a lot harder to compete and all your potential clients will look at only price—you know, the tire kickers that show up wanting only to know what you charge or that do not show up at all.

Now, think of it this way: If you could do something in your business significantly different from all your competitors and they could not copy it, what would it be?

Take a blank piece of paper and spend thirty to sixty minutes coming up with different ideas on what you would want to say and what you could back up with proof, something that is different from everyone else who is an Orthodontist or a general practice Dentist.

I have developed a powerful, proven system called PFO (Positioning for Orthodontists). I charge my clients a minimum of $65,000 to do this for them. Today I am going to give it to you for a significant discount. Do you think I am crazy? The reason I am giving it to you at such a deep discount is that I want to prove to you that you can become #1 in your market and you can make as much money as possible. To apply to get the system please visit www.WealthyOrthodontist.com/PFO_System.

You can get the system immediately and it will definitely help you eliminate the need for general practice Dentist referrals. I am making this available to only the first fifteen Orthodontists who respond.

Grabbing your ideal client's attention in the first few seconds is a must. If you don't, they will gladly leave your website and go to your competitors. This is why it is important for you to have your USP right up front for them to see. It will engage them, and they will continue to read and explore your site; it will bring trust and show you are different from everyone else.

I would present my USP as a video. You should speak about your practice and share how you are different and what you have to offer compared with Dentists and other Orthodontists. Of all the Orthodontists out there, 98 percent do not share how and why they are different from a general practice Dentist who is offering the same services.

Now, I want to ask you: Is the Dentist really offering the same services? You need to let your ideal client know why you are different and what exactly they are going to get working with you.

Some facts you should state are horror stories of the Dentist who worked on a client's braces and did such a poor job that you had to redo the entire procedure. I can tell you stories of my clients who have had such procedures done that they had to completely do over. The poor client has no idea the training the Dentist receives does not even compare to the training an Orthodontist—you—had to go through.

It is like buying a Rolls Royce at Chevrolet prices; you get what you pay for and your clients need to know.

The second way I would have my USP up front and on every single page of your site is in your web copy. Put your USP up front, explaining why you are different and why your clients and prospects will be making the right decision going with you.

Go online and search for an Orthodontist in your area. Look and see if they have a USP right up front or if they even have one listed anywhere. You will find that they speak and act like everyone else. You don't want to do that. After going through this remarkable book, you will be way ahead of everyone else.

Trust is what your ideal client is looking for to make their decision and to give you the YES you want. Your prospects must think you're likeable and caring; in return, you just have to obtain their trust. This is why it is important that you have a devoted section or pages on your website for testimonials and positive stories from your current and past clients.

Did you know that over 78 percent of consumers trust someone else's opinion online when it is given? This study was conducted by Social Media Today. Most people want to know they can trust that you are going to give them what they want. If you give them what they want, everything else will fall into place.

Now, your stories should be in video format first. Get your clients to share their stories in video. You can have a flip video or a handy cam ready to go at your practice. Just videotape your clients talking about how happy they are with your service. They should give their name and what service you performed for them.

If they can't be on camera, get their testimonials in writing, sharing their entire experience. Video stands out because it gets your ideal client engaged and shows them what someone like themselves achieved by working with you. Most people want to do business with someone they like and trust and you can gain their trust and become likeable by showing them that someone just like them achieved exactly what they wanted.

Here is the sad part: Of those of you reading this, 98 percent will not do what I just outlined because of fear or fear of intrusion on your client. The other 2 percent that do follow my guidelines will enjoy a steady flow of new clients coming into their practice who are more than happy to share their story.

I guarantee your clients will become evangelists for your service and share their experiences with everyone they meet. Don't put this on the back burner—start it right now. You should do this after every single client visit. The more testimonials you have the better. It will just overwhelm your ideal client that you are a trusted advisor and know exactly what you are doing.

Search engines love credibility and so does your ideal client. When designing your website, you should have the following seven things to increase your trust, credibility, and honesty with the search engines and your ideal client.

1. **Policy page:** Make sure you have a policy page which explains the policy of the website, the dos and don'ts, and what exactly you will do with the information potential clients and clients provide to you through your website.
2. **A site map and an xml site map:** With so many changes occurring with Google and the other search engines it is important that you have a site map that lists the various pages and content throughout your site.
3. **Contact page:** You would be surprised how often this page is not completely clear and helpful to your ideal client. I have done audits on Orthodontists' websites where they don't provide a contact telephone number, a mailing address, street address, hours of operation, or a form to submit for additional information. All these things must be on your site. It also helps you gain exposure in the search engines.
4. **Services page:** You must list all the services you perform. As I said before, many of your clients will look at the services page to find out what exactly you offer. This seems so obvious, but it is most often overlooked when a site is being designed.
5. **About the doctor or doctors:** List your credentials in a way that shows the client the benefits of working with you. I would use this opportunity to have both a video and web copy that explains and provides your credentials. Remember, it is

about the client. Show them what they will get if they work with you. They care only about What's In It for Them, their favorite radio station WIFM.

6. **An opt-in page:** This provides a valuable report or video that can help you build your list and provide crucial information that will assist your ideal client in choosing you over your competitors.
7. **Before and after pictures of your clients' work:** Show them what they will get along with a testimonial from the ideal client (preferably on video) with the before and after pictures.

Engaging with your ideal client, as you probably know by now, builds trust and provides a huge advantage to you because you are doing something completely different from your competitors. Studies have shown that more people are watching videos online than the combination of viewers of the big three networks.

Tapping into the market with the right message at the right time and providing valuable information will put you ahead of the general practice Dentist and other Orthodontists.

The other huge advantage you gain by having videos on your website is you can be ranked organically in the search engines for certain topics that you know will provide you with an income and that will drive money into your practice.

If done correctly, a well-optimized video can be ranked in the search engine on the same page as your website. Here are a couple things you want to make sure you do to optimize your videos:

1. The city and/or location of your practice
2. The topic—make sure your keyword tags are set up correctly.
3. A call to action—make sure all your videos provide the opportunity for a free report, white paper, or DVD to build your list.
4. Keep your video at three to six minutes in length; any longer and you start to lose your ideal client.

5. Do a link-building campaign to your videos to increase your rankings in YouTube search and organic search for Google, Yahoo! and MSN.

The second advantage of using video on your website is it allows you to effectively test your marketing message. With your video hosted on YouTube on your own YouTube channel, you can see exactly where people drop off from watching your video. This will tell you how effective the information and the marketing message you are providing to your clients and/or ideal prospects are.

If they are leaving at a certain spot in your video, you can quickly redo the video to grab their attention and provide exactly what they are looking for. Of all the Orthodontist out there, 99 percent do not use this tool to their advantage. It is available to you when you set up your YouTube channel. (Please see the picture below.) You want to track this on a weekly basis as you drive your ideal client to the page to view.

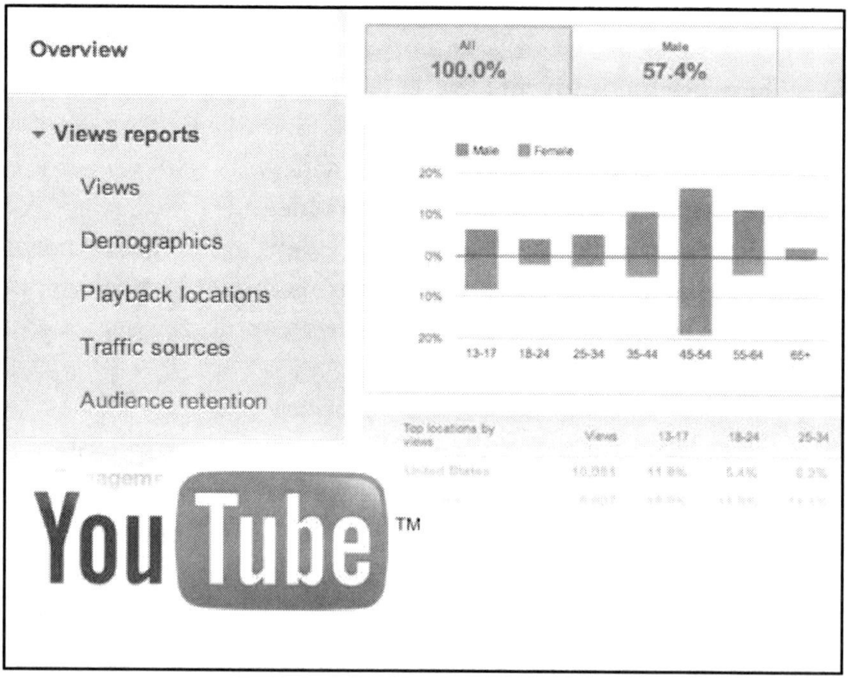

Directing your ideal client or clients to a page you want them to read or that they land on specifically is called a landing page. This particular page will be relevant to the needs and wants of your prospects and it will provide them with the direction and a call to action to pick up the phone and call your office to book a consultation.

The goal you should have for your landing page is to engage and entice your prospect to take advantage of what you are offering to them. It should be compelling; they should feel that if they leave, they are making the wrong decision. This is why we started off by doing the ideal client system—to drive home to the emotions, needs, and wants of your prospect.

When using your landing page for PPC, it is important all these elements are there. As you read earlier, human reviewers go through your site and grade your site accordingly. They look at the content to see if it relevant; they look at your design to see if you and your practice are credible; they check to see if the page and the site are honest and truthful.

So you have two individuals you must abide in order to drive as much traffic to your site and get as many leads as possible. You have Google to please and you have your potential clients to please when designing your website. Do both correctly and you will have nothing worry about.

Clients and the search engine want easy access to your products and services. They want to know where to go on your site and they want to know it is visible and easy to find. Category pages provide detailed answers regarding your product and services for anyone who visits. It builds credibility and trust that you are a real business and you know what you are doing.

If you were searching for a product, would you not find it strange when you hit the site if there was no information on what exact services and merchandise they carry and offer to the public? Well, many sites miss this all together.

Having worked on hundreds of Orthodontists' sites, I can tell you they totally miss listing the services they provide; they don't put it up front for everyone to see. When I ask, "Do you perform X service?" They say, "Yes, I do." Then I ask, "Why isn't it on your website?" They look like a deer caught in the headlights. Thankfully, you are not going to have that problem.

First, get a blank piece of paper and list all the services you perform and all the products you have for sale to your prospects and ideal clients. They need to know what you carry, and you should sell it to them.

Once the list is created, put it in order from the product that has the highest margin (the one you make the most money from). Remember, you want to sell as much as possible. The name of the game is to sell more to your ideal client and clients, and if they don't know what you are selling, how can they buy from you?

Now make sure the list is visible on your site under the services you provide.

This should also be listed in your site map as well, to help the search engines know exactly what you offer and the business that you are in. Remember, Google's human reviewers will visit your site and they verify:

A. If you are a real business
B. If you are relevant
C. If you are trustworthy

Another metric many Orthodontists don't check or do not know about is the bounce rate. The bounce rate = results that you are looking for. The bounce rate is how long a potential client or your ideal client stays on your site. As I said before, you have fewer than seven seconds to make an impression and grab your ideal client's attention. If they leave the site before reading and moving on to other pages on your website, the bounce rate is high. It is calculated by how many visitors hit your site and leave within one minute. If they do not go to any other pages, this means the marketing message /web copy does not provide what they are looking for.

Here's the thing: Google is now calculating with a new proprietary technology how long and where someone stops reading and leaves your site. They use this information to help them decide if your website is helpful and valuable to those to whom you are marketing; if it is not, your rankings in the search engine will drop.

Now, if your site is already designed and you're saying, "Oh man, I already spent so much money designing my current site and I don't want to do it over again," my question to you is how much money is it bringing you now? Are you getting the results that you are looking for? Most likely the answer will be no, but you can change this right now. The following checklist will help you develop the right site for the ideal client you are going after. This will increase the bottom line in your practice with more leads coming in requesting a consultation and more money in your pocket.

Checklist for Redesign:

1. Is your USP up front and everywhere on your site?
2. Are you using video?
3. Do you have a policy page?
4. Do you have an e-mail policy page?
5. Do you have a "Contact Us" page with a map with directions, telephone number, address, hours of operation, and form for them to complete?
6. Are you providing valuable, unique content on every page of your site?
7. Do you have a category page?
8. Do you list all your services and products?
9. Do you have a site map?
10. Do you have an xml site map?
11. Are you using pleasing graphics that sell your product and services?
12. Is it easy to navigate your site? (Get a usability test done.)

Unique selling proposition + Trust + Testimonials + Services = The Radio station WIFM. What your clients want to see and know about is, "What's in it for me?" This is the only thing they care about; your ideal prospects and clients tune in to this radio station 24/7. As the director of your radio station, you must play the music and advertisements they want to see and hear.

This means your positioning statement or your unique selling proposition must be up front and clear for everyone to see. You must have convincing testimonials in video format which outline exactly what everyone is saying about you and your practice. They want to see all the services you offer.

The success of your practice relies on you putting this together. I can't harp on this enough: The more you target and provide valuable unique content in your marketing message to your prospects, the more they will stick around and pick up the phone and book a consultation with you for your services.

Anything else is a waste of time and is not making money for your practice. Don't deviate from what works and say, "Oh jeez, this is too much work to do" or "I don't have the time to do it." Make the time; it is going to increase your bank account. If you don't have the time, you can hire me to do it for you. (Please see the back of the book.)

Website testing is often forgotten, but it is a safe technique to make sure your clients and your prospects are getting everything you offer. I can tell you horror stories of clients forgetting to test their site before going live, which cost them dearly. One company lost $175,000.00 in a month because they did not test how their site looked on Internet Explorer. They were getting leads, but no one could buy. Let this be a learning lesson.

What you want to do is test your site on all browsers to make sure your site is readable and all the content and pages are accessible. Test all the forms to make sure you are receiving requests from prospects. Also test your opt-in box. Put yourself on your own list to make sure you are receiving e-mails. Test all three major e-mail providers (Yahoo!, Gmail, and Hotmail). You would be surprised to find out your e-mail is going into spam and your prospects will not be able to read it.

The following list should take care of the things you need to test before you make your website live. You don't want to leave money on the table where your competitors can come and steal your clients.

Don't skip over this at all; it might be tedious, but it is 100 percent worth it. Don't rely on your website designer or webmaster to test everything; you too should go and test it before going live.

Website designers and webmasters tend to forget some of this or they assume everything is fine. Please use the following list:

1. Test your website for viewability in Internet Explorer, Chrome, FireFox, and Snow Leopard—all the major search browsers.
2. Test that all pages are linked properly back to each other so that if you go to one page you can get back to the page you came from or any other page by hitting the back button.
3. Test your "Contact Us" page form; make sure that you are receiving the messages sent by potential clients and/or clients.
4. Test your free offer for report opt-in box; join your own list and check your e-mail account on all the major e-mail providers (Gmail, Yahoo!, MSN, and AOl).
5. Test to be sure all buttons on your site and links work, especially on your site map and category pages.

Blood = life and so it is with leads. If you don't have a steady flow of leads coming into your practice, you will not grow and your practice will fail. Don't believe me? Try to go a month or two without getting any leads for your practice and tell me what your reaction is. I once had an argument with a client who stated he did not need any more leads. I said to him, "Oh really? Well, give it try for a month and call me and tell me what happens." Within two weeks I got a call back for me to help him start generating more leads in his business. You see, leads = sales and growth. You don't want to be at the end of the stick of getting what is yours.

Your website goal is to generate as many leads as possible and you do so by offering your potential clients something of value in exchange for their name, mailing address, phone number, and/or e-mail address. You want to build a list. There is a saying which states the money is in the list or the money is in the leads.

Once you have those leads, you can continue to market to them over and over again, selling your products and services as many times as you want. By the way, you never want to sell your client just once. There are three ways to grow your business: Get new customers, increase the frequency of when they purchase, and raise your prices. Does it not make sense for you to focus on all three to take your practice above and beyond where it is right now?

Now, you're probably wondering, "Great, Teran, what should I provide to potential clients to generate a constant source of leads?" You are on the right track for asking. Here's the thing: With so many changes occurring in the Orthodontic industry and because you are competing with the general practice Dentist who is taking weekend courses or a one- to three-month course to try to do what you do, you and I know your prospects have no clue if they are getting what they pay for. I am sure you have heard of or worked on horror stories of what Dentists have done only to have you fix the situation. Don't get me wrong—I'm not bashing Dentists, but if you don't let your ideal client know the difference between your capabilities and the capabilities of a general Dentist, you will be out of business.

You should provide a report or video on how to choose an Orthodontist, a report on how to get the right braces, and/or a free report on the difference between an Orthodontist and a Dentist. The report should provide important material which assists your ideal client in making the right decision—the only decision—choosing you as their trusted advisor to help them get the results they are seeking.

If you do this, I guarantee you will be ahead of 99 percent of the other Dentists or Orthodontists out there marketing their services because they are not doing it at all. You, on the other hand, will provide exactly what the client wants.

Value is what your ideal client is seeking in order to part with their money and give it to you. When you provide value up front, you have built trust and credibility. The main thing you also want to concentrate on is the quality of your lead. By using the ideal client profile we created, you will craft all your marketing messages and free reports around what your prospects want.

Once you have created the report, you want it to be visible on all your pages of your website. They will get the free report by providing their e-mail address, mailing address, and name to you. Remember, the report must provide the desires of your ideal prospect (WIFM) and a call to action to contact you for a consultation and/or additional services.

It does not make sense to provide the free report and not ask for the consultation to sell them. The quality of your lead is going to be much better than the price-shoppers you were getting before because you are connecting and engaging in the radio station WIFM.

Please see the following example of what an opt-in box form providing a free report would look like.

You want to make sure you have a series of e-mail or autoresponders set up introducing yourself and soft selling your ideal prospect about you and your services. We will get to how to do exactly that in Chapter 11.

The free report should be up front and available on every page on your site. You are giving your ideal client the opportunity to make the right decision. And the right decision is you!

CHAPTER 6

Shock and Awe

SURPRISE! EVERYONE LOVES A BIG SURPRISE. Even those who say they hate a surprise—deep down they love it. The shock and awe package will provide overwhelming proof and credibility to your prospects and your clients. It is a box filled with marketing material and your credentials that will put you ahead of your competitors and get your ideal client to say, "YES! I want you to be my doctor and trusted advisor."

The shock awe package was created based on the 2003 US war in Iraq. It was the big surprise the US military used when they started their attack campaign on the country.

This technique is used to sell high-priced items to your ideal prospects. The package—just like the war—will overwhelm your prospect with so much material and proof that it will get you the ultimate response you are looking for.

As the Orthodontist, you must use every single weapon that you have in your arsenal to provide exactly what the client wants. You want to leave them with no other choice but to go with you after they have looked at so much overpowering material.

If you remember, within a couple of days, the war was over and Iraq was defeated. The US military was victorious with their plan. With this technique you are going to do the same thing, but you will not be using military weapons to get the job done.

Credibility can be gained instantly by using the shock and awe technique against your ideal clients and referrals. When done properly, it completely shows your expertise and closes the sale.

None of your competition is using this technique to close the sale and convince the client to make their decision. Don't hesitate or think twice about using this strategy in your practice; just do it and send me a message thanking me for sharing it with you.

When your ideal client gets the shock and awe package, they are going to compare it to everything else. Fortunately there is nothing else to compare it with because your competitors have nothing available and they are not willing to go the extra mile to close a sale.

Now, you also want your staff to know about the shock and awe technique as well. This will let your staff know you are serious in building your practice and it will get them on board.

Your client consultation will no longer be a hit-or-miss opportunity and neither will requests or referrals when you use the shock and awe package. The technique should be used right after the consultation or during the referral process.

After speaking with your ideal client and following the TDCS System and the ideal client form, using this package will be the icing on the cake to seal the deal for you. The package will overwhelm your prospect with so much proof that they are making the right decision they will show it to others, including the decision maker if he or she is not present during the consultation.

When providing the shock and awe package, let the client know they should also get the decision maker to review the material in the package. Leave a little hand-written note as well if the ideal client is not the decision maker so that the husband, wife, or partner can see that you are going the extra mile and making sure they make the right decision.

You do not need to give the package to everyone who has a consultation with you. By following the TDCS and the ideal client system, you will know which prospects to provide your shock and awe package to.

Shock and awe is what you want to achieve with your ideal client. That being said, you should have an elegant box to hold all your marketing material and other goodies you will put in your shock and awe package for your prospect.

The typical cost for a high-end shock and awe package will run you around $100–120. Now, do not balk at the price—it is well worth the investment. To get a closing sale that is worth a minimum of $5,000, the rate of return is well over 500 percent.

There are companies out there that will create a custom box for you, or you can get one picked out or made by your staff. You can get the material for the box itself at such stores as Michael's Crafts, Bou Clair, and Home Sense, to name a few.

A nice, elegant box will stand out it, and it lets your potential client know you are a professional, well-organized practice. Remember, it is all about perception. If you do not come across as the right doctor to your ideal client, they will go down the street to the next doctor or, even worse, to a Dentist. You will be doing them a disservice by not providing the right perception so that they can make the right decision to choose you as their doctor.

Industry statistics will definitely highlight your expertise, along with a powerful sales letter, testimonials, and published articles, books, and white papers that you have written. The main thing you must have is a video testimonial of all your clients on a DVD for the client to watch. You should also have a powerful sales letter outlining the benefits that they are going to receive by choosing you as their doctor. You can also add treats, such a gift card to Starbucks, Best Buy, or Amazon. This will put you ahead of your competitors because no other Orthodontist is going to put together a package such as this for their potential clients.

The package should be packed with information that will overwhelm the prospect to the point that they say, "Damn! This doctor sure knows his stuff!" Also, put a tracking number on each package because you want to track the results to see which potential client was persuaded to go with your services. Tracking results is crucial because you might want to tweak the content that is in the shock and awe package.

Don't hesitate to put everything in the package about you and your credentials—including any interviews that you have done or awards you have won at school or in your community. It all counts toward getting your ideal prospect to say YES.

Measuring results in your marketing campaign leads to success in the growth of your practice. If you do not measure the results of your shock and awe package, you will not have a clear conclusion as to how effective your package is with your ideal prospect.

The first step when measuring results is to track every single package that you give out to your ideal prospects. You can do this by numbering the shock and awe box or labelling the box and taking note of whom you have given the box to.

This allows you to test the contents and the box itself quickly and effectively for higher conversions, meaning the clients are responding with a resounding YES for you to become their trusted advisor and doctor.

Later on, we will discuss on the process of following up with your ideal prospect after the shock and awe package is given to them. I am really surprised how often Orthodontists do not follow up with prospects who book consultations. This is free money on the table—all you have to do is ask for it.

Do not make the mistake of not asking for the sale. It is the only way to truly grow the business.

You might face this challenge: The ideal prospect may not accept the shock and awe package right on the spot. Not a problem! You can send it to them via mail or you can send a letter regarding the consultation that they had. It is a very quick and effective way to get the sale back.

Positioning your practice differently from your competitors makes you shine. You are building proof, credibility, and authority that you are the only go-to doctor in your area.

This differentiation is exactly what the shock and awe package will provide, making it possible for you to charge higher fees for each case that you take on. The majority of Orthodontists do not position themselves differently from their competitors. If everyone has the same price, how can you take a bigger chunk of the market? The only way is to make your practice and service different from everyone else's.

The shock and awe package provides so much overwhelming proof that you are the expert that your ideal client will have no other choice but to go with you. If you follow up correctly, getting the sale becomes so much easier because you are hitting the wants and the emotions of your ideal prospect.

Put the work into setting this up correctly and witness the huge benefits you will obtain. Don't just take my word for it. Try it out and let me know how well you do.

Remember too that charging higher fees means fewer clients to handle if you choose to do so. That means you have more time to spend with friends and family and to do the things that bring you joy and happiness.

Differentiation can greatly assist you when it comes to cornering your local market. The shock and awe package will be part of that and the element of surprise in your marketing will provide trust and proof to your ideal clients.

If someone else in the market starts to copy you with a shock and awe package as well, do not worry because they will not have the TDM two-step process to increase the opportunity of the sale once they have given the package out.

They will also not track the results or make necessary changes to increase profitability by providing the package. Rarely do practices track and measure the results of their advertising dollars. However, after reading this chapter, you know this is a big mistake.

You see, your ideal client is going to see you as the first person to offer the shock and awe package, so you are positioned as the first one out of the gate. In marketing, the person that does it first and does it correctly is rarely overtaken by their competitors when they continue to build upon their results.

Never be satisfied with the numbers that are coming in; you can always tweak your marketing to achieve higher conversions and sales. It is up to you—it is your business and future.

Engaging with your ideal client is a must because it builds credibility and it shows you care. Adding a video showing you welcoming your prospect and including testimonials and stories from your clients will build your prospects' trust and help them achieve a rapport with you as well.

Marketing has shifted with engagement devices that help show prospects and clients what is really going on in a business. Everyone loves to watch a video, but in your case make sure the video is no longer than six minutes and it is not boring. Your prospect does not want to watch a boring video or engage in a video which does not provide value. Your goal is to take your client from the stage of wondering if they are making the right decision to "Yes! This is the doctor I am going to go with."

Always test and track your videos as well. With YouTube analytics, you will be able to see exactly where your clients drop off from watching your video. This will tell you what you need to do to fix a particular spot and/or message in your video. Quickly reshoot the video and test it to see what results you get after you do.

Continue to test and redefine your message until you and your ideal prospect are on the same page. Selling will become so much easier—effortless even.

Tooting your own horn is not a bad thing when it comes to providing the shock and awe to your prospects and referrals. They are looking for your expertise, proof, and credibility that you can give them what they want.

The first thing you want to have in your shock and awe package is industry statistics and articles regarding procedures and information regarding the cheaper aspect of going with a Dentist versus going with you, the specialized Orthodontist. Also include any articles and white papers that you have written and published.

This is the time for you to shine and provide as much material as possible. Let's put it this way: Your shock and awe package should make a large *thud* when you drop it on the ground. It should contain all the elements your prospect wants to see so that they can make the decision to choose you.

The articles and white papers written and published by you show that your peers consider you important as well. If you have not written any articles or white papers, now is the time to do so. This can make a significant difference in your prospect's decision making process and how your practice is perceived in the public.

It won't take you more than an hour to write an article on a particular subject. Write the article on the subject your prospect continues to talk to you about during the consultation process.

Don't worry—you don't have to be an excellent writer; you just need to show you care and you are on their side.

You see, a sales letter technique I have developed is the next step to reaffirm to your ideal prospect they are making the right decision. This two-step method should occur two days after your ideal client has received the shock and awe package after their consultation.

The letter should outline that you are sending the letter because you have not heard from them as of yet and you're a bit surprised they have not moved forward. It should contain all the benefits and the desires the ideal prospect is looking for, which you know because you conducted the ideal client profile and the closing system we discussed in Chapter 2.

After three days, you send the letter via Federal Express; it will get their attention and show you truly care. The reason you want to send it via Federal Express is that 98 percent of the time when we receive a FedEx envelope, we open it.

If three days have passed since you sent the letter and you have not gotten a response, make a call to follow up to ensure they did receive the letter and ask if they have any additional questions and/or concerns.

After seven days, follow up with a postcard reminding them

of the benefits they will obtain by going with you and that they are missing out on the benefits.

Think you're done after this? You're not. You need to repeat the process two to three more times. Studies have shown it will take a minimum of asking fourteen times to get the potential ideal client to say YES.

Do not just send the one sales letter and fail to follow up with the phone and postcard. It won't work if you are not committed to the process. This is a case which could be easily worth a minimum of $5,000 or more for a small investment of $30–50.

Systems are great because they help build and structure a successful practice. The system I am going to discuss with you will assist you in building your practice on a daily basis. Remember, the goal of your practice is to continue to drive in as many leads (i.e., ideal prospects) as possible on a daily basis.

Another way to use the shock and awe package to your advantage is to allow your employees to share the shock and awe package with any of their friends and family members who are in need of your services.

You should then reward your employees for each referral they bring in. You have to look at the big picture here. What is the lifetime value of each client that comes into your practice? You must know these numbers or it is going to be very hard for you to grow your practice.

You can provide monetary rewards, gift cards, baskets, movie tickets, dinners, or a day off. All these things add up and build a rapport with your staff. They will be more than willing to go the extra mile for you because they know that you care about them and it is not about just the money alone.

Remember to track and measure the results from allowing employees to provide the shock and awe package to referrals or to anyone they come into contact with that asks. Always ask for their feedback as well; they are the first line of contact with your ideal prospect. Their input will be valuable.

Positioning is the ultimate tool to get the sale, and when it's done right, it oozes trust and expertise to your ideal prospect. Credibility building is done just by providing the information to your prospect so that they can evaluate it for themselves. It tells them they have made the right decision to just sit down have a consultation.

In an economy which has slowed down, trust and credibility are essential in order for any business owner to grow and maintain their business. In the Orthodontic industry, it is even more important because you are going up against not only other Orthodontists, but also general practice Dentists who are stealing your clients. Credibility, trust, and being totally different—the shock and awe package truly does achieve these things.

Your governing body is not going to do anything about helping you build your practice and neither are the general practice Dentists a majority of you have been so heavily relying upon for referrals. Now it is your turn to move in and get what is yours.

Growth in your practice is not something you should put off any longer. It should be high on your priority list. If you refuse to use the shock and awe package, I can guarantee you will not succeed the way you should.

The shock and awe package builds:

1. Trust
2. Credibility
3. Authority
4. Differentiation
5. Positioning
6. YES
7. Which leads to the CASH

Do not forget these seven things. Each time you refuse to use the shock and awe system, remind yourself of the seven keys of successfully growing a $2+ million-dollar practice. It can be done, but it is all up to you. This book has provided you with the tools to get started. Don't let the information sit on your shelf and collect dust. Put it to use and witness the cash pouring into your bank account.

Providing fun, surprises, and happiness are excellent ways to get a YES from your ideal prospect. This is what you will witness once you give the shock and awe package to your prospects and referrals.

They will be astonished by the amount of information you provide to assist them with their decision. They will be impressed, especially with your video testimonials and stories from your clients, along with articles, books, and white papers that you have written.

It provides the fuel to justify their decision to choose you as their doctor. Think back to when you purchased a car you wanted. What persuaded you to buy the car from the salesperson and their location? This is the approach you must take when you are speaking and working with your prospect.

The justification of the purchase is no longer an issue. Your prospect will see it as an excellent investment to obtain what they want. You are providing value to them, which the other doctors could not provide.

CHAPTER 7

Google Local+ for Your Business: Get Your Bank Account to Shout for Joy

LOCAL SEARCH COMBINED with social search gives you the best of both worlds. As a business owner, you can now have a single page that outlines your services and provides information in great detail and pictures of your staff and location with a social network. Google+ does just that. It uses the local search elements (what you see and type in Google each day for product and services) and combines that with its own social networking site, Google+. Here you can have your clients join as a network of friends and provide feedback about you and your services with reviews and testimonials about your practice.

Your Google Local+ website will show up in the search engine results for local searches on keywords related to Orthodontists in your specific area. The beauty of using Google Local+ for business is that Google is now allowing more local results in the search engine, so your prospects and clients can find you a lot easier than with the typical Yellow Pages where you constantly have to do battle with all the other Orthodontists listed.

There a total of seven results that show up in the local search results. Your goal is to make sure you are well optimized to show up in the premium spots to get high-paying prospects searching for your services. To get started, sign up and claim your Google Places account first at *www.google.com/placesforbusiness.*

Example: Google+ page in search:

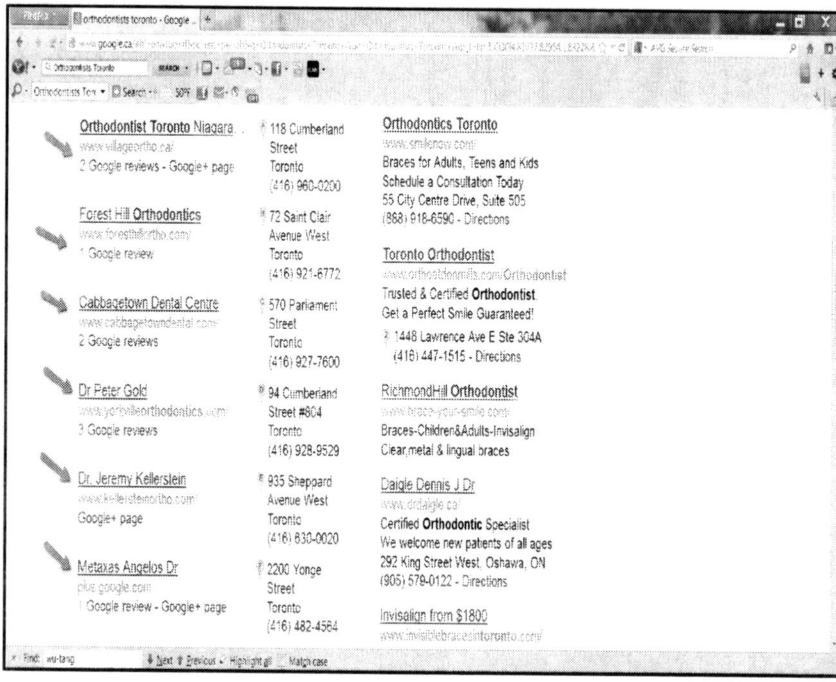

Combining both the Google Local search and the Google+ social network can provide huge success for you if set up correctly. The best thing you should do once you have your account is to invite all your clients to your Google+ listing page. We are going to talk about that a lot more in greater detail.

When your clients and ideal prospects see the results, reviews, and testimonials, your phone will be ringing off the hook. Not many Orthodontists have a Google Local+ business page, which is free. Your goal is to take advantage of the free offer and build and track the results that you get by using this new and great service.

As you know, Google owns over 70 percent of the world's search results, which means this is where all your clients are going to search for you. If you are not showing up in the results, your clients can't find you at all.

Combining the social search results so that others in your group can find you is one of the best advantages you can use. It is another form of word-of-mouth advertising that can quickly increase your lead flow and spread throughout the social network.

Do not discount Google Local+ for your business. It is free; the only work you have to do is optimize it to get the results you want to dramatically increase the leads coming into your practice.

A single page listing your services with a brief summary of your product, reviews, pictures, and testimonials is controlled by Google, but it is your listing page. Your website is totally different; there you own the domain name and you control the content and what and how much you want to say and place on your website.

Your website itself should be more than one page, and it should provide valuable content that helps your potential ideal client make their decision to go with you and you alone.

However, you are limited as to how much information you can place on your listing page with Google. It is not as graphic as your website and it contains less information, which means there are fewer opportunities to capture leads as freely as your own website.

However, it is still powerful to have the listing page because it greatly complements your website, making it possible for you to get double results. This means your website is also ranked on the first page of Google along with your Google Local+ listing. This builds credibility and authority in the eyes of potential clients searching and looking for you online.

Your website has a policy page, testimonial page, "About Us" page, "Contact Us" page; braces, Invisalign, and any other products that you offer can have their own page.

Search engines continue to change their algorithms constantly and it is becoming a lot harder to use SEO than it used to be. This is one of the main reasons it is important for your practice to have a Google Local listing as well. It helps bring reviews and results for your practice right up front for your prospects to see for themselves.

As things change, Google continues to pour millions of dollars into the expansion of Google Local+ for business. They know that a big chunk of searches taking place are for businesses that are local to the searcher's area.

They want to provide high-quality information to everyone that searches, and if they ignore it, that makes them irrelevant. If you are not there, it is no loss to them—your competitor will gladly take your spot and your clients as well.

You should also know that Yahoo! and MSN also have a free local listing service that you can use to your advantage as well. Your goal is to get as many avenues of leads as you can generate for your practice. Do not leave it up to your client to find you; make sure you are playing your part—that you are seen and known as the go-to doctor in your area.

Too many times I hear Orthodontists state they don't have the time. Well, if you don't have the time, I can tell you that you will be out of business shortly. Do the things that make you money and that make your clients happy; that is what you should be focusing on.

Ideal prospects, information seekers, and clients are the groups that use Google Local+. Your goal is to make sure you hit each client with the right information. Do not ignore the three groups. Not everyone will buy immediately; however, some will want more information. This is why I stated that you must make your marketing material valuable. It must provide value all the way through, and that goes for the information seeker too who is looking for information in order to decide who they are going to pick up the phone and call.

The ideal client knows what they want, but they need backup information from clients that are happy with their results. Testimonials and reviews from past clients weigh heavily on whether or not they make the decision to go with you as their doctor.

The potential client does not know you, but they know what they want. They have not heard of you before, so they will gather as much information as possible to learn more. This individual should not be ignored; sometimes it will take you three to four contacts in order to land the sale. Use a lead capture technique such as providing a free report or video to help them gather the information they need to move up the buying cycle and get the YES.

Confirming and claiming your Google Places page first www.**google**.com/**places**forbusiness and then launching into your Local+ page is quite easy to do and it is free. The first thing you should do is go to http://www.google.com/+/business/. From there you can sign up with a Gmail account to get started. If you do not have a Gmail account yet, you should get one for your business and name it the name of your business. It will identify you with your ideal prospects and clients.

Once you sign up with your Google Places page, you will be asked a series of questions for verification to get started on building your page out.

Once you have claimed your listing, the next step is to confirm that you are an actual business and the information that you provided to Google is truthful. If you own more than one business, you can set up a separate business for each location. Google will confirm this by sending a letter or a postcard to your business address to confirm the location and the request to set up the local listing page. You will get a confirmation number that you will then enter to confirm your listing, which now gives you the opportunity to make changes to your listing and to start providing relevant information so that your prospects and ideal clients can see it.

From there you can start to add your clients that have a Google+ account to join you on your new Google Local+ page.

Setting up your Google Local+ business page starts off with you entering the business information of your practice. Please see the following figure:

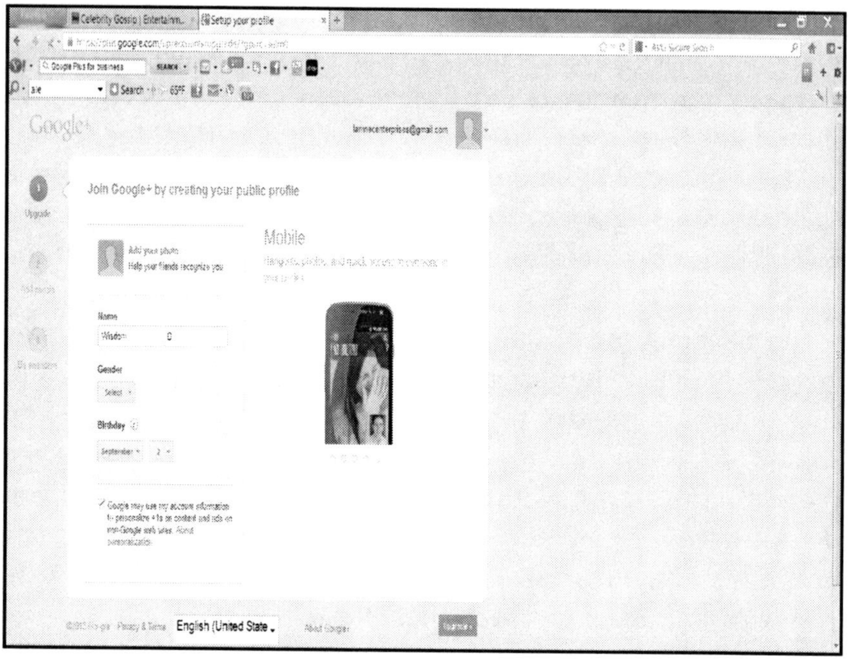

One of the most important things that you must remember when using a Google Local+ listing page is that your information must be consistent. Google will verify the information across other sites and directories to make sure that (1) You are a real business; and (2) Your business name matches up with all the other directories and listing on the Internet, such as the Yellow Pages, local directories, Yahoo!, Bing, Yelp, Superpages, etc.

If the information that you provide is incorrect or mistyped, you will jeopardize your rankings in Google because it is not consistent across the entire network. Please make sure you have spelled the business name correctly, and that the address, location, telephone number, and hours of operation are also correct.

Next, you want to gather as many pictures as possible of your practice, your happy clients, and your staff and you. Google will allow you to place pictures on your listing page for your prospects and ideal clients to view.

The third thing that you want to do immediately is to get and add reviews to your listing. Reviews are essential when it comes to rankings in the search engine. They also help your prospects make the right choice—you and not your competitor. Start asking your clients to place reviews on your listing page to help you optimize your listing.

Step 2

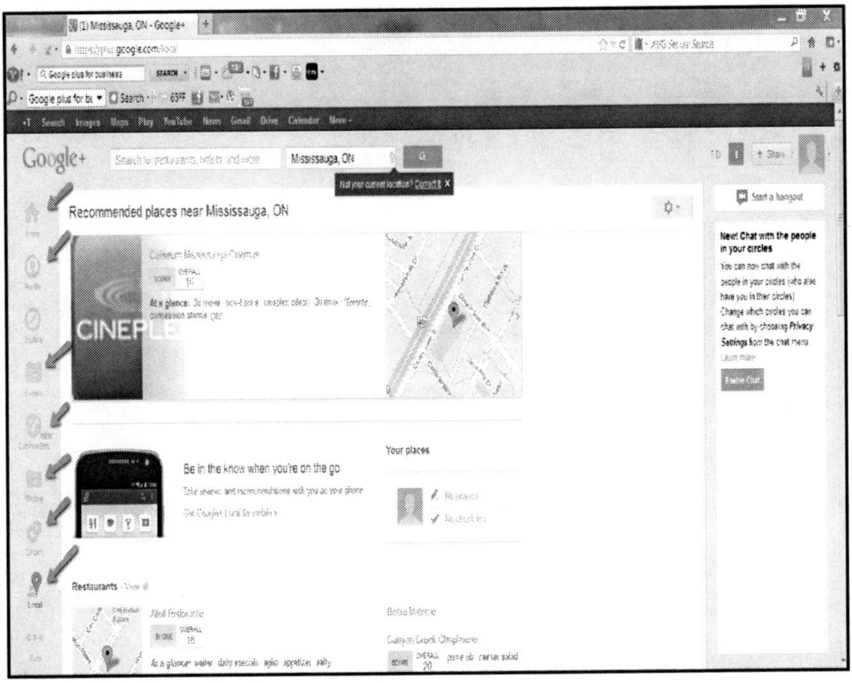

STEP 3

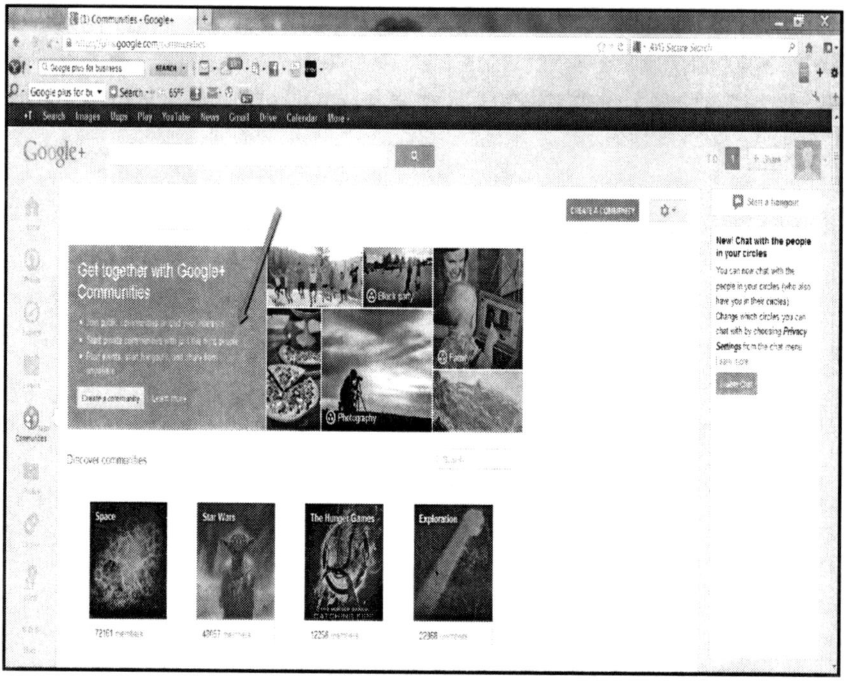

STEP 4

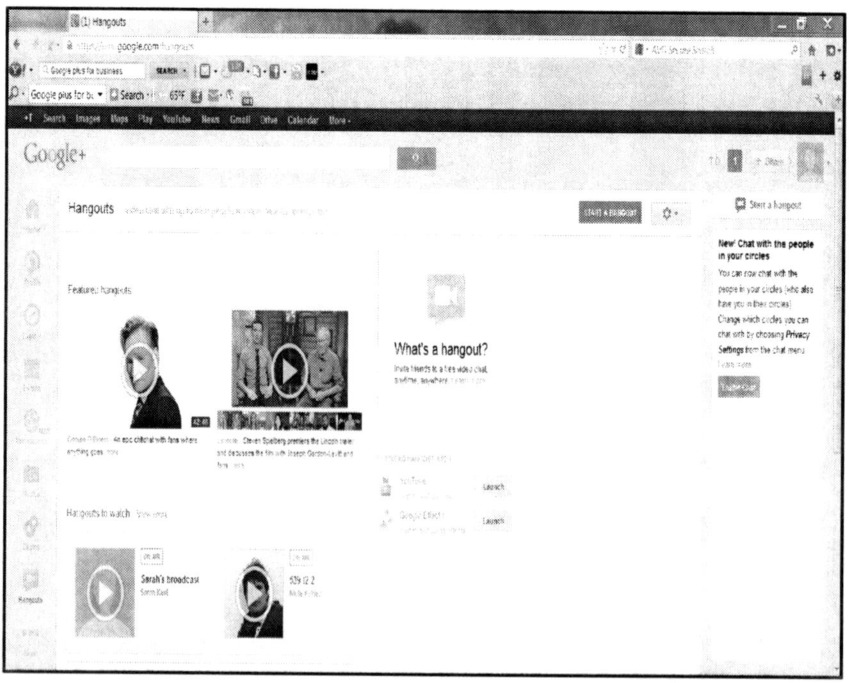

Step 5

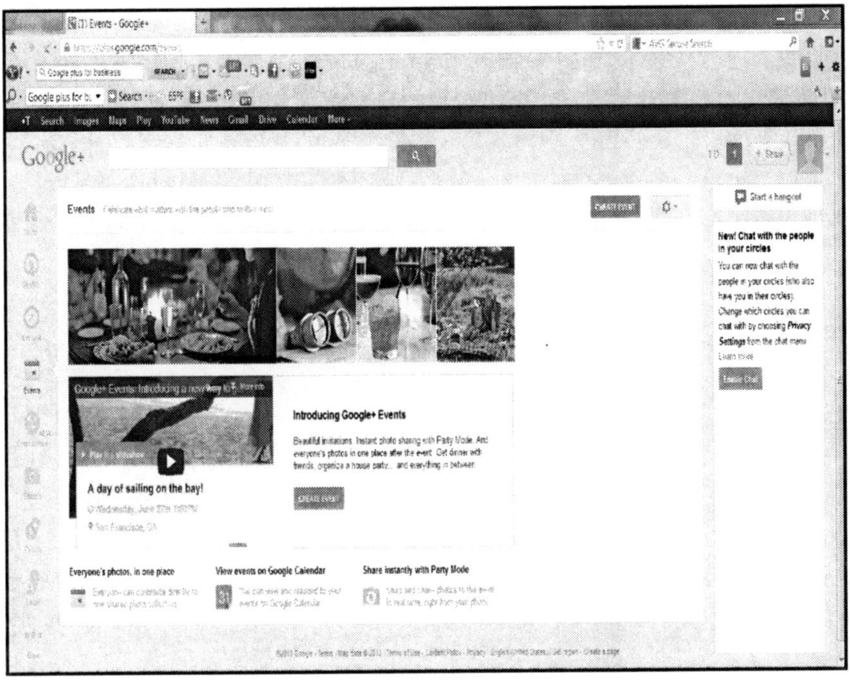

Information about your practice is crucial to the success of your Google+ listing page. Mainly, you should have as much data about your practice on your page as possible. You want the information to come across as valuable not bland and in a way that shows the benefits that your ideal prospect will achieve by picking up the phone and calling you. Take a look at your competitors' listing pages; I guarantee they will not have anything like what you are going to put together.

The next step is to make sure your reviews are in place for your listing page. The more positive reviews you have on your listing page, the better. Google relies heavily on reviews to adjust your rankings and move you up in search results. It is part of the optimization process for the success of your listing page. You should let your clients post their reviews praising your practice and the end result they achieved. You should have a review for each service that you conduct at your practice. Again, when you look at your competitors' websites, they will not have any of this set up.

Third, your pictures should be crisp, clean, and provide a clear image of what your potential client should expect and experience when they come to your practice. You want your prospects to feel welcome and that you are a trusted source as their doctor. You must come across as likeable and caring.

Gaming the system is a big no-no with Google and with Google Local+. Providing the wrong info will automatically penalize your listing in the search engine.

Over the past year, Google has come down extremely hard on those that use dirty tricks and tactics in order to get their listing and website in the number one position. Many Orthodontists are promised their site and listing will be number one, but they have no idea what exactly was done to do so. The technique used by those that call themselves SEO experts is "black hat." Black hat optimization will leave you out in the cold if Google catches you. In 2012, Google penalized the huge retailer JC Penny for using deceptive practices to gain results in the search engine. If you use this technique in Google for your website or listing, you may be delisted, which will mean you just lost a massive load of leads for your practice.

So, to recap, do not try to game the system by stuffing your content full of keywords or providing irrelevant and/or wrong information. Always do things on the up-and-up and Google will reward you. You will notice a significant increase in calls and new client consultations when you set up your account properly.

Gaining your ideal prospect's attention starts with knowing what they want and providing valuable information right up front.

The three main things that your ideal client wants to see once they hit your local listing page are:

1. USP = what makes you different from everyone else. I can tell you right now 98 percent of people in the Orthodontic Industry do not have this right up front for potential clients to see on their listing page. When you apply this to your listing page, you will be way ahead of the competition.
2. The second thing your prospect would like to see is reviews. They want to know what others are saying about you and your practice. Influence from others online weighs heavily toward getting your phone to ring as the prospect calls to book their consultation. Get as many of the right reviews front and center as you can to build overwhelming proof.
3. Next, you want to make sure that you have as many pictures as possible that showcase you, your staff, and how happy and successful your clients are with the results they have achieved because of you.
4. They also want to see the right information, a map and location, and a telephone number for your practice. The more information you provide, the better for your listing and your ideal prospect.

Credibility + Trust = Success and Cash. Google loves reviews and so does your ideal client. The more reviews you have, the better overall presence you will achieve in Google and Google +. Always strive to obtain client reviews. Here are few things that you should get your clients to do to put you ahead of your competitors:

1. Get a written review from every patient that you have serviced over the years. Reward them for providing the review because this is going to be huge surge of cash for your practice.
2. Next, you want to get every single client to provide a video testimonial of their story that tells how happy they are after using you as their doctor and trusted source.
3. Third, you want to have a binder full of letters and pictures

of your happy clients. This binder should be presented to the prospects to read while they are waiting for their consultation. You can include this in your shock and awe package as well.

4. Let your clients join and friend you in Google+. Let them add their review to their listing and have them set up a map to your practice as well.
5. Have them post their story of your practice in their Google+ network. This will help increase in your rankings in Google and Google+. Combine these techniques and your practice will become unstoppable in your area.

Optimization is one of the keys to success using Google+ for your business listing page. A well-optimized listing can bring you thousands of prospects every month. Providing the right information and reviews can dramatically increase your rankings.

To begin the optimization process, look at your competitors and take notes on what exactly is missing from their listing page. Then, look at their page and see if they have a USP front and center.

The third thing to look for is a well-suited link campaign for their listing page. Building a link campaign directly to your listing page means higher rankings. The techniques that I have shared with you will not only bring you higher rankings, but more cash into your practice.

You see, the biggest mistake many Orthodontists make is that they think they need to be number one in the search engine. What they should really look at is whether they are providing valuable information to the prospect, are they connecting with the prospect, and are they providing what the prospect wants? If not, it makes no sense to strive to be number one because no one is going to pick up the phone and call you for a consultation because you have not connected with them. You have not given them a reason to trust you, and you are not different from everyone else that has a Google+ listing page. If you combine that with being number one, though, you are definitely on the right track.

Your goal is to outshine your competitors and become the only choice for the trusted doctor to every client that steps into the office. You are offering what they want and desire. Remember, it is all about the end results. If you provide a high-quality end result, your practice will be making more cash than it can handle—guaranteed. Either you or your competitors are going to take the money. Make sure that it is YOU!

A successful Google Local+ page should have your practice information on a single page, along with maps, reviews, and a USP that stands out. It should provide valuable information that puts you and your practice above the rest. Please take a look at some Google Local+ pages that have gone above and beyond in different industries that you can model from.

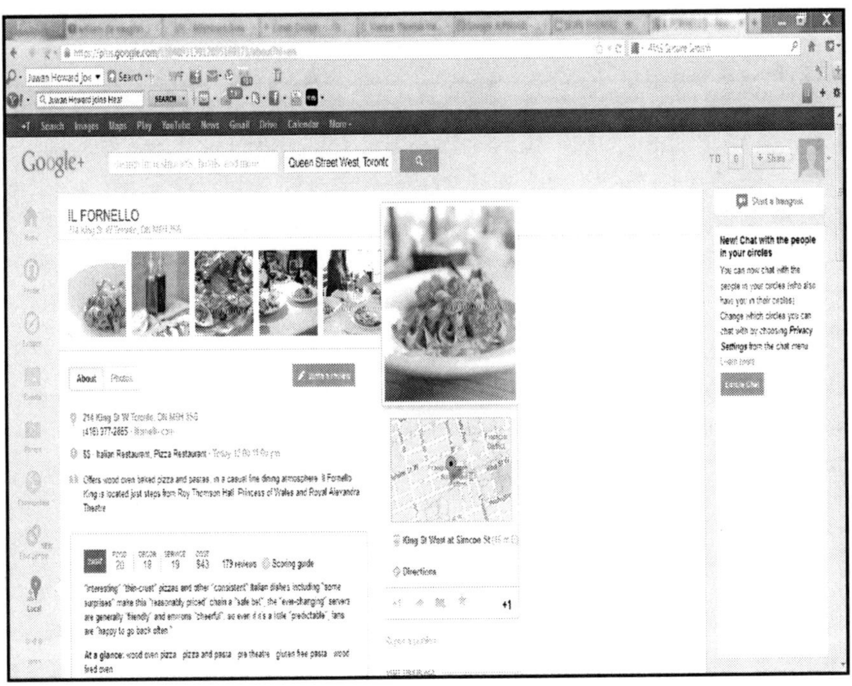

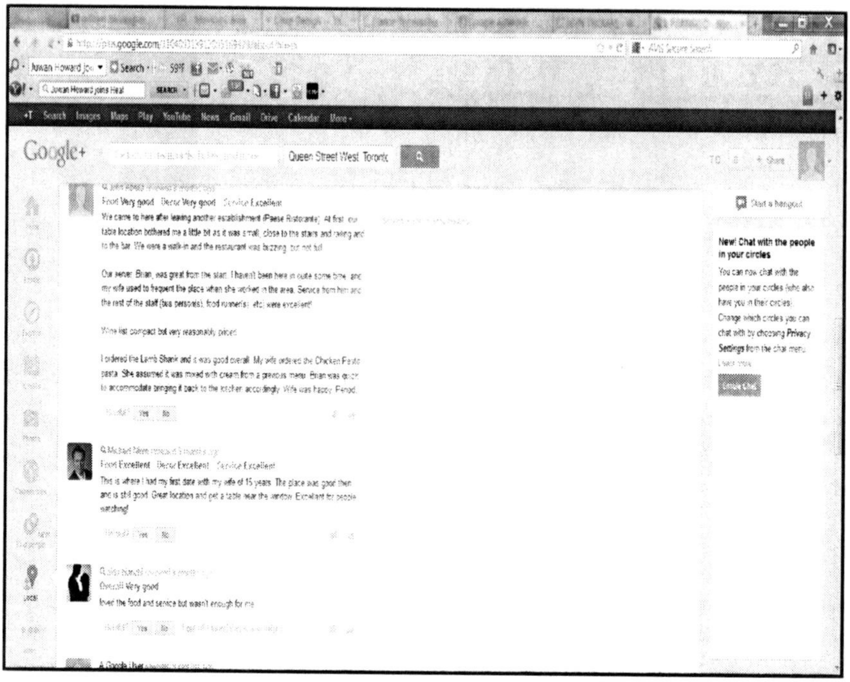

Do not copy what they have; model what they are showing. Your goal is to be the king in your area; do not strive for second place. When you do this, you will no longer need to depend on a general practice Dentist for referrals. Do you want to continue to leave the future of your business in the hands of another person, dependent on them to send you clients? I hope you answered no to that. If you're thinking, "Yes, Teran, I understand, but my guy will not turn his back on me. He is not interested in providing braces or orthodontic care to his patients." My statement to you is—it is only a matter of time. Stop relying on him and start building your own flow of leads for your practice.

It will leave you stress-free and headache-free, no longer thinking, "Man, what am I going to do this month?" and "I don't have enough patients. My overhead is high and I need to pay my staff."

Don't let this be you.

CHAPTER 8

PPC: The Secret on Using Google AdWords Pay-Per-Click

Targeting your ideal client can be as easy as 1-2-3 by using Google AdWords. Google AdWords are what you might call tiny classified ads that show up on the right-hand side or at the top of the search engine results page when you are searching for a product, service, and/or additional information.

The beauty of using Google AdWords is that your target market is using the search engine as well, searching for your product and/or service. You as the Orthodontist and advertiser can now write ads to introduce yourself or to capture your ideal prospects' attention. The AdWords program charges you only when someone clicks on your ad. Otherwise, you do not pay for your ad to be shown. It was an ingenious idea that started back in 2001. Many searchers were looking for information and they wanted it right now. Google noticed they could profit by providing relevant information to its users and decided to start the program.

If put to use correctly, it can dominate your competition because the majority of your competition has no clue how to use the advertising platform successfully. One of my clients is using the program to generate over 175 new leads each month. It is something that you should look at now if you want to grow your practice. Before we dive into using Google AdWords in more detail, take the time to familiarize yourself with what the ads look like. See figure 1.1 below or you can go directly to Google and type in Orthodontist ___ (city name) to see the results and the ads on the right and at the top of the page. Take notice of the ads.

EXAMPLE:

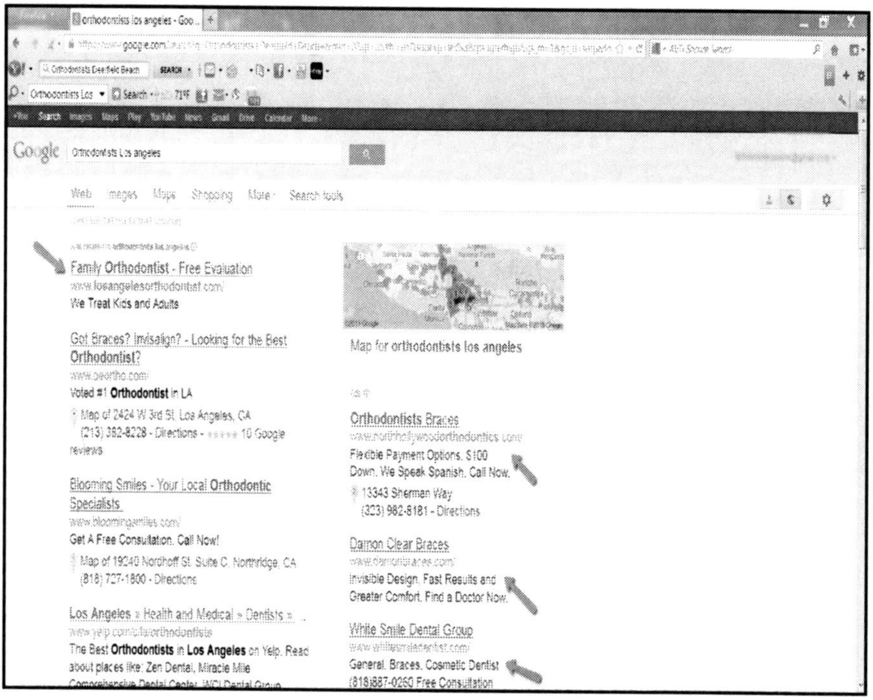

Paying for your advertising with the right message at the right time—but only when someone clicks on the ad—is a huge advantage to you and your practice. Google AdWords provides not only this advantage but many others as well.

For example, as an advertiser, you can decide what time and day to show your ads. If you know that your ideal client searches for you at a specific time of the day and on a certain day, you can show your ad to that ideal client or prospect when you want. The other advantage is that you can target clients based on geographical location. I have worked with so many Orthodontists who have been targeting the wrong client at the wrong location. You can set up your targeting to focus on zip codes/postal codes, cities, a surrounding area or a radius around a location. It is up to you. However, the best way to use Google AdWords to your advantage is to implement the client profile we created in Chapter 1. None of your competitors are using this technique to their advantage—I guarantee it—and when you do, you should see a flood of new leads calling and booking consultation visits to your practice.

The other advantage of using Google AdWords is that you can talk directly to your ideal client with the right message. By using the ideal client technique, we can craft the right ad that speaks to their wants and desires. Many ads, as you will see, do not focus on what the client wants; they are very generic and do not get the results that the Orthodontist is after. Focus on the client first.

Consumers search on Google AdWords every day. Over a billion searches are conducted on Google. The majority of the searches that are conducted are focused on local products and/or services that the consumer is looking for. My question to you is does it not make sense to be where your target market is searching, where they hang out and gather information to spend money? I hope you said yes, it does make sense. The Google AdWords program is a platform that allows advertisers to target those consumers who are interested in their products and services at the right time with the right message.

Let's give an example: Say that a mother is searching online for an Orthodontist in her city. Let's use Los Angeles. What show up are ads that state what she is looking for. An advertiser's job is to attract your ideal client to click your ad so that they can find out more information to make their decision.

Google will show that ad to the consumer only if they type in the word that you wish to advertise on. We will get into that later on—how to set up a profitable campaign that will drive more leads to your practice than you can handle.

Your goal as an advertiser is to please Google by providing relevant information to the consumer who is looking for your product and/or service. In addition, you have to make sure that you please your ideal client and provide the right information at the right time that will get them to pick up the phone and call you.

Targeting your ideal client results in success in any marketing campaign. What we are going to focus on is using the ideal client profile we created to target our potential client that is looking for us online. The research we conducted gives us a complete breakdown of what our client wants. So now we need to think like our ideal client.

Have you ever decided to search for a product or service online? How did you go about doing so? How did you come up with the word or phrases that drove you to look for the product or service? That is what we have to do; we are going to think like our target market.

What would your ideal prospect or client type if they were looking to fix their crooked teeth? Would they type "fix crooked teeth"? It is possible that the client used that phrase to purchase your service. That is what you are looking for when designing your campaign.

The next step is to sit down with a blank piece of paper and use the TLMC (Think Like My Client) technique. You know your industry and you know what your clients are looking for. I want you to make a complete list of keyword phrases that your potential client would use to search for you (besides the name of your practice).

Hint: What are some of the products and/or services you offer? Start there. Also, make it a practice to ask potential clients how they found your services. Take note of their responses; this gives you a huge advantage over everyone else.

Signing up for a Google AdWords account is quite easy. All you need is your credit card and your website. Please see figure 1.2 below.

Once you click the sign-up button, Google will ask you if you would like to register using your Gmail account. If you do not have a Gmail account, you can use your own e-mail from your website. Example: John@OrthodontistsinLosAnges.com so your e-mail would be your name@yourdomainname.com.

Then it will prompt you to start your campaign. Skip that for now; it is not necessary to build out your campaign yet. The next step is to enter your credit card information. This is straightforward; please see the figure below.

To get a complete step-by-step guide on how to set up your AdWords account and campaign, please go to www.Wealthy-Orthodontist.com/Adwords-Videos. I will give you the step-by-step process for setting up your AdWords account to drive leads to your website.

Now that that step is completed, we are going to move to the exciting part, setting up your campaigns to start flooding your office with new prospects looking for your services. Get ready to take your practice and your income to the next level.

Step 1 – Setting up your first campaign:

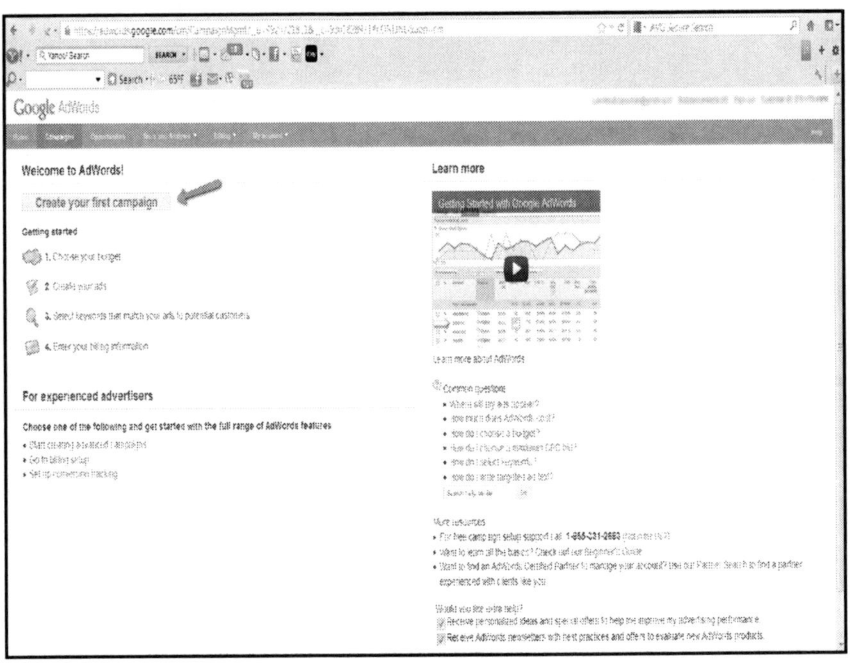

Step 2

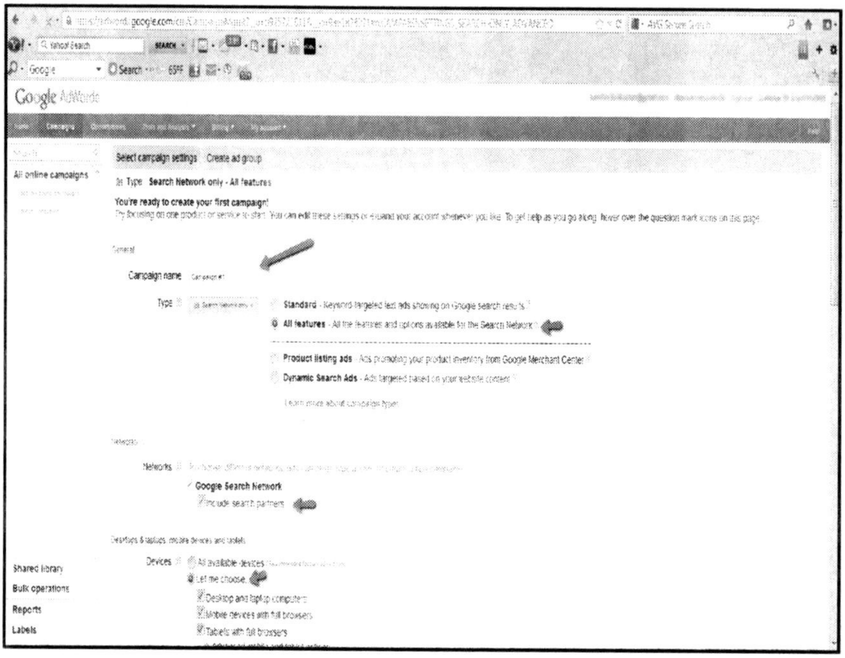

Step 3

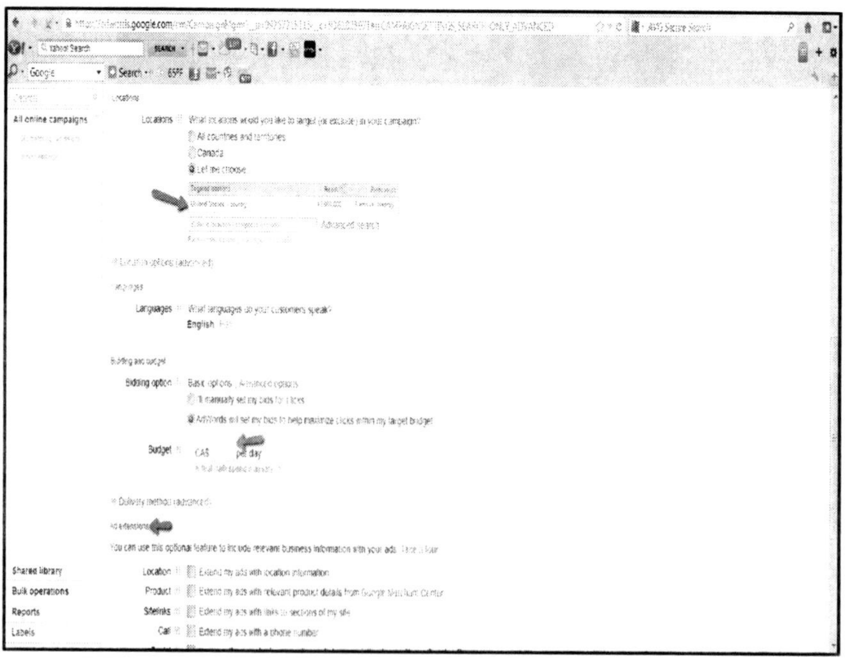

Step 4

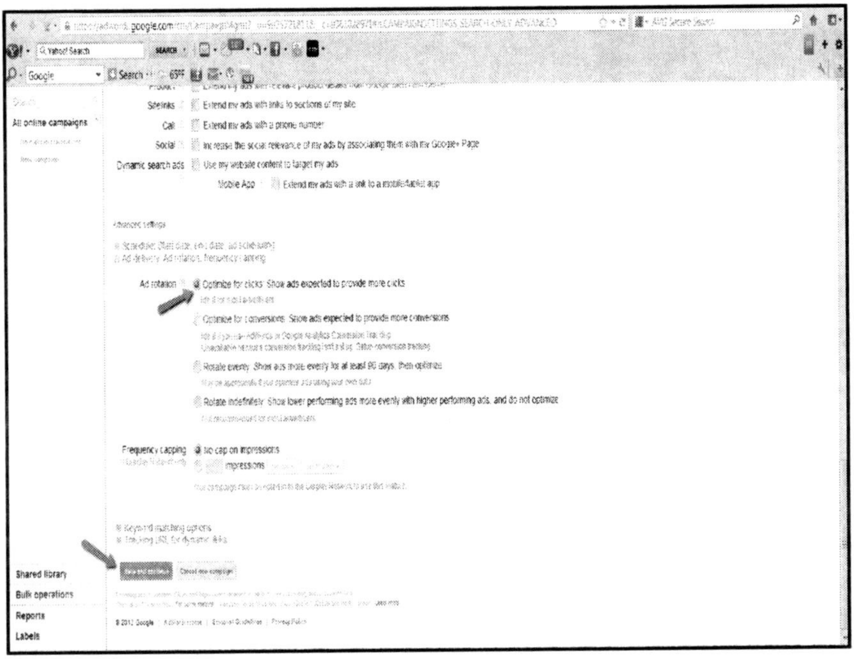
Sitelinks
Extend my ads with links to sections of my site
Call
Extend my ads with a phone number
Social
Increase the social relevance of my ads by associating them with my Google+ Page
Dynamic search ads
Use my website content to target my ads
Mobile App
Extend my ads with a link to a mobile/tablet app
Ad rotation
Optimize for clicks: Show ads expected to provide more clicks
Optimize for conversions: Show ads expected to provide more conversions
Rotate evenly: Show ads more evenly for at least 90 days, then optimize
Rotate indefinitely: Show lower performing ads more evenly with higher performing ads, and do not optimize
Frequency capping
No cap on impressions
impressions
Shared library
Bulk operations
Reports
Labels

Step 5

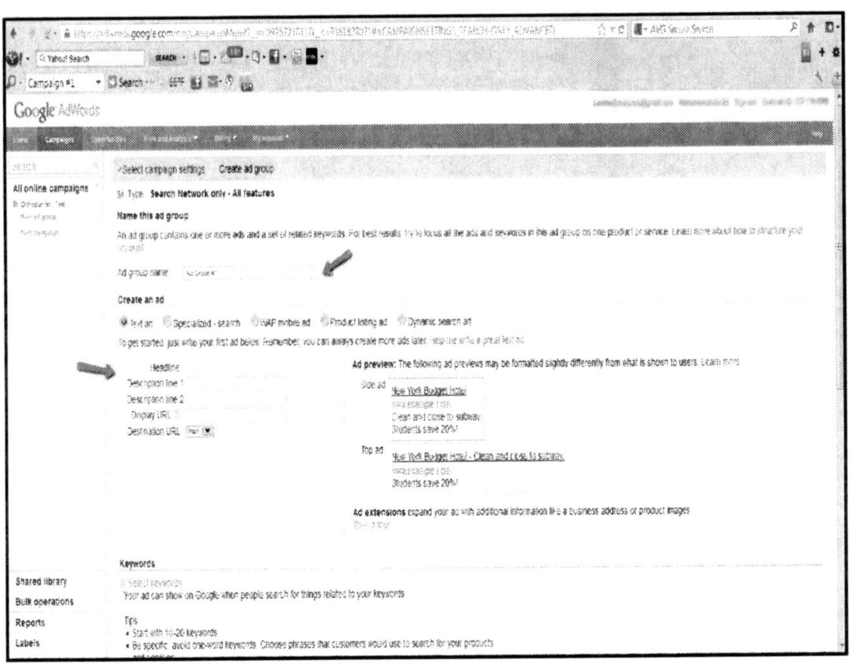
Select campaign settings
Create ad group
Type: Search Network only - All features
Name this ad group
Ad group name
Create an ad
Text ad
Specialized - search
WAP mobile ad
Product listing ad
Dynamic search ad
Headline
Description line 1
Description line 2
Display URL
Destination URL
Ad preview: The following ad previews may be formatted slightly differently from what is shown to users.
Side ad
New York Budget Hotel
Clean and close to subway.
Students save 20%!
Top ad
New York Budget Hotel - Clean and close to subway.
Students save 20%!
Ad extensions expand your ad with additional information like a business address or product images
Keywords
Your ad can show on Google when people search for things related to your keywords
Tips
• Start with 10-20 keywords
• Be specific: avoid one-word keywords. Choose phrases that customers would use to search for your products
All online campaigns
Shared library
Bulk operations
Reports
Labels

Step 6

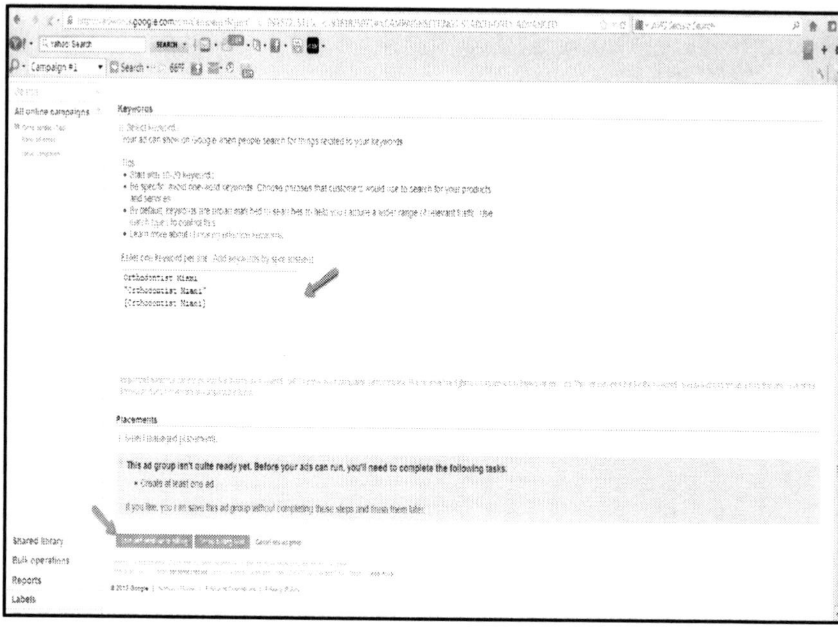
Keywords
Orthodontist Miami
"Orthodontist Miami"
[Orthodontist Miami]
Placements
This ad group isn't quite ready yet. Before your ads can run, you'll need to complete the following tasks.
Shared library
Bulk operations
Reports
Labels

Step 7

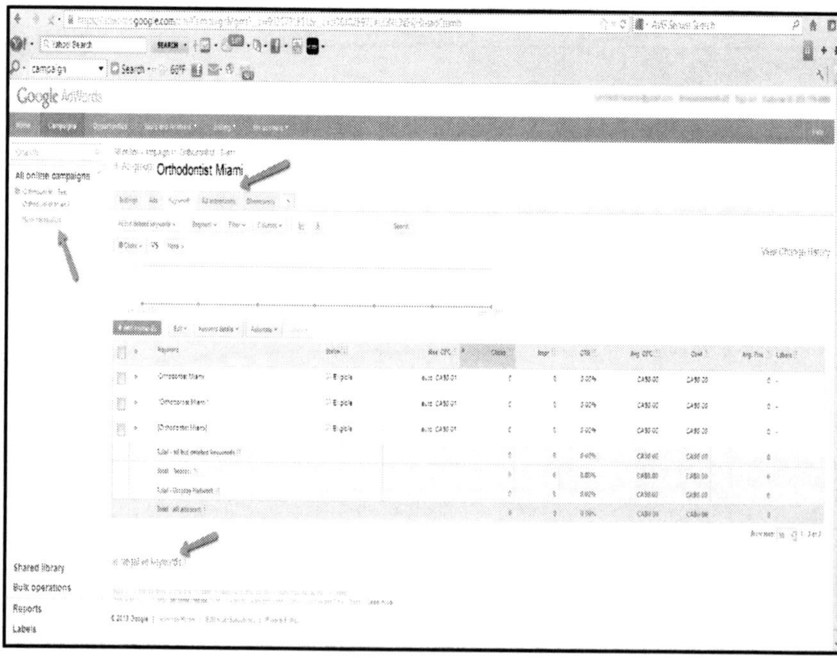
Google AdWords
All online campaigns
Orthodontist Miami
Shared library
Bulk operations
Reports
Labels

Step 8

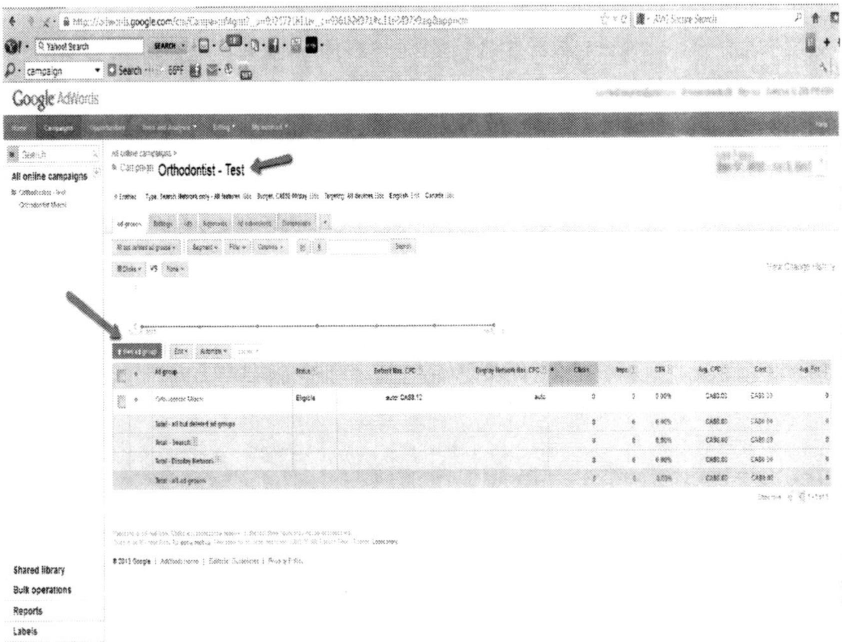

Structure, Structure, and Structure. You will hear me say that often in this chapter. The success of your AdWords campaign is going to depend on structure as well as your ad groups and ads that you write to get your ideal client to pick up the phone and call your practice.

Google loves structure. Structure to Google means success, and it also tells Google you know what you're doing. It is going to ask you to start a campaign. It is important that you name and start your campaign correctly. If your main focus is going to be on the keyword phrases that contain "braces," you are going to name your campaign "braces." That will tell you that all your ad groups and keywords will be built around the word "braces."

Don't worry—we are going to go into detail on what an ad group and keyword phrase is all about.

Campaigns help drive the leads to your website, and they

also let you develop the right account structure when it is time to get things going. Campaigns can be of various sizes; they can big, holding more than 100 ad groups, or they can be small, holding just one ad group.

The size will be up to you. I am going to show you how to set things up so that you can start getting new leads on day one without relying on a Dentist for referrals—guaranteed.

Keywords are the lifeline to your AdWords campaign. Along with the ads and structure, your keywords will make your phones ring with new patients wanting your services. Have you ever watch *Jeopardy*? It is the game show where they give you the answer and you have to provide the question. In the game there is a board, and at the top of the board, you have the categories (which we would call the campaign topics) of all the questions. Then, inside the categories you have the questions (which would be the ad groups).

This is how the ad groups are set up in Google AdWords. You have the campaign that lists the theme of the ad groups within the campaign itself, and then you have the ad groups, which would be the keywords that are in the campaign, along with all the ads for each ad group.

We will discuss further in the book how to structure your account correctly so that you please Google and get the results that you are after. The ad group is what Google looks at on a constant basis; they check to see that your ad group, keywords, and ad copy match the landing page or the website that you directed your client and/or ideal prospect to.

If things do not match up or if there is a problem, you will see it in various places.

Please look at the next image for what an ad group and campaign look like as well as various problems that may arise when you do not set up your account correctly.

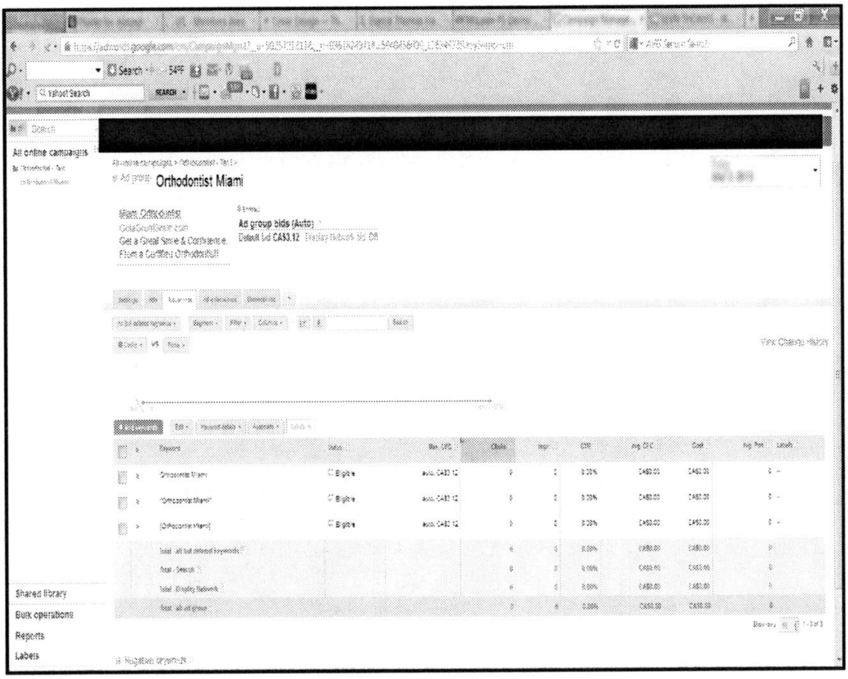

Not using the correct format for setting up your ad group will penalize you in two ways. One is that you will pay more to advertise on the Google AdWords platform.

Keyword phrases are the engine for your campaign. Without keywords, your campaign will fail and you will not receive the just rewards for your advertising dollars. Remember, your ideal client uses keyword phrases on the search engine to find you. If you do not have the right keywords in your ad groups, you will leave money on the table.

Researching the right keywords is extremely important. In this section, I am going to show you step-by-step how to conduct keyword research that blows your competition away.

What I want you to do first is to think like your prospect. Do you remember the exercise we conducted? Great! Start from there with a blank sheet of paper. Next, I want you to go to your website and read through your website for any additional keywords that you can find that you believe your ideal client would type in the search engines to find you.

Next, get another blank sheet of paper (or you can use a

spreadsheet program such as Excel) and I want you to set up your ad groups.

Now that you have done this, I want you to go to a free tool that will tell you exactly what people are typing into the search engine to find your product and service. This tool is called AdWords Keyword Tool. You can go directly to the tool at Adwords.google.com/tools.

As you see in the figure below, you have a box where you will enter more than one keyword phrase.

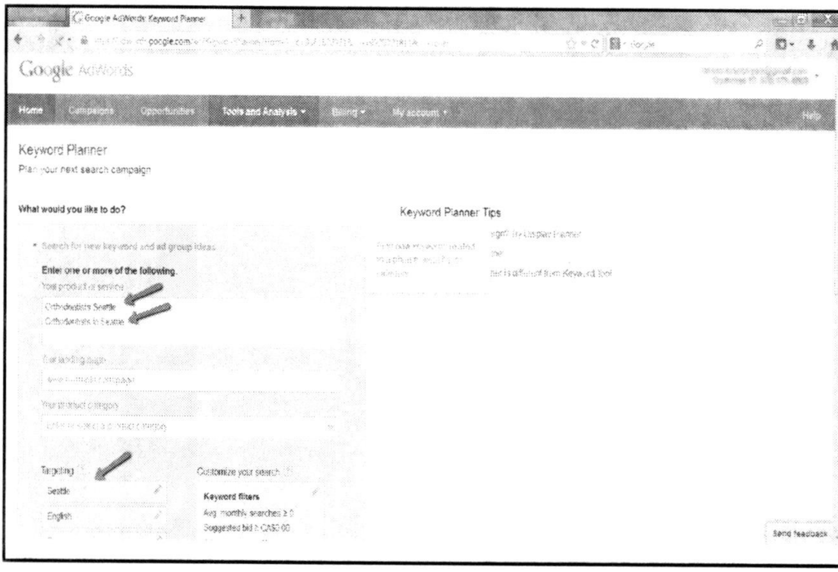

Enter one keyword phrase at a time. This tool is going to give you suggestions for the keyword that you entered based on what people are looking for. You should start off with the keyword phrase "Orthodontist _____ (your city)." Example: Orthodontist Seattle.

Then you want to make sure you select the right country. The program defaults to the area where you are using your computer or laptop for the research.

Once you enter the security image and hit "Enter," you will see a list of keywords and your keyword phrase as well as the number of people who are searching on that phrase globally and locally.

Beside the keyword, you want to select "exact match search."

We will talk about the different forms of keywords so that you understand this when setting up your account. To purchase a detailed starter package of this, visit www.WealthyOrthodontist.com/Keyword-Research.

This will give you a complete picture of how many people are typing that exact keyword into the search engine locally. It will also show you the cost-per-click, meaning the cost you will pay each time a potential client clicks your ad.

Setting up your budget is simple in Google AdWords. If you click on "your campaigns," you will come to a tab that says "settings."

Click the settings tab and scroll a little farther down the page, and you will see the "budget" tab. You can place the amount of money you would like to spend on a daily basis in this box.

Keep in mind, the higher the budget, the higher the exposure your ad will receive on the Google network. Start your budget the following way: I advise my clients to spend a minimum of $4,000 to $6,000 per month on advertising with Google. That works out to roughly $133 per day on up to $200 per day at $6,000 per month. Remember, you can always increase or decrease your budget anytime you want.

Note that your bids, what you are willing to pay for your ideal client to see your website, must be lower than your daily budget.

Google will not go over the total monthly amount calculated for your daily budget. So do not worry if you see that you have gone over your daily budget amount; they will average it out for the total monthly budget.

The budget will give you a good idea as to what you should do with your campaigns—whether you should increase it if you are not getting results or decrease it and tweak and optimize additional things within the campaign itself.

Your keyword phrase, the benefit your offer, and a call to action in your ads are ingredients to the secret sauce to get your ideal client to click your ad. The secret is to make sure that you have the keyword phrase in the headline, and, if possible, also in the body copy. You also need to mention the benefit, the end results they are going to achieve from using you as their doctor, and a call to action that will get them to pick up the phone and/or click the ad to call you now.

Before you begin your journey of writing your own ads, you want to get a blank piece of paper and a pen to take down details about your competitors' ads. This is a simple trick that none of your competition does that you can use to your advantage.

After you do that, go to Google and type in the keyword phrase you would like to use in your campaign. Example: "fix my crooked teeth." Now look at the results on the right and on top of the SERPS. Take note of which ad is #1 and write it down.

Next, I want you to do the same thing, but this time add the following to the keyword phrase you typed in previously: "fix my crooked teeth&?$12" and see what ad comes up.

Is it the same as the first ad you wrote down or is it different? If it is different, and it is #1, write it down. That is the ad that is getting the most clicks and it is the best ad for that keyword by your competitor. All you have to do is use it as an example and write a better ad as I outline below.

Designing your ideal-client-targeting (ICT) plan is the next step to really knock out your competitors (i.e., the general practice Dentists and other Orthodontists). Of the Orthodontists' campaigns I have looked at over the years, 99 percent leave money on the table because they do not follow the ICT system.

They would usually just dump a bunch of keywords into their campaign and hope for the best, which does not work. When they do that, they come back and say, "I have wasted my time and money" and "Google AdWords or PPC does not work."

Well, my friend, this will not happen to you. The first thing you want to do is target the city where you practice or reside or the cities where you offer your services. It does not make sense to target the GTA or an entire city when you do not provide services for that city or if your ideal client believes it is too far to travel there.

To change your targeting, go to "campaigns" and then click on "targeting." Here you have the choice to target by city, radius, zip code, postal code, country, state, or province. It is up to you.

Here is the million-dollar answer to making your campaigns profitable and successful. Start two separate campaigns: one targeting the city and the other targeting the zip codes of your clients.

The zip code or postal code of your clients will yield a huge advantage and success for you.

Relevancy is the name of the game with Google and the success you will achieve with your marketing. When you implement my RQCL system, it will put you ahead of your competitors. The RQCL system stands for Relevancy Quality Conversions Landing page.

Your landing page must be relevant to the keyword or theme of the keywords that you are advertising with. If the keyword does not match the theme or if the keyword is not on the landing page, the quality of your page will be low in Google's eyes and also to your ideal client because it does not match what they are looking for. This ultimately leads to zero conversions, meaning no calls for consultation and no forms being filled out for a free report or an appointment.

It is very important that your landing page have all three elements to be successful. Your landing page is where you are going to direct your ideal client after they have clicked your ad. You want to make sure that you bring them to a page that shows them exactly what they are looking for because if you do, you will pay a lot less to Google. They will actually reward you because you are more relevant than your competitors.

Your landing page should have the following:

1. The keywords or themes of keywords you are advertising with in your campaign and ad groups
2. Quality information and value so that your ideal client can make a decision
3. A good design and easy navigation to find information
4. Exactly what your ideal client and prospect wants and desires

Getting leads is the name of the game; this is why you're advertising on the Google AdWords platform. Now we are going to put everything together and build you a successful campaign that will get the phones ringing in as few as fifteen minutes. Yes, that is right—in only fifteen minutes. We are going to combine structure, relevancy, and keywords and make a campaign that will have your competitors quaking in their boots.

The first thing we are going to do is take your website URL or the landing page you want to send your ideal client to and go to the Google AdWords Keyword Tool. You are going to see a box that says "website." Enter your landing page URL or your website address in that box, then the security code, and click "answer."

Google is going to come back with what they think your landing page or home page is about. Look through the keywords that return back to you. Do they match what you want your ideal clients to think about your site and do they match what the ideal client is looking for?

If not, you have to tweak your landing page and make sure those keywords and themes are there. If they do match, you are going to copy the keywords and put them as ad groups in an Excel spreadsheet and name it your master file. (Using MS Excel spreadsheets is going to assist you in building out your campaigns.)

High importance should be paid to CTR or click through rate. Click through rate is how many times someone clicks on your ad when it is shown. The calculation is as follows:

Clicks divided by impressions x 100 = the percentage

Now, the higher the percentage, the better it is for you. Here's why: A high percentage of clicks means that your ads are relevant and that you are attracting the ideal client to click on your ad. In return, Google will reward you for achieving such a high rate by lowering the cost-per-click that you pay for each client that clicks your ad; it will also increase your ad position and show your ad more often than your competitors'.

The second thing that you get with this is you are showing your target market that you know exactly what they want and are looking for. They too will reward you by picking up the phone and calling for a consultation or by filling out a form for additional information.

There are other factors that come into play as well, such as a quality score for the keyword itself, the landing page, and the ad copy.

Google will actually tell you if you are on the right track and if your ad is relevant.

You should strive to achieve a click through rate of 1.50 percent or higher. The higher the better because you are basically wiping out your competition—they will have to pay more for the same keyword to advertise, and you will pay less because you are more relevant and have a higher click through rate. (Note: there are exceptions to the rule.)

Measuring results is also important to the success of your campaign. When you measure your results, you will know what is working and where to direct your advertising dollars to generate more leads to your practice. Google will actually track your results for you for free with a conversion tracking code. This conversion tracking code is in the "tools and analysis" tab; click on the "conversion" tab link and you will be able to generate a code to be placed on the page or pages you would like to track for results.

You can track to see how many forms or requests for consultation are filled out. This will help you develop the right form to increase leads. It will also track calls as well as how many times someone has called for a consultation or additional information. This can be set up in the campaign setting called "site extensions."

Please see the figure below of site extension and how to access it.

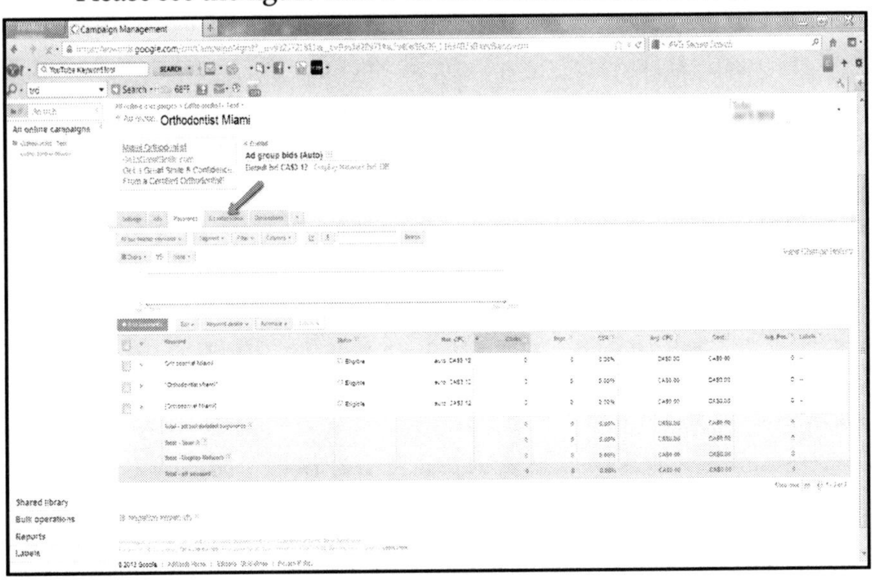

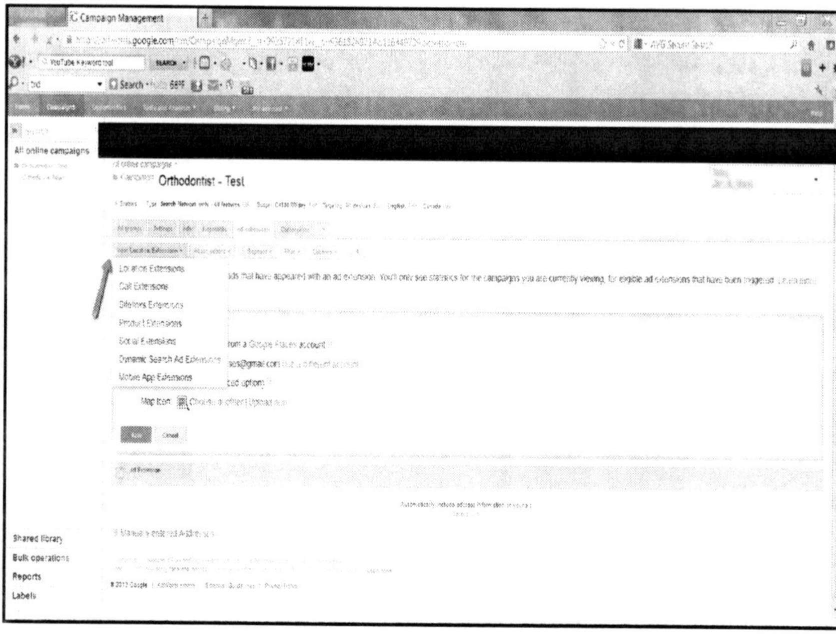

You can also use Google Analytics (which I highly recommend) for free. This tool will allow you to see where the holes are in your website, how long someone is staying on your site, and if they are engaging with the marketing material and information that you provide to them.

This will help you make additional changes or split testing to find the optimal way to show your ideal client the best information.

All of this is to your benefit, even though 99 percent of Orthodontists and general practice Dentists do not track or seek out information on making improvements to increase their lead flow online.

Campaign optimization will lead to more money in your practice and more leads than you can handle if you do it correctly. The majority of Orthodontists totally forget to do this on a weekly basis and do not have any clue as to what exactly they should be doing.

Remember, the system is RTELP, and if you follow it to a T, you will not have to worry about losing leads or your competitors overtaking you using Google AdWords because they do not know about optimizing their campaign.

The first thing you want to look at is each ad group and the keywords in your ad group. Is the keyword getting impressions? If so, how many? Are you getting clicks from your ads? If so, is the CTR higher than 1.5? Is the keyword quality score lower than 6? Is the quality of your ad showing low relevancy or below average? Is your landing page showing below average?

If any of these things show up, you have to address them immediately or else:

1. Google will charge you more to advertise and they will not tell you. You will only see it in the cost-per-click and in the ad position that you get on the Google network.
2. You will bring down the results not only for the campaign, but your entire account.
3. Your ads will be shown less because they are less relevant and your leads will start to drop.

The success of any of your pay-per-click campaigns is going to ride on the ongoing optimization of your account. Once you start advertising on the platform, your competitors are going to react. On top of that, Google is going to make changes. In fact, Google wants you to go into your account and make changes to your campaigns that are beneficial for you. If do not go into your campaign and optimize on a regular basis, you will eventually pay more than you have and your leads will start to dwindle. Get started today flooding your office with new, high-quality leads.

CHAPTER 9

Facebook Advertising

SOCIAL NETWORKING SITES are some of the most visited sites in the world. The number one social networking site in the world is Facebook. More people spend their time on Facebook than any other site in the world. The beautiful thing about Facebook is we can target our ideal clients by using Facebook's advertising program.

The Facebook platform lets us tap into the demographics, the likes, and the interests of our ideal clients based on their geographical location. We are going to use our ideal client profile here as well to target the exact clients we want to build your practice.

Facebook has various advertising products. For example, we can use their pay-per-click platform, their sponsored-stories platform, and you can also start off by using their post-advertising platform, which allows you to advertise based on a story or based on a single post.

Facebook advertising can be very lucrative when used correctly; however, it can take some time to target your ideal prospect if you have not set up the ideal client profile that we described in Chapter 1.

If for some reason you have not completed that profile yet, please go back to Chapter 1 and start the process immediately. You will gain a lot more knowledge about getting the right client into your practice.

Facebook advertising also allows you to see how your client truly feels. You won't have to guess anymore about the conversations they are having; you will be able to witness their likes, their dislikes, and the process they go through when making a decision to buy products and/or services. Many advertisers have no clue how to use this advertising platform correctly. This chapter will teach you how to tap into one of the biggest websites in the world.

Knowing the exact demographics of your ideal prospect will put you far ahead of your competition. Imagine that you have the opportunity to get into the conversations they are having about your products and/or services. Knowing right away what they like or do not like will give you the opportunity to make changes in your marketing, your website, and your practice.

The distinctive advantage of using Facebook is you can connect to your clients and ideal prospects on a social level. If you sit back and observe their topics of conversation and their interests, you will be able to expand your marketing reach into the Facebook advertising platform.

The second advantage you will have with your prospects and ideal clients is that you can target those who are in your local community and surrounding area for your services. You will not be wasting advertising dollars by targeting those in areas that are not interested and areas you wish not to service.

The greatest advantage you have using this platform is you are eliminating the guesswork when it comes to what your client wants. You can now participate on a higher level regarding their thought process and provide the exact, detailed information they need to make a decision.

On top of that, they will spread the news of your services and practice once you have connected with them and built a rapport by communicating and providing value.

Targeting your ideal prospect and gaining a connection with them is easier when you use the Facebook platform correctly. Results are what you are after, and results you shall get when you use the client profile to set up your campaigns.

This is why I stress so much that you do the legwork to find out as much information as possible on who exactly you are selling to. When you know who you are selling to, it becomes so much easier to get the sale and the ultimate YES.

The purpose of the client profile is to grow your practice to $2 million or more. The decision to grow it further is all up to you. When you set up your campaigns with the right data, it becomes very difficult for your competition to gain a piece of the market share.

If you can pay more than your competitor for a prospect and still make money, you will basically eliminate the competition in your area.

Use it to your advantage and continue to improve your ideal client profile. Facebook will surely help you do just that because now you have the opportunity to not only engage in the conversation that your ideal prospect is having but you can also provide so much value to them. In return they will greatly reward you with loyalty and money.

Social connection with Facebook is totally different from using the Google AdWords platform. With Facebook you have the opportunity to enter the conversation your ideal prospect is having with friends, family, and loved ones. With Google AdWords, you do not have that opportunity to see what the client is really thinking.

However, entering the conversation your ideal client is having is a delicate matter and must be done elegantly and without upsetting your prospect. This is where a majority of advertisers get it wrong when they use Facebook to generate leads.

With Facebook, you can target and promote a specific post that you write that provides value and which your ideal prospect would be interested in. The other advantage you have is you can create stories (in this case, client testimonials) that will get your prospect's attention. You would only have to pay if your prospect clicks on the story or post.

Facebook truly has a very tight range on helping you achieve success by providing the right mix of demographics to build a successful campaign. For example, while observing your ideal prospect, look at what magazines, TV shows, personal interests, and sports they watch or engage in. This is an opportunity to expand your targets in these specific areas on Facebook. You can create specific ads around their interests to gain their attention so that you can get high-quality leads. Signing up for your Facebook advertising account is quite easy to do. All you need is your ideal client profile and your credit and billing information to get started.

The following steps will guide you through setting up your campaign:

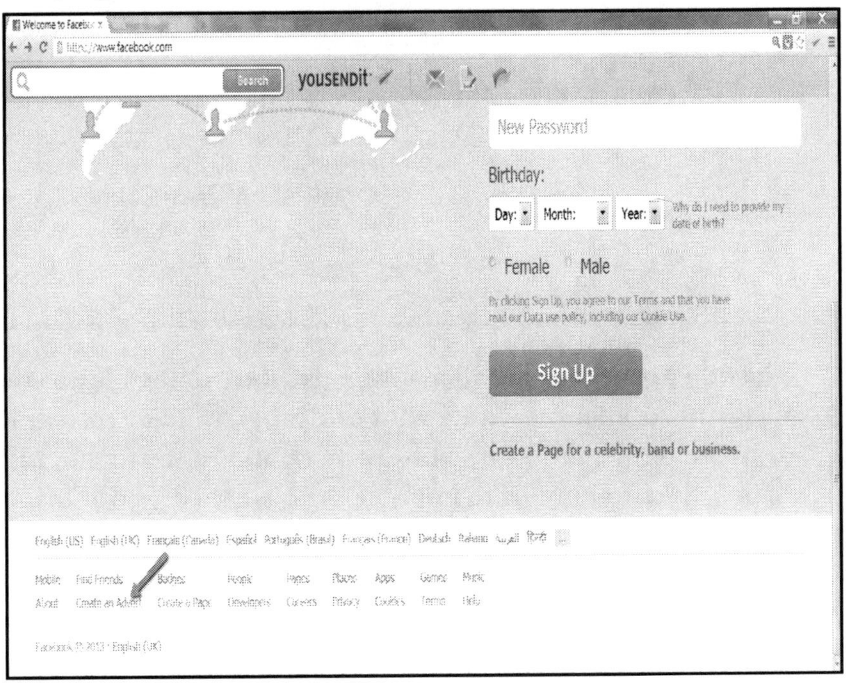

You can track your advertising results and manage your reporting in your own personal dashboard. This dashboard is called "ad manager." It gives you a complete breakdown on how many people clicked on your ads, sponsored stories, and/or posts. It provides in detail how many times your ads, stories, and posts have been seen. It gives a complete breakdown of each campaign you set up with all the bidding options you have selected.

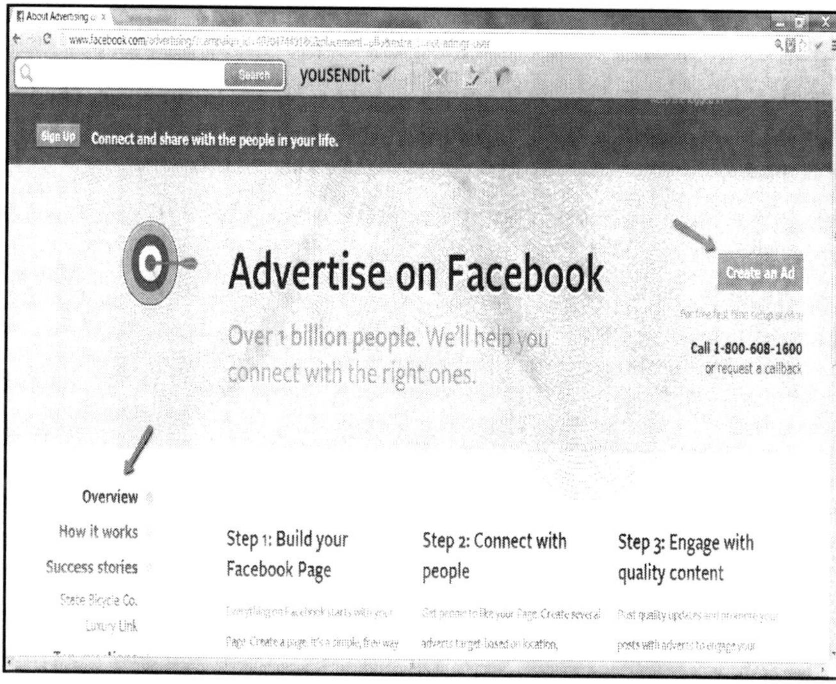

The other benefit of the ad manager dashboard is it allows you to quickly make changes within your campaign by going to specific ads to see results. You can pause, cancel, and re-start your ads. You can split test your ads to improve the quality of your leads. It gives you the direct information and a summary of the breakdown of your ideal prospect that you set up for each campaign. This dashboard is the main area you will be working from on a daily or weekly basis. Play around with it and become familiar with where things are listed and what you can do and not do.

The following figures provide greater detail of the ad manager platform. Please take the time to look at them and to implement the information I have provided.

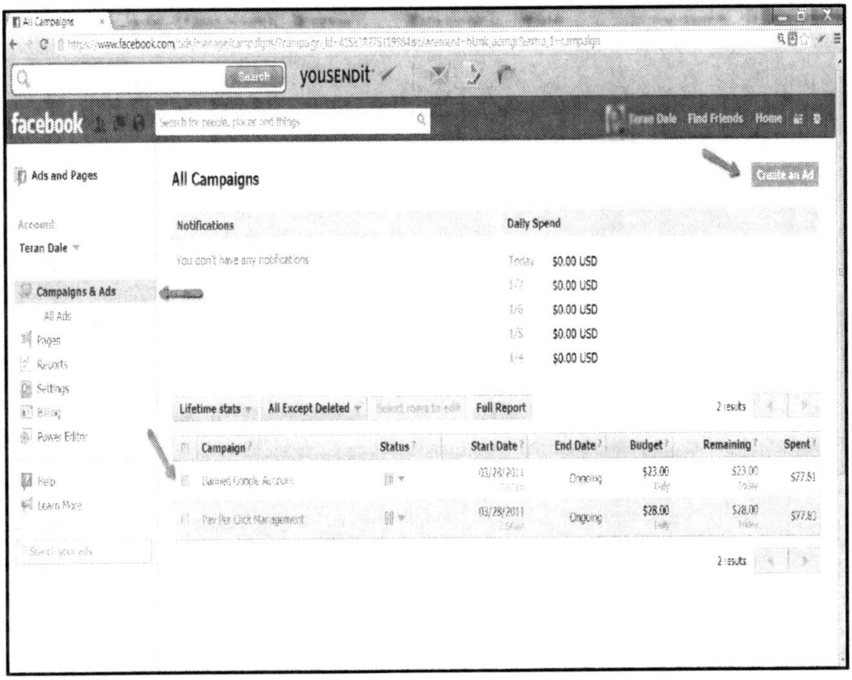

Testing is the name of the game when it comes to using Facebook advertising to bringing as many high-quality leads into your practice and sales funnel. You should have at least ten different ads for each campaign you set up.

The reason you want to start with ten or more different ads is your target market will quickly get used to the ad copy and image. You want to continue to provide a fresh image and message to entice your prospects to pick up the phone and call you to book an appointment.

With Facebook ads, you are going to notice right off the bat that you have a lot more space to write what you want to say to your prospect. This is the time to use your ideal client profile and the research you conducted with the TDCS System to develop the right marketing message to hook your clients' attention.

You can start off with ten different images; five should have the same message and the other five ads should have a different message. Remember, your ad must provide a benefit and a call to action to gain your prospects' attention. Unlike Google AdWords, your keyword phrase does not need to be in your ad. We will explain how to set up your Facebook campaign properly to ensure you are maximizing your advertising dollars and getting a high return on your investment.

Using the right image is a huge advantage when it comes to designing your ad for the sole purpose of enticing your ideal client to click your ad or pick up the phone and call you. Your ad should have a beautiful woman that is related to the subject matter you are advertising on. This is not a chauvinistic thing. Studies have shown that an ad on Facebook featuring a beautiful woman that is highly targeted to the subject matter on which the advertiser is bidding outperforms the majority of the other images. An example you can use is an attractive, smiling woman with ad copy about braces, Invisalign, diamond braces, etc.

You should have different images to use for designing your ad. You are doing this to split test which ad provides the most clicks at the higher click-through-rate and at the lowest cost-per-click.

All your advertising on Facebook and the other platforms should be measurable and trackable, and it should provide evidence you are receiving a high return on your investment. I am a strong believer that if you can't effectively track the results of your advertising, you should not use that platform because you will have no clue what your advertising dollars are providing to you to build your practice.

Targeting is the key, and aligning your campaign with the right interests, topics, and gender of your ideal client when setting up your ads is a must if you want your ads to be profitable.

Figure 2.1 will show you exactly how to set up the target-

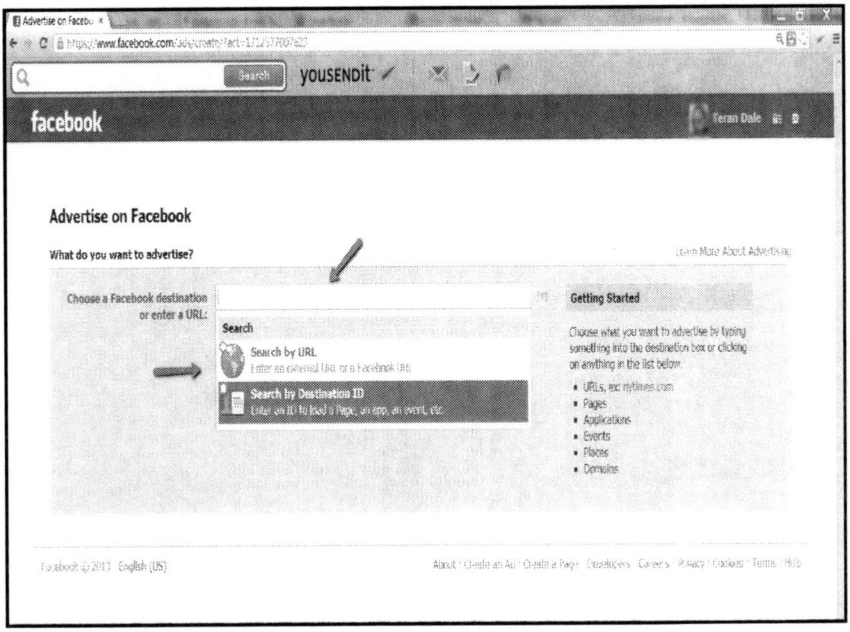

facebook
Teran Dale
Advertise on Facebook
What do you want to advertise?
Choose a Facebook destination or enter a URL:
Search
Search by URL
Search by Destination ID
Getting Started
Choose what you want to advertise by typing something into the destination box or clicking on anything in the list below.
URLs, ex: nytimes.com
Pages
Applications
Events
Places
Domains

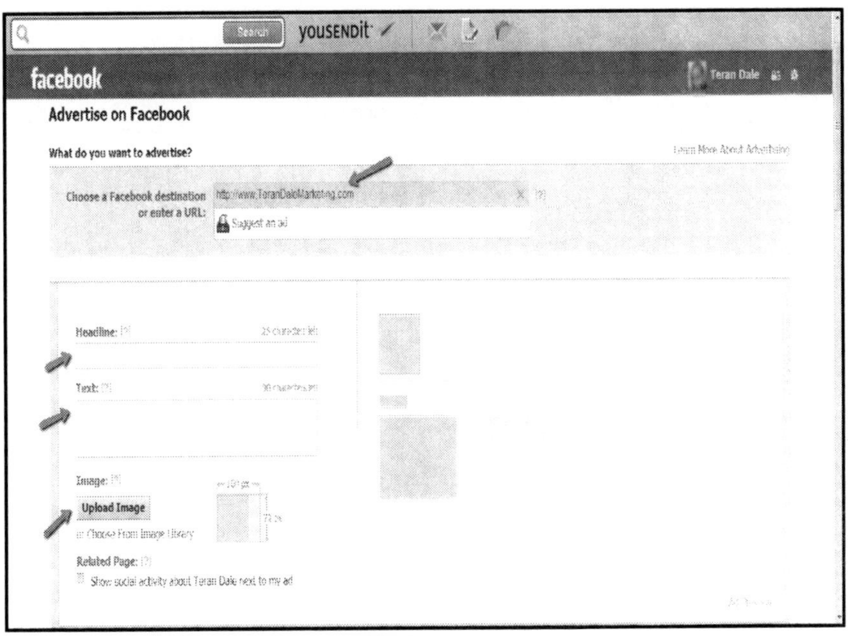

facebook
Teran Dale
Advertise on Facebook
What do you want to advertise?
Choose a Facebook destination or enter a URL:
Suggest an ad
Headline:
Text:
Image:
Upload Image
Related Page:
Show social activity about Teran Dale next to my ad

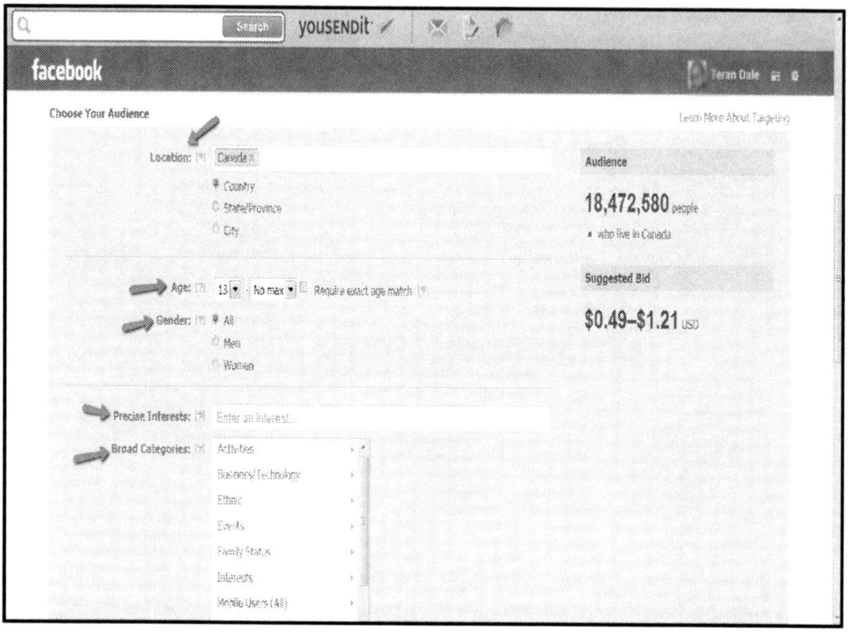
facebook
Teran Dale
Choose Your Audience
Learn More About Targeting
Location:
Canada
Country
State/Province
City
Audience
18,472,580 people
who live in Canada
Age:
13
No max
Require exact age match
Suggested Bid
$0.49–$1.21 USD
Gender:
All
Men
Women
Precise Interests:
Enter an interest...
Broad Categories:
Activities
Business/Technology
Ethnic
Events
Family Status
Interests
Mobile Users (All)

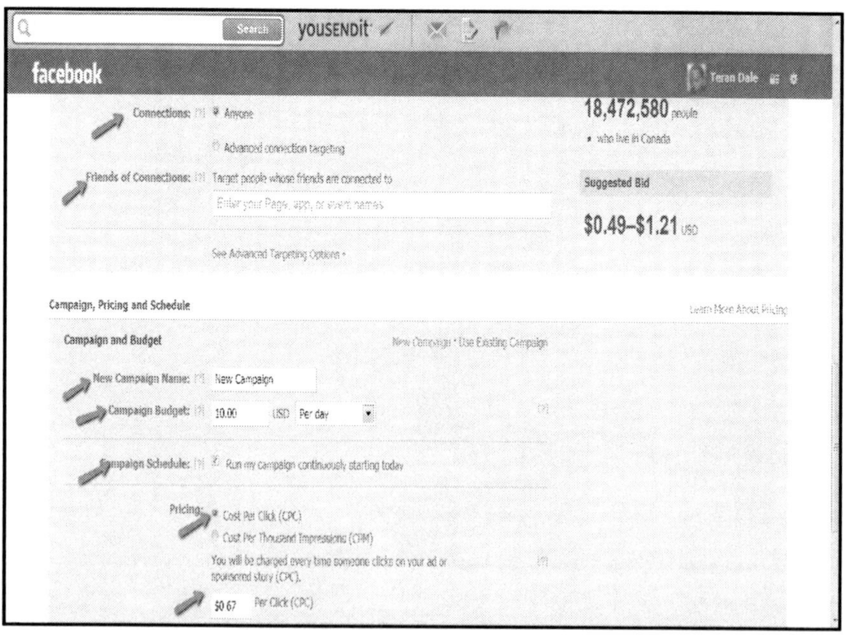
facebook
Teran Dale
Connections:
Anyone
Advanced connection targeting
18,472,580 people
who live in Canada
Friends of Connections:
Target people whose friends are connected to
Suggested Bid
$0.49–$1.21 USD
See Advanced Targeting Options
Campaign, Pricing and Schedule
Campaign and Budget
New Campaign · Use Existing Campaign
New Campaign Name:
New Campaign
Campaign Budget:
10.00
USD
Per day
Campaign Schedule:
Run my campaign continuously starting today
Pricing:
Cost Per Click (CPC)
Cost Per Thousand Impressions (CPM)
You will be charged every time someone clicks on your ad or sponsored story (CPC).
$0.67
Per Click (CPC)

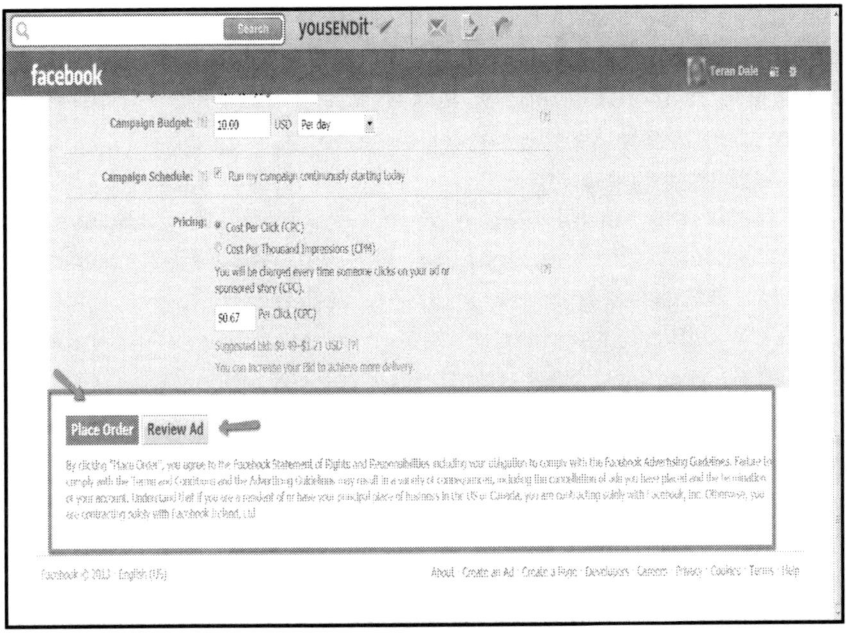

The location and demographics of your ideal client are the next elements you must build upon to effectively develop a winner. You see, if you know exactly where your clients are located, you will not waste your time and money trying to figure out if this person wants what you have to offer. When you know where they are, you can provide the offer to them immediately because you know that they want what you have.

Now here's a secret that no one talks about when using Facebook targeting:

You should break up your campaigns: one targeting only men and the other targeting only women. This technique will give you a clear picture regarding (1) who books more appointments on the Facebook platform; (2) who the decision maker is in the family; which allows you to (3) put your advertising dollars into the campaign that is providing the biggest bang for your buck.

All your competitors are going to group the men and women together. Don't do this because you will not know which ad resonates with each targeted ideal prospect. Maybe men will like one ad compared with the women and maybe women will prefer another ad more than the men. This will also allow you to effectively use your marketing budget wisely and cut costs in all three major areas while at the same time gaining high-quality leads at the lowest cost possible.

Images of beautiful women placed in ads with the right message increase your CTR. Your goal (just like with AdWords) is to get the highest CTR possible for each ad you design. The higher the CTR (click through rate, meaning how many times your ideal prospect has clicked on your ads), the better it is for you overall.

A high CTR indicates to Facebook that as an advertiser you know what you are doing. You know what your target market wants and you are on the right track. In return for gaining such an impressive CTR, Facebook will reward you by showing your ads more often to your ideal prospects and you will start to see a significant difference in cost and results in your cost-per-click.

Put it to good use and eliminate ads after three to five days that do not have a CTR of 0.20 because they are costing you money. Go back and re-evaluate your ad copy and make sure that it has the following:

1. Attractive women related to the subject matter
2. Benefits (what the ideal prospect is going to get—their ultimate desire)
4. Call to action to take the steps to pick up the phone and call for a consultation

Apply these four things when you are testing and tweaking your ads. You can also look at the interests and topics that you currently have. Look to see if you can expand on them by observing the conversations your ideal client is having on Facebook.

Setting up your budget is fast and easy to do. You can start off by using your ad manager dashboard to change your budget for each campaign, add a new budget to a new campaign, or pause your campaign and the budget anytime that you want.

When setting up your Facebook ad campaign, start off with

a monthly budget of $1,200 and break that out for thirty days to come up with your daily budget. In this example your daily budget will be $40 dollars per day.

Now, this does not mean that you will hit $40 per day because, when you are starting out, it is all based on the clicks. You want a budget that is high enough to ensure that your ads are being shown to everyone in your campaign.

Facebook will also provide you with the maximum amount you can spend for each day. This might be higher than your daily budget, but once you have established your campaigns, the magical number of how much you can spend will increase (based on Facebook's discretion).

The following figure will show you where to add and change your budget within the ad manager platform.

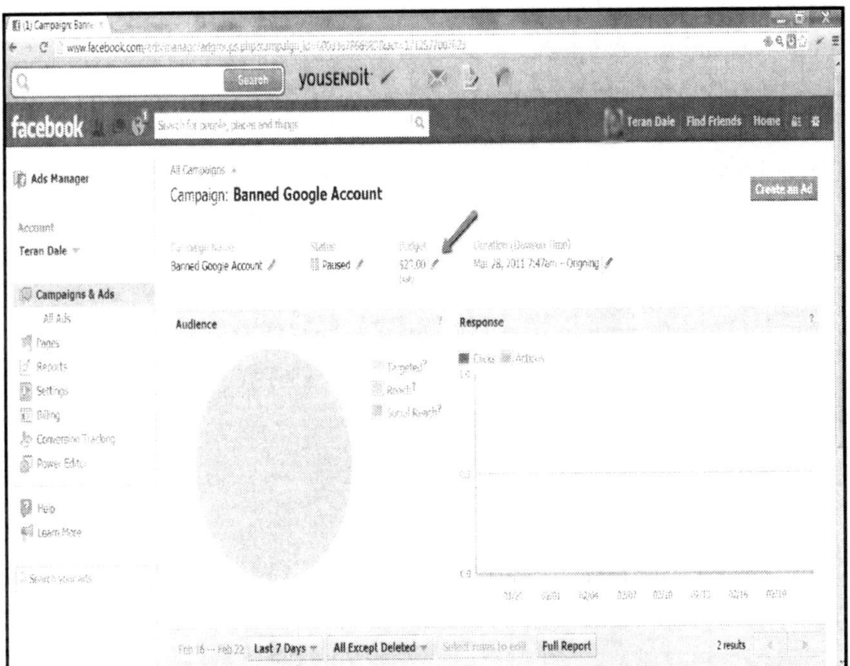

Directing your ideal prospect to the right landing page will definitely increase your bank balance and get your ideal clients to say YES. You first achieve this by building a rapport and connection with your prospect in your ad. From there, you continue to provide value, and you continue building the connection, driving them directly to your website.

The landing page (or the page where you send your ideal client after they click your ad) should match the ad that they are coming from. It must be relevant, it must provide value, and it must have what the ideal client would like to achieve.

Do not forget your landing page should have your USP front and center for them to see. This will put you in the right light, aligning your prospect so that he or she will pick up the phone and book a consultation.

Most advertisers direct their clients to another Facebook page or a fan page. Your goal is to get them off of Facebook and onto your website. You are looking to move the conversation into your arena where there is less distraction and competition. This is a golden nugget and an opportunity to get a high-quality lead who is ready to buy.

Bidding strategies in Facebook can yield a significant increase and more high-quality leads flooding your office. When starting out with your campaign, the bidding strategy you should use is the CPC = cost-per-click. This is when you pay only when someone clicks on your ad. This model will tell you if your ad, image, and message resonate with your ideal prospect.

The second bidding strategy you can test out is the CPM model, meaning you are charged for every 1,000 impressions of your ad (i.e., for every 1,000 times your ad is shown, you are charged a set amount).

There are advantages and disadvantages to using the CPM model. Many times I have gotten high-quality leads for my clients at a lower cost than CPC. However, it is better to know if your ad is working now than to wait for a certain number of impressions to take place before you make a decision.

What I also want to share with you is a ninja bidding strategy that I have developed called PLPL = Pay Less Per Lead. This technique is unique and gets results in as few as seventy-two hours when implemented correctly.

This is what you are going to do with your CPC campaign: After running your ads for seventy-two hours, you are going to look at the average CPC that you are paying. You are also going to look at the CTR of your ad. For any ads in your campaign that have a high CTR (0.20 or more), you are going to lower the bids to the three-day average.

Next, you are going to monitor to see if you are getting the same number of clicks and quality of leads at a lower cost. Once you know the answer to this for sure, the next steps is to run the cycle for another three days and lower the CPC to the average once again. You are testing what is the lowest CPC you can pay to obtain a lead or client at the same quality.

When you obtain the information, you increase your budget so that you can generate more high-quality leads from your ideal prospect.

It is only worth creating a huge following on Facebook if it provides a ROI and you can move your fans from your own Facebook fan page or Facebook business page to your website. Remember, moving the conversation from Facebook to your website is important because your ideal client will have fewer distractions and there is less (no!) competition on your own website. You want their full attention on the offer that you are presenting to them.

You can create a following by having a Facebook fan page or business page. The name means literally what it says: You have your own practice page that you can direct your clients to that are fans of your service.

On the fan page, there are so many things that you can do to increase the flow of leads and cash into your practice:

1. You can conduct surveys to find out what other additional services and products your clientele would like to buy from you.

2. You can build your list and provide messages with offers and surprises to build a rapport and get the phone ringing during slow months, weeks, or days.
3. You can instruct your following to spread the news about your services to their friends and family members who need your services.
4. You can observe, listen to, and hear exactly what your ideal client is talking about, leading to the opportunity to enter the conversation and provide value to your client.
5. You can get all your present clients and ideal prospects to like your posts and fan page.
6. You can start a group for your clients and prospects so that you can keep in contact with them.

Creating your Facebook fan page or business page:

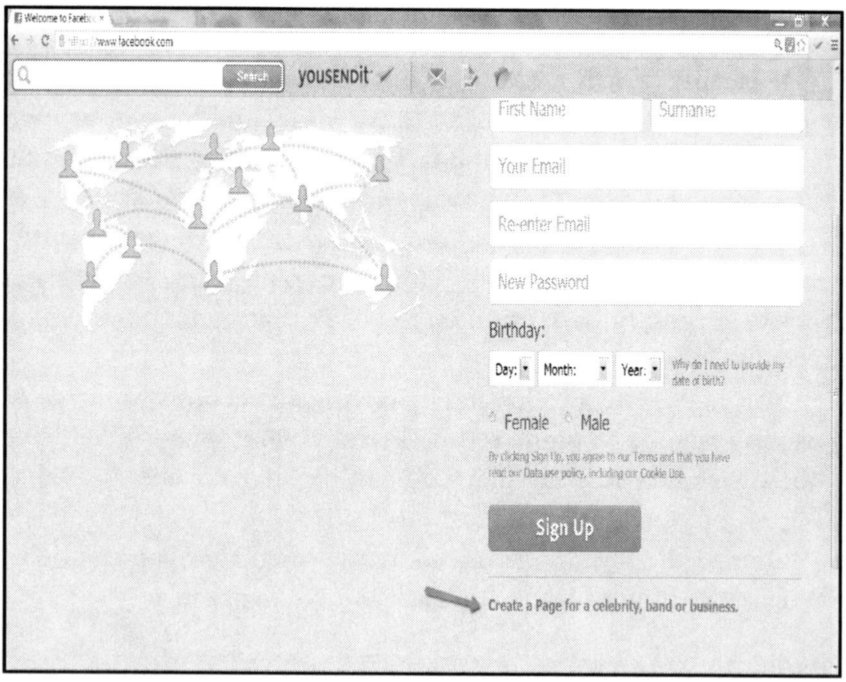

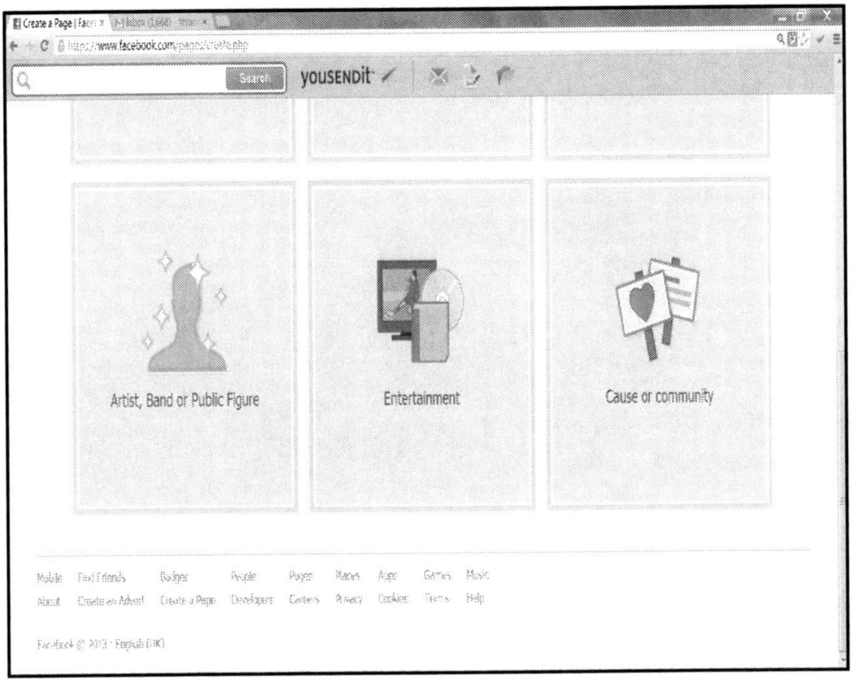

Use the same process on your fan page: provide value and show how your product and services offer a solution to their problems.

Take a look at various Facebook fan pages. You want to get your fan page designed and provide a lead-capture system on the fan page. Also, consider providing a free report or video that will help your ideal prospect. And always be list building to keep the flow of leads coming into your practice.

CHAPTER 10

YouTube Marketing

VIDEOS HAVE TAKEN OVER THE INTERNET. Everywhere you go online, you see businesses and the general public using videos to engage and excite their audience. YouTube is the third-most-visited website in the world—over one billion videos are watched every day. In fact, YouTube's viewership is larger than the three major TV networks combined. Marketing with videos is the next step to capturing high-quality leads, which will put more money into your practice. The source you are going to use to do just that is Google and YouTube.

On YouTube, you can view any type of video that you wish, and every day your ideal client goes to YouTube to search for videos to enjoy. We are going to take advantage of this and create effective videos that capture your ideal prospects' attention and give them the opportunity to pick up the phone and call your for a consultation.

YouTube can be very effective when it come to helping you meet your goals. Your videos can be listed in YouTube search when optimized properly and can also be ranked on the first page of the search engine results. You also have available the Google YouTube PPV program, which you set up within your AdWords account and which drives your ideal prospects and clients to watch your videos.

Differentiation is a concept and a system that has been talked about a great deal in this book. In order for your practice to survive and thrive, it must differentiate itself from its competitors. One sure-fire way to do that is to use videos on your website, on YouTube, and on any other third-party video site.

Videos build trust when used properly and engage your ideal prospect when you provide value and the exact information your client wants. If you do not use videos on your site or on YouTube, you are leaving a ton of money on the table.

To create a video that engages, builds trust, and is different from your competitors, you must start researching what your current competition is offering. If they are using videos to market their services, watch the videos and take note. List what you do like about the video and then list what you do not like; create a plan for the beginning of your script for your own video.

It is almost like building the client profile with this technique; your competition might use videos, but 99 percent of the time they are not doing it correctly. The rest of this chapter will break down the techniques of creating an effective video that will give you a HIGH return on your investment. This is the only reason you would invest your time and money into a proven marketing medium that gets results.

Let's dig deeper into the effectiveness of using videos for your practice. When using YouTube, you can track and measure the results of your video script and find out what your ideal prospects and clients will watch.

YouTube has a free tool that will analyze your video and show you exactly where viewers have left your video to the exact second. By using this information, you will be able to see why your ideal client decided to stop watching your video and go elsewhere.

This is an effective tool that hardly anyone who markets their product or service uses to their advantage. With this newfound information, you can create videos that excite and engage your ideal client to watch your full message so that you can start generating higher quality leads.

When done correctly, YouTube can help your videos to be ranked higher in the YouTube search engine. They also offer a free keyword tool that allows you to research the tagging of your videos to drive more targeted traffic to your videos and/or YouTube channel.

Because YouTube is an authority site owned by Google, your videos can also have the distinct advantage of not only playing on YouTube, but on other associated sites that are linked to YouTube. This allows your message to be shown across an entire network of ideal prospects that want and need your services.

Pay-per-view is a very unique and effective way to generate a boatload of fresh leads for your practice. YouTube has a program that is linked with Google AdWords called YouTube PPV. This is very similar to Google AdWords and the option is in your AdWords account. You can also set up the account via your YouTube account.

PLEASE SEE FIGURE 1.1 BELOW:

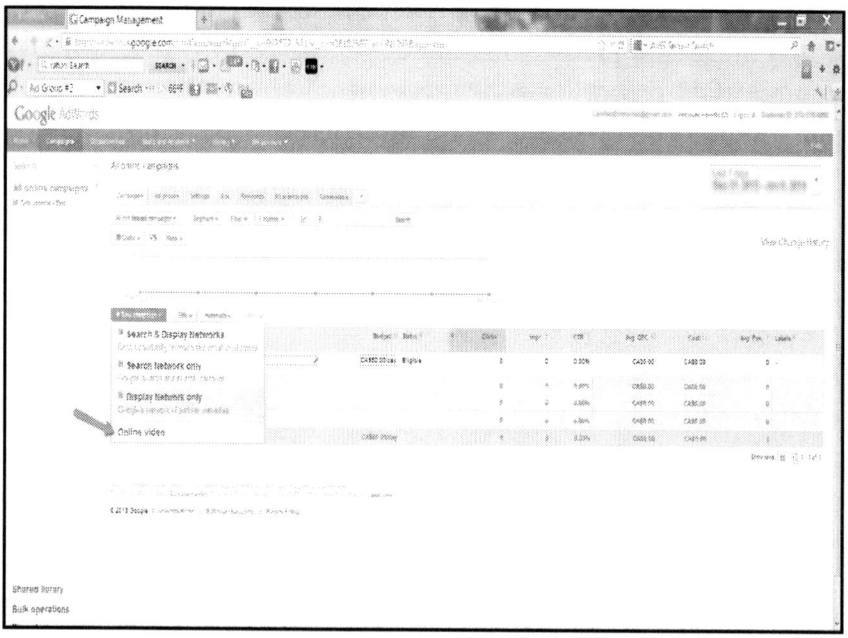

only once your ideal prospect watches your video; this is very similar to PPC when you pay only once someone clicks on your ads. You can have ads on the YouTube network that are shown on the side and above the fold just like AdWords, and you can also have your regular video shown in the YouTube search and other third-party sites.

FIGURE 1.2 YouTube Search:

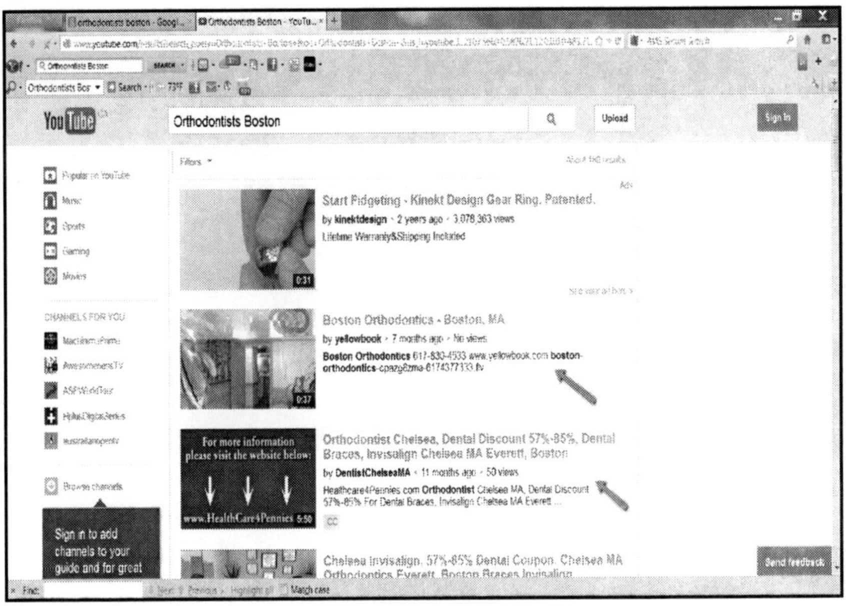

A huge advantage is this builds credibility in the eye of the consumer and it shows you are everywhere. They will consider your video important and liked. We will discuss likes and favorites in more detail later on in this chapter, as well as the importance of building a campaign for each video you upload onto your own YouTube channel.

Your video marketing message should match what your ideal prospect desires, wants, fears, and needs. This will engage them to watch your entire video and to take action by contacting your office.

Your video ad can be placed in two different places on the

YouTube platform. It can be placed along the side and above the search results of other videos. (This would be for paid ads where you pay for each view of your video.)

The second way your ad can be shown is on third-party sites that are part of the Google and YouTube network of sites that have content related to the video that you are promoting.

The third way you can have your video ad shown is on the YouTube platform itself within the search results. A well-optimized video ad can show up for the specific keyword term that your ideal prospect is using.

The fourth way is to have your video ad show up in the original Google search engine results. When optimized correctly, your ad can show up on the first page under videos and/or in the search results themselves.

Please see figure 1.3 below:

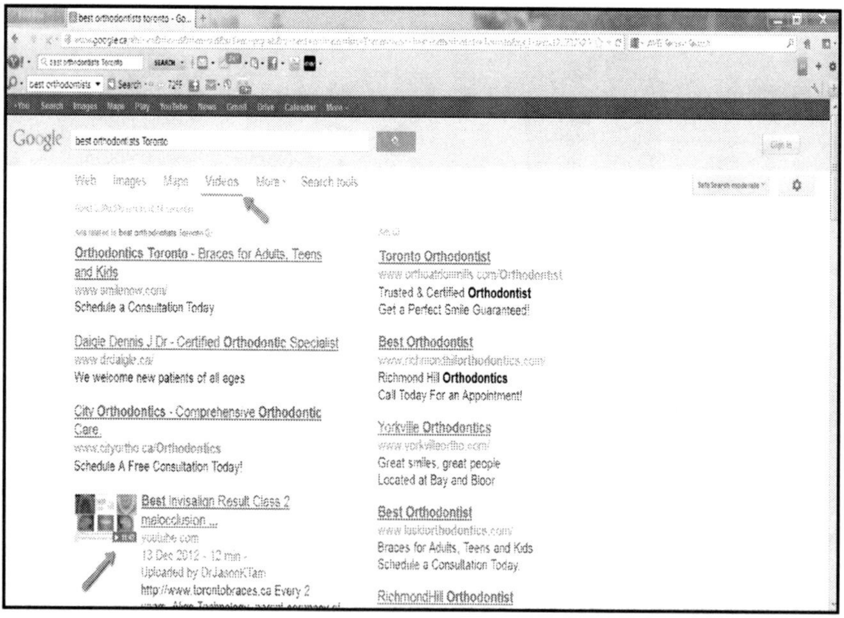

Your goal is to have your video ad on all four places; the more exposure you gain, the better the results and the quality of leads—if you are giving the right message to your ideal prospect.

Structuring a powerful, very profitable YouTube PPV campaign starts off by having the right ad groups and the correct video and designs to take advantage of the low cost and high return on investment of using the marketing platform of YouTube PPV.

The ad group is very similar to the ad group set up in Google AdWords, with a few exceptions. You name the ad group the same way, but the design and implementation are different. You can also set up your ad group via YouTube. However, if you are just starting out, I would insist you get comfortable by using the Google AdWords interface and having your YouTube account linked to AdWords.

Google will ask you if you wish to link your account to AdWords; reply with a "yes" and the transition should go smoothly.

The keywords you should use in YouTube and the structure of the group of keywords themselves can be set up slightly different. You should use all broad match keywords and you should have a minimum of six keywords per ad group.

Branding is a must in the new era of marketing. The three major search engines are shifting that way, and the biggest shift is taking place with Google. Now, as a small business owner you are probably saying, "Teran, how the heck am I supposed to brand my practice against the bigger guys?"

The first thing is that you need to optimize and build a complete system and network for the major digital platforms, and YouTube is definitely one of the platforms you should be using right now.

With a YouTube channel you can start to build your brand and become the go-to doctor in your area. Here are the steps to take to get started with your branding:

1. Have your USP front and center in all your videos. It should be easy to repeat and be memorable and different from all your competitors.
2. You should have as many videos as possible on your YouTube channel, and they should all provide valuable information

to every client and prospect that gets the opportunity to visit and watch the videos you have on your channel.

3. You must build your list of subscribers on your YouTube channel. It is imperative you offer something of value for free in exchange for their contact information (their e-mail address, mailing address, and/or telephone number).
4. Continue to build upon your list, keep in contact with all subscribers, and provide value and your USP. Repeating your USP constantly makes it forceful and memorable in the minds of your prospect. This is a technique that politicians use so often and it works like a charm.

Use all four techniques with your YouTube channel, and you and your practice will spread across the net as the go-to doctor and practice that delivers exactly what their clients want.

Creating your YouTube channel is the smart way to build a successful lead-generation system. To get started, log into your YouTube account and follow the instructions below.

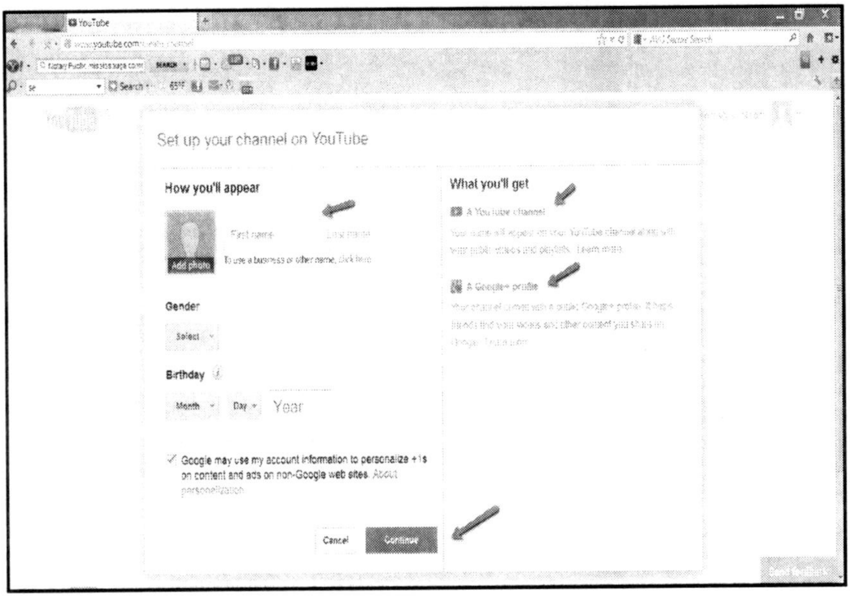
YouTube
Set up your channel on YouTube
How you'll appear
First name
Last name
Add photo
To use a business or other name, click here
Gender
Select
Birthday
Month
Day
Year
Google may use my account information to personalize +1s on content and ads on non-Google web sites. About personalization
Cancel
Continue
What you'll get
A YouTube channel
A Google+ profile

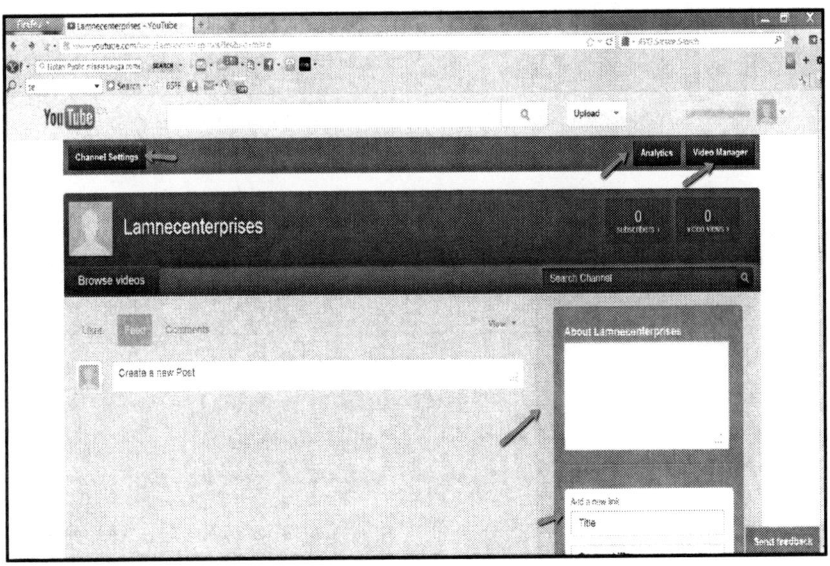
Lamnecenterprises - YouTube
Upload
Channel Settings
Analytics
Video Manager
Lamnecenterprises
0
0
Browse videos
Search Channel
Comments
Create a new Post
About Lamnecenterprises
Add a new link
Title
Send feedback

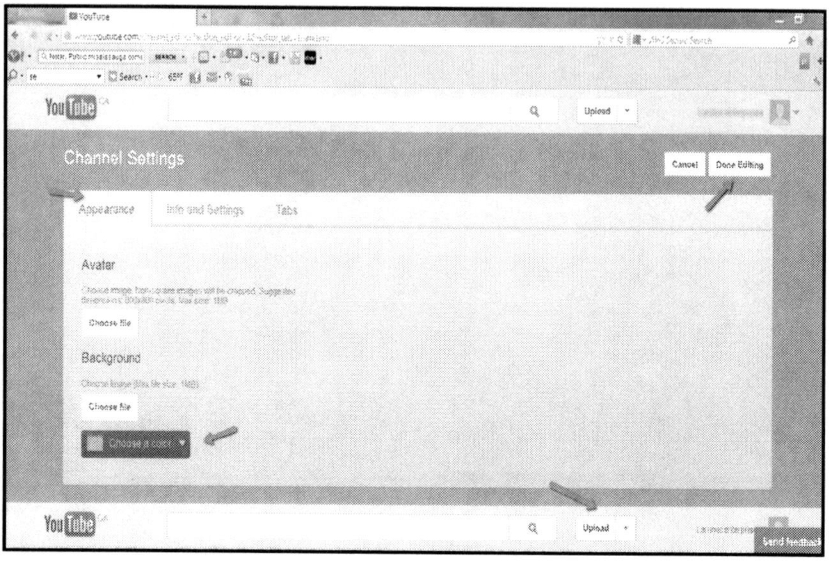
YouTube
Upload
Channel Settings
Cancel
Done Editing
Appearance
Info and Settings
Tabs
Avatar
Choose file
Background
Choose file
Choose a color
Upload
Send feedback

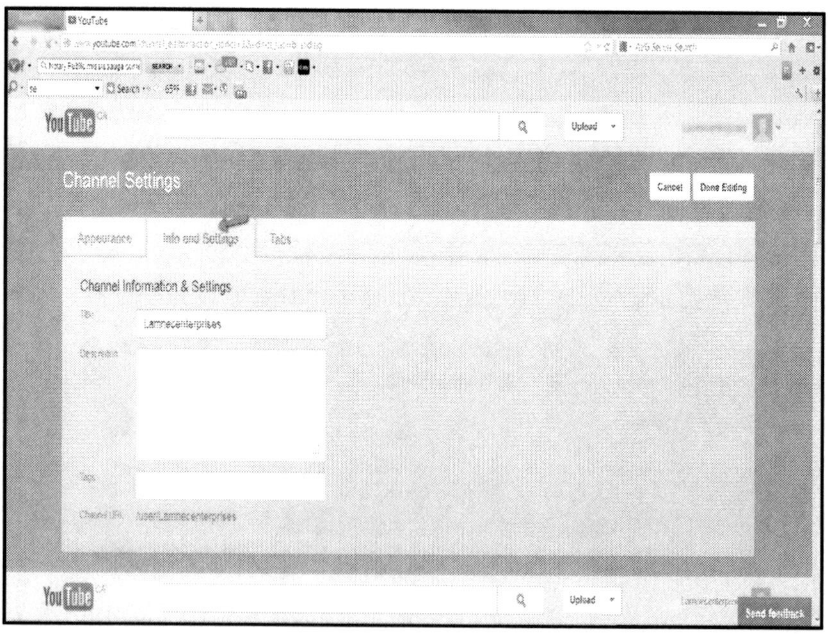
YouTube
Upload
Channel Settings
Cancel
Done Editing
Appearance
Info and Settings
Tabs
Channel Information & Settings
Lamnecenterprises
/user/Lamnecenterprises
Upload
Send feedback

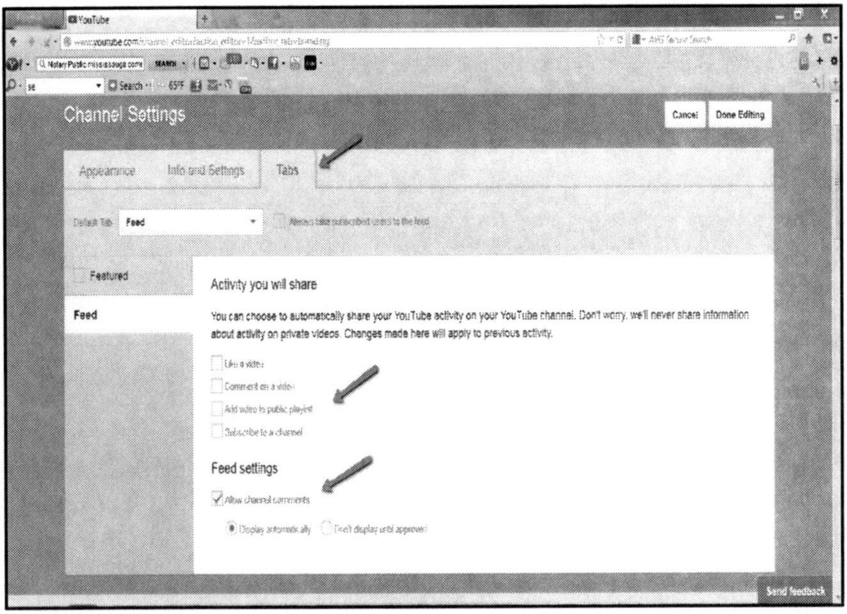

The right marketing message should also have the right design that engages and increases the lead quality of the ideal prospect you are going after. With your YouTube channel, you want to create the right design that draws your prospect into watching and subscribing to your videos.

1. Your channel should stand out and have a powerful design; it should have colors similar to your website.
2. You should have testimonials, pictures of happy clients, and stories on your template so that your prospects can see exactly what they will be getting by going to you for their orthodontic care.
3. You should have your address, a map, telephone number, and office hours on your template. (Note: if you have more than one office, list them as well.)
4. You should also offer a free report in exchange for their contact information. Remember, always be building your list.
5. Your Unique Selling Proposition should be front and center for all your prospects and clients to see.

Use all five elements and you will have a winning YouTube Channel design that will generate huge amounts of cash for your practice—guaranteed.

Describing your office and its atmosphere and showing your prospects and clients around the office should be part of your first video. You should also have footage of testimonials from happy clients singing your praises. The staff should be smiling and talking about the practice and the care their clients and prospects will get once they visit your office.

You should sit down and write out your script and practice what you would like to say in front of the camera. This is very important; the more you practice what you want to say, the better the video will be when you upload it to your YouTube channel.

Don't worry, you do not need to create a Hollywood motion picture; it has to look and be authentic and honest. If you are having a hard time coming up with a script, think of the following: If you were a client, what would you want to see and hear about someone's practice? What would make you decide to pick up the phone and call for a consultation?

The more information you provide, the better, and yes—do not forget—your USP should be front and center. It should seal the deal and get your prospect to call you immediately for a consultation. If you have not done so yet, make sure to go through the exercise questions in Chapter 1 on USP. That chapter alone is worth millions of dollars to your bottom line if you implement the system correctly.

In all your videos, you should have a couple of testimonials and images of your office and staff. As for the testimonials, your clients' testimonials and/or stories should match the subject of the video itself. What you are doing is building your credibility and your branding, and providing the social proof that you are the expert and the go-to Orthodontist in your area.

The continuous use of testimonials in your video just hammers away, providing proof that "Yes, I am making the right decision to use this doctor for my Orthodontic care." This also diminishes your client's concern about price. As I said before, we do not buy on price—we buy on value. If you do not show your clients and prospects the value they are going to get, price becomes an issue. The videos you use should always provide value to the client. They should give them enough information that they will pick up the phone and call you and no one else.

The steps to follow for your PPV advertising campaign are as follows:

1. Testimonials in all your videos
2. Pictures and comments from your happy staff
3. You on camera explaining and guaranteeing your USP
4. Offer a free report on the subject matter in exchange for their contact information; direct them to your landing page that has the report for FREE.

As an example, you could have a video about Invisalign. You should have testimonials from Invisalign patients—teens and adults, both men and women. Put this to use and witness the results as your PPC YouTube campaign generates a boatload of high-quality leads for your practice.

The YouTube AdWords platform is built on a pay-per-view model. The strategy I am going to present to you knocks your competition out with one powerful, vicious uppercut. They will have no idea what hit them.

Once you have set up your campaign and it has been running for a week, you want to look at the following and take down notes for each ad group in each campaign.

1. Keywords
2. CTR for the ad
3. Cost-per-click for the keyword
4. Results you are getting for that keyword (Is it providing a high-quality lead to your practice)

You are going to use this technique to optimize your campaign to generate more quality leads without paying a high cost for the lead. You are going to reinvest the money back into the budget to continue to increase the flow of leads to your office.

You need to look at each ad group, the keyword, and the CTR for the keyword over the past seven days. You want to have the following: 1.5 or higher CTR, a quality score of 8 or higher, and you also want to know if that keyword has generated a lead.

Next, and if all the above align correctly, you are going to lower your CPC to the seven-day average. And do the same thing again until (in some cases) you are paying one penny for a high-quality lead. (This is the first time I am sharing this secret out in the open.) Then you increase your budget so that Google will continue to show your ads more often across the network, getting you more high-quality leads at a lower cost. You can do this all day until you can't handle any more leads coming to your office. Please use it to your advantage—you will not be disappointed.

Keywords, description tags, and a highly relevant link-building campaign are the three components to getting your videos ranked in the Google search engine.

Let's start with keywords you can add as tags to your video. One of the best ways to add the correct keyword phrases to your video is by using the information you have developed in your AdWords campaign in Chapter 8. Once you have identified the keywords that are driving in new leads and making you money, these are the keywords that you should tag in your video because they will bring you additional high-quality leads without spending more on advertising.

When you upload your video, your description of it should contain the keyword phrase and the full description of what is in the video. Another secret tip is to upload the transcript of the video as well. This way your video is completely optimized for the search engine. Your description should also include your address and telephone number.

You must develop a highly relevant link campaign to each of your videos. You have to be careful when developing your link campaign because Google has made significant changes to the quality and procedures of sending links to websites and videos. If you violate any of their terms and policies (i.e., black hat techniques), it will be extremely hard to get back in their good graces.

The links should be natural and linked not only to a specific keyword, but also to links with the anchor text of your business. If it looks like you're gaming the system, Google will not show your videos in the search engines.

Crushing your competitors using videos as a marketing tool is a lot easier than you think. To make the most of using videos to drive more traffic to your website and provide high-quality leads, you should always, always have a call to action at the beginning, the middle, and the end of your videos and a caption at the beginning, middle, and end of your videos.

Having a call to action brings more cash into your business along with higher quality leads. It shocks me when I critique videos that Orthodontic practices put up with no call to action. Then they wonder why they haven't received any calls to their office.

You always want to ask for the sale. Once you have provided valuable information to your prospect, you are providing a disservice to the client and your profession if you do not ask for the sale. Strong words? Yes. However, they are true. The only way you are going to grow your practice is to ask for the sale after you have provided value to your client.

Captions in your video build your brand and help the client to remember where exactly they saw the video and it will make them think, "This is the right doctor for the job." A caption also allows you to differentiate yourself from your competitors because they are not asking for the sale.

Remember, in all your videos you must add a call to action along with captions to get the sale and high-quality leads.

YouTube has a keyword tool that you can access in your account that will help you develop the right keywords for your ad groups and campaign.

The lifeline for any successful pay-per-click campaign is the keywords and demographics of its ideal client. What you want to do is use the keywords that generate high-quality leads and eliminate those that do not. It is very important that you track and measure the results that you are getting from your campaign. Go to www.ads.youtube.com/keyword.tool

Step 1 – Got to the tool:

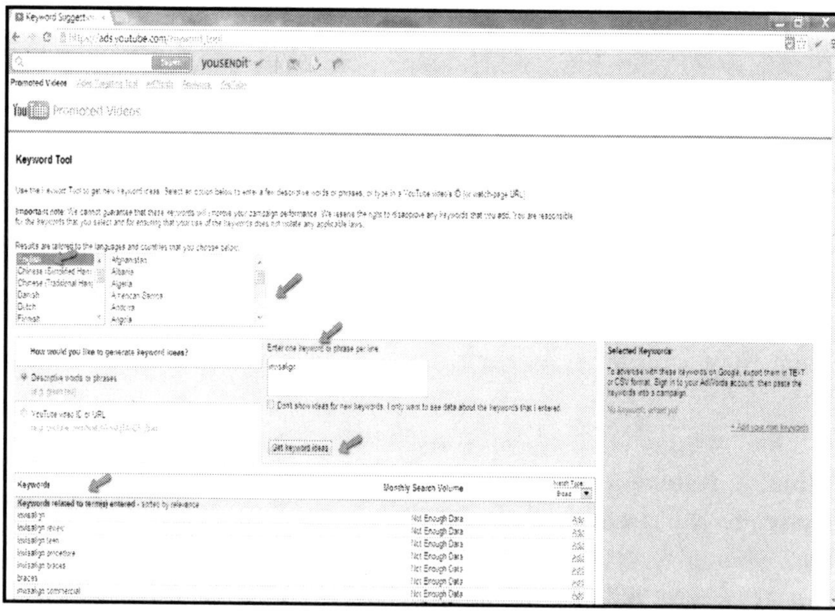

Step 2 – Create a master file like we did in Chapter 7 and have a separate tab as a keyword on YouTube.

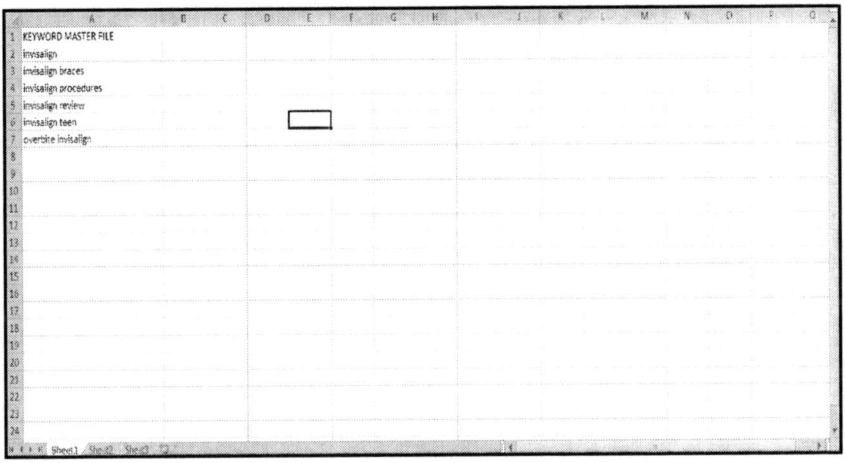

You are going to use these keywords to help you build a profitable campaign for your practice. Get familiar with the tool—please do not skip this process. The better you know how to use this tool, the more of an advantage you will have against your competitors—I guarantee it. They are not using these free tools to help them develop winning campaigns.

Developing a successful YouTube channel is the first step to becoming a YouTube partner. A YouTube partner has a huge advantage over those who are not. Being a YouTube partner builds the credibility and branding of your practice.

The following are four advantages you will get from becoming a YouTube Partner:

1. YouTube will provide in-depth advice on video equipment, production quality, and distribution of your videos. (They have the data regarding what is working and what is not working, which they will share.)
2. They will provide guidance in building a larger audience with certain promotional tools that are not available to the general public.

3. You can earn a lot more money with your videos. This is a side benefit—you can join if you wish. It has its advantages and disadvantages. You have to know how to set this up correctly so that your competitors do not gain market share.
4. You can have clickable banners and links on your template where you can direct your ideal prospect to specific landing pages to generate a high-quality lead.

All the videos that you upload must be owned by you; you must have full rights to the videos on your YouTube channel. You also must have a number of views, likes, favorites, and subscribers to your videos.

To sign up to become a YouTube partner, you can go to the following page and read their policy and guidelines. http://www.youtube.com/yt/creators/partner.html.

Video marketing is extremely important and profitable. What you have learned in this chapter is the foundation for developing a winning campaign that generates as many leads as possible. If you want to take it to the next level, go to www.Wealthy-Orthodontist.com/Video-Marketing.

CHAPTER 11

Email Marketing

STAYING CONNECTED WITH YOUR PROSPECTS and clients is a must if you are looking to build a profitable practice. It amazes me that over 98 percent of Orthodontists do not stay in contact with their clients and prospects. They are basically running their business as a onetime shot—get the money once and move on. This is the wrong approach if you wish to take your practice to $2 million-plus. You will hear me say in this chapter over and over again: The money is in the list. You need to cultivate and nurture your list to get it to grow. You need to have high-quality clients who are willing to pay for your services and high-quality leads that continue to come into your practice for consultation and then for treatment.

E-mail marketing is effective when you send marketing messages that provide value to your list on a regular basis. This can take the form a daily, weekly, or monthly newsletter or coupon. Your messages should provide marketing material and valuable information that will get your prospects to pick up the phone and call you for your product and services.

There are several ways you can approach the setup of your messages and content you send out. It is very important you test and measure the response you receive when you send out your e-mail message to your list.

E-mail marketing is extremely cost effective; however, it also can take time for your clients and prospects to respond because they get bombarded with other marketing messages on a daily basis. This is why your e-mails must be persuasive and must provide valuable content to get your clients and prospects excited to read your e-mails and to do business with you.

Getting your clients and prospects to read your e-mail is the first step to an effective email. Your e-mail message should convince your client and ideal prospect to take action. The first step is to ensure your e-mail gets opened.

Your e-mail draws upon the desires and wants of your ideal prospect and client and provides an overwhelming value and proof of what you are selling. The effective e-mail is crafted with the sole outcome in mind of getting your prospects and clients to pick up the phone and give you a call to buy.

Your e-mail subject headlines (which we will talk about in greater detail) should stop them dead in their tracks and compel them to read what you have sent them.

An effective e-mail accomplishes all these things; it is also trackable and measurable, providing you with insights on what is working and what is not working. With these insights, you can make additional changes and tweaks to get higher quality leads, which increases your bottom line.

One single, good e-mail can bring in tens of thousands if not millions of dollars. This is another reason we conducted the ideal client profile at the very beginning—to make sure we get the prospects and clients we want, the ones who want to buy from you.

Can you think of an e-mail that stopped you in your tracks and got your attention? That is the approach you need to take when sending e-mails out to your clients and prospects.

A caring and authentic doctor brings more cash into their practice. There are various types of personalities you can use when crafting your e-mails to send to your list of clients and prospects. You can come off as being empathetic and caring. You can have a humorous personality and let that attitude shine in your e-mail. It is basically up to you what type of personality you would like to portray in your e-mails.

This attitude should also carry over to your face-to-face correspondence with your prospects as well. The persona you create in your e-mails must be shown in person. If you use a persona you do not like, it will be obvious and it will come off as if you are trying too hard and are not authentic.

Your goal in your e-mails is to build a working, friendly relationship with your clients. You don't want your prospects to look at you as just the doctor; you want them to look at you as a friend. As I said before, most people want to do business with people they like, a person they consider a friend.

When you become friends with someone, it is a lot easier to influence their decisions and make recommendations in their life. I am sure you have friends you have listened to throughout your life. If they say, "Go see this movie!" and they provide a background story about the movie and how good the movie is, most likely you are going to go see the movie.

This is the type of relationship you want to build with your prospects and clients and it can be accomplished through e-mail when done correctly.

Great content is king when it comes to your e-mail. The content you include should be valuable, and it should focus on the services and products you offer as well as testimonials from your past and present clients. The content should drive home each service you offer, and you should tell a story that connects with your clients and ideal prospects.

Stories sell—the right stories engage your clients and get them interested in what you have to say. If you provide great stories, your prospects and ideal clients will be waiting for and eagerly anticipating your e-mails.

You're probably saying, "Teran, I have no stories." My response to you is "Yes, you do have stories you can share with your prospects. They need to connect with your audience and provide—in great detail—the benefits and the end results they will achieve by coming to you for their solution."

Your e-mail must ooze evidence that you're their trusted advisor. You must show yourself to be an advisor who cares about their well-being and who looks out for their best interests. Your competitors will not use these powerful techniques to grow their practice.

How many Orthodontists do you know who are using e-mails to generate new leads and to provide great stories to keep their clients and prospects engaged, compelling them to take action and pick up the phone and call? Not too many. Here is your opportunity to continue to gain a bigger piece of the market share.

Engaging with your prospects and clients and keeping them excited is a must if you want to be different and make a lot more money for your practice. One of the ways to do just that is something that hardly any Orthodontist is doing right now—video e-mails.

A video e-mail message has the same concept as your text e-mail. You can send your prospects and ideal clients to a specific section of your website for them to watch your message. This allows you to truly track your ROI.

Your message should have the following at all times:

1. Exceptional value
2. Great content
3. Captions at the beginning and the end
4. A call to action to get your clients to do what you want them to do

Your video should be just you sitting at your desk and talking, or you can have one of your staff members talk as well. You should be smiling and friendly, and you should look like you care about the topic and the message you are sending out to them.

Nothing screams boring more than you, the doctor, just reading from the script and not showing any emotions or enthusiasm in what you are presenting. It will kill the sale and the content you deliver to your clients and prospects.

You should also track and measure how many people watch the video and how many clients and prospects pick up the phone and come in for a particular product and/or service. The more information you have, the better the results you will achieve because you know what is working and you can make the necessary changes for it to work better. Always strive to improve each marketing message so that you can gain a higher return on your investment.

Building your list should be priority number one. The goal is for your practice to generate and expand the lead flow of new clients coming into your practice. You start to build your list by providing a free report or video on a particular topic that your ideal prospects and clients would be greatly interested in.

For example, you can develop a report on "How to Choose the Right Orthodontist" or you can develop a free report on "The Truth about Dentists Providing Braces." This will portray you as the expert and the go-to doctor who is providing extremely important content to help them make the right decision—and the decision should be to use you and only you for their Orthodontic care.

Building your list starts with the following steps:

1. Create a free report or video for prospects and clients that come to your site and/or office.
2. In exchange for providing the report, your ideal prospects and/or clients are going to give you their e-mail address or mailing address and mobile number.

3. You deliver the report after they sign up, and you let them know they should label you as a safe sender in their e-mail program. That way the e-mails you send them will not end up in their spam or junk box and they will see it is coming from a trusted source—you.
4. You continue to follow up with your prospects and clients with additional information and a marketing message to get them to take action on the products and services you are selling.

It is that simple: You keep track of who is reading what, what is your open rate, how many people clicked a link, and how much money you made from each e-mail that had a call to action to buy. Note: not all e-mails are targeted to get your client to purchase something from you. Some emails can be just pure, valuable content that builds your credibility and trustworthiness, which stills brings more money into your bank account.

Connecting with your clients is different from connecting with your ideal prospect. Crafting your e-mail for clients will require a different message because they have already established a relationship with you. The things that will stay the same are the following:

1. Excellent content
2. Continuing to build on the connection (friends)
3. Excellent value

Where the e-mails are going to be different is that you have already built the rapport and you have the connection established. Each e-mail will bring out the things that your client is happy about. Each e-mail you send out can make a particular client the star of the month or the client of the month, sharing their success story. This is where you want to make your clients the star of your practice. This will get them to continue to read your marketing message, and it will continue to strengthen the friendship you have with each client. How powerful is that?

Well, it is extremely powerful. This technique—making the clients the stars—took a failing toy business from bankruptcy to over $250 million.

You want to use this technique with your e-mails when you are writing to your clients. You also want to segment your client list, which we will talk about in greater detail later on. You want one list of your clients and another list of your prospects.

Providing satisfaction up front is a must when crafting your e-mail messages for your ideal prospect. This is the time when you are building the rapport with your prospect; you're looking to gain their trust and to show that you care about their needs by being different from all the other Dentists and Orthodontists and providing the right education for the prospect to make the decision.

Your e-mails for your ideal prospect should always contain your USP. What makes you completely different from your competitors? It should be front and center so that your prospect will never forget it. You are positioning yourself in the eye of the prospect; their only decision should be to use you as their trusted advisor.

Your content should also show empathy and caring. If you tell stories and provide testimonials from happy clients who have gone through the same situation, this shows you are connecting with them on a different level compared with your competitors.

One technique you should definitely use is telling horror stories of clients that have gone elsewhere and used a Dentist instead of an Orthodontist, only to have things completely redone by an Orthodontist later. You are not bashing Dentists; you are just showing one has more expertise than the other. One of your e-mail messages that you send to your ideal prospects must contain such a story if you have one.

Effective e-mails need to be sent by an excellent service provider who can deliver your e-mails without any major hiccups. One of the services you should sign up for to get your messages delivered is Aweber.

Aweber is extremely effective, inexpensive, and easy to set up for delivering auto-responder messages to your clients and prospects. Once you have signed up for an Aweber account and have exhausted their service, you can move up to another provider that will do wonders for your business: Infusionsoft.

To sign up for Aweber, please go here: http://www.aweber.com.

To sign up for Infusionsoft, please go here: http://www.infusionsoft.com.

Both e-mail service providers have videos that show you step-by-step how to set up your e-mail campaigns.

You can find more details on using effective e-mails to gain more prospects by going to www.WealthyOrthodontist.com/Effective-Emails

Success with your e-mails starts with an important metric called "open rate." To obtain a high open rate for your e-mails, you must have the right subject headline which will stop your prospects and clients right in their tracks and compel them to open and read your email.

The formula for having a successful headline is AIDA:

1. It should grab their ATTENTION.
2. It should be INTERESTING to your client and/or prospect.
3. It should appeal to their DESIRE.
4. It should compel your prospect and clients to take ACTION.

This all starts in the subject headline.

Your subject headlines can be funny, curious, or challenging. You can ask a question and/or provide facts. Your main goal is to get your prospect to open your e-mail. If they don't open your e-mail to read your message, you are not using the AIDA formula correctly.

Here are several profitable headlines you can use:

- Bad News
- Good News
- (Client's Name) I want to let you know...
- Thank You
- Ooops
- (Client's Name) this is for...

Keys open locked doors. To open the door to success with your e-mail campaign, you must start testing and tracking results in order to make more money for your practice.

Testing is essential, and the majority of Orthodontists and even advertisers in other industries never test their marketing material to improve their results. Your goal is to obtain the highest conversion possible, which includes sales of your products and services, the open rate of your e-mails, and your marketing message as a whole.

Tracking what is working and not working is the first step. Aweber has the ability to help you track the open rates of your e-mail and the click-through rates of links within the e-mail you send to prospects and clients. In other words, you will be able to find out exactly how many people open your e-mail to read it and how many people clicked the link that took them to your website for additional information or to book an appointment. You could also track by a telephone number in your e-mail to see if the message you crafted connects with your prospects or clients.

Here are few things you should test after setting up a series of auto-responders for your e-mail campaign.

1. Subject headline
2. The message or copy of your e-mail
3. The offer you present to your prospects or clients
4. Video e-mail vs. text e-mail
5. Short e-mail vs. long e-mail
6. Call to action
7. P.S.

These seven elements will get you started in testing and compiling your data so that you can create an effective e-mail campaign that adds a significant amount of cash to your practice.

I also want to help you crush your competition and make more money than you can handle by using the valuable secret technique of list segmentation.

List segmentation is when you divide your list of prospects and place them in certain sections within your business. It is a technique that no one in the Orthodontic Industry is using to dramatically increase their lead quality and the amount of money flowing into their practice.

Today I am going to reveal to you exactly how to set up and take advantage of this technique to bring in the highest quality leads and build a rapport with your clients and prospects.

As you probably remember, I talked about having a list of e-mails that are directed to prospects and the other list directed to clients. Using Aweber, you can create as many lists of names as you want.

PLEASE SEE FIGURE 1.1 BELOW:

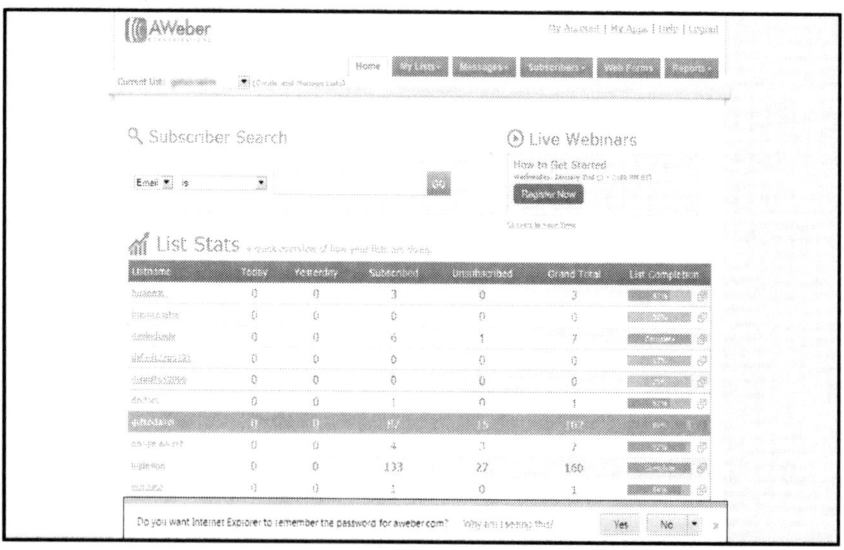

Having different lists allows you to craft the right message for each segment of your prospects and clients (e.g., your prospects that contact you). Some might be interested in Invisalign only, so you would create a list and send messages to the people on that list about the use of Invisalign and nothing else. Being specific to their wants and needs increases the quality of the lead and the money coming into your practice.

As for your clients, maybe you have clients that are over fifty and are interested specifically in Invisalign. You would need to tailor your message differently when you speak to an older crowd than you would when you speak to a younger crowd.

THE ADVANTAGES OF USING THIS TECHNIQUE ARE:

1. You show that you care about the client or prospect.
2. You are building rapport and credibility.
3. Your connection will become unbreakable because you are providing high-quality information.
4. You are giving them exactly what they want.

Please use this technique to your advantage; your competitors will have no idea what hit them. There are many other ways you can use list segmentation for your practice, but you should start off by breaking down the different type of clients that you have and prospects you would like to have for you practice and deliver the right message to them at the right time.

Checking for spam is a smart and essential way to make sure you will not receive any complaints from your subscribers. One of the ways to quickly to check to see if your e-mail will be flagged as spam and/or placed in the junk section of your clients' and prospects' e-mail accounts is to have your e-mail checked and verified before you send it out by Aweber.

Aweber has a free function that will check the content of your e-mail to make sure there are no words that will stop your e-mail from being delivered.

If you do receive a high spam warning, you must rewrite your e-mail in a way that will get your e-mail message delivered. You should also set up your e-mail accounts so that clients have to verify only once instead of twice when they sign up for your free report and/or newsletter.

It is also a law that you must give those on your e-mail list the opportunity to unsubscribe from receiving any future message from you if they choose to do so. However, if you have the right content and are providing value to your prospects and clients, you will have nothing to worry about.

Please see the following Figure 1.2 regarding checking your e-mail message for spam before sending it out to clients and prospects.

FIGURE 1.2 – CHECKING E-MAIL FOR SPAM

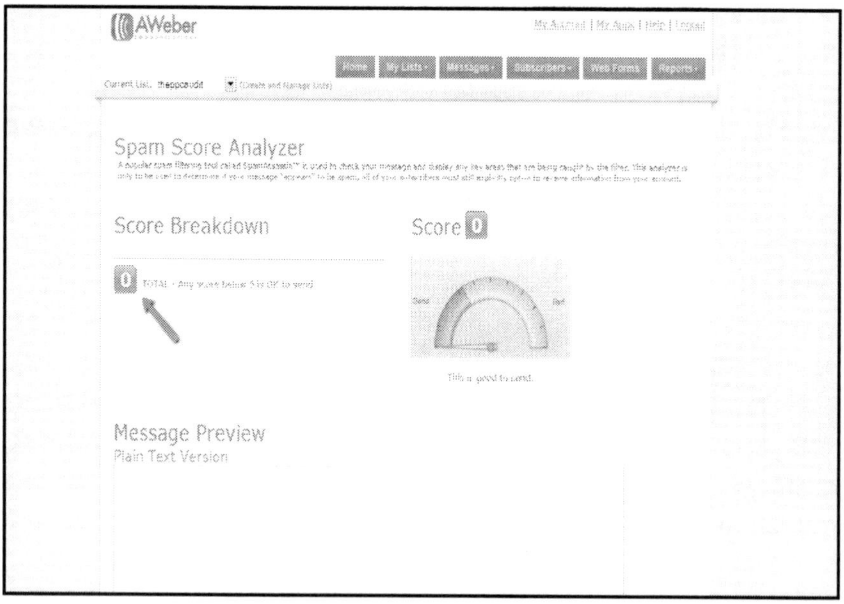

FIGURE 1.3 – RESULTS FROM CHECKING FOR SPAM

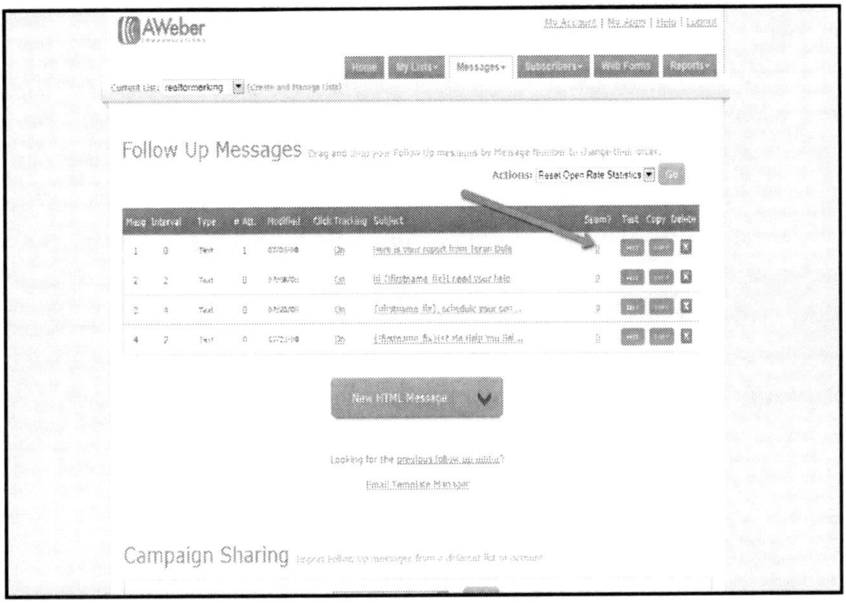

The money is in the list. Repeat after me: The money is in the list. Do not forget this golden rule. The one thing to remember is the more high-quality leads coming into your customer database and potential customer database, the more money you will make.

It is a fact that it costs more money to obtain a new customer than it does to sell more to your existing customer. Continue to build upon your list by using online and offline strategies. Don't just focus on one solution; use all solutions to your advantage.

The strategy you want to use is to provide valuable content—free reports and/or videos—that educate and provide the exact information your client wants in exchange for their contact information.

On every page of your site, you should give your prospects and clients the opportunity to join your list. You should also have two monthly printed newsletters that you send out to both prospects and clients. You should have one monthly newsletter going to your clients. This newsletter reiterates why they have decided to stay with you as their trusted advisor. You should also feature a client of the month and write a small article about the client. Appreciation goes a long way.

Your second newsletter should provide high-quality information directed to your prospects. It should show them what they are missing by not using your services. You should include industry statistics and new procedures in the newsletter, and your USP should be front and center in both newsletters. Invite your prospects and clients to share the newsletter with their friends and family as well.

The second highly effective and profitable technique for building a highly responsive, quality list of clients and prospects is to start blogging.

Create your own blog to connect with your clients, referrals, and prospects. And remember, they are looking to see if their doctor is likeable, authentic, and honest.

Engage with your prospects by telling stories of your clients' successes—the problems and the solutions that your practice has provided over the years. Include interviews with your clients about your practice and let them provide a powerful testimonial to build your list.

You should give the opportunity to those who read your blog the privilege to request additional information about a product and/or service. It is all about providing value to the client. The more you provide, the better the quality of the lead and the more cash you will have in your bank account.

You have nothing to lose. Implement these powerful, money-making techniques now. The longer you wait, the more money you are letting your competitors take away from you.

Auto-responders help make an effective e-mail campaign because you can create as many e-mails as you want for your segmented list of clients and prospects and have them sent in a series on the day and at the time you want to certain individuals. It is all up to you.

I provided the process for setting up your list earlier in this chapter. An effective e-mail campaign can be measured, tracked, and should show a ROI for the time you spent working on your e-mails.

It is valuable to get feedback from both sides of your list, so you should provide surveys in exchange for rewards such as a discount on certain products and services, which all lead to higher revenues. However, do not discount your prices. You have the formula that gives you permission to increase your prices without upsetting your clients while at the same time you are providing an extremely valuable service.

The effective e-mail campaign also tells a story and hits all your clients' and prospects' emotional buttons. We buy on emotions, so tap into the emotion of your prospects and clients and back it up with credibility, authenticity, trust, honesty, and value.

If you do this, you will create an effective e-mail campaign. Your prospects will be eager, willing, and excited to get an e-mail from their trusted advisor. Become their friend, give them what they want, and you will get the reciprocity back plus more as well as a practice you and your family can be proud of that generates lifetime earnings.

CHAPTER 12

Mobile Marketing

OVER 85 PERCENT OF THE WORLD'S POPULATION has a mobile phone and that number is still growing rapidly. As an advertiser, this means you have the opportunity to target a huge segment of the population who are constantly on their phones and who share and read each other's messages.

The beauty of mobile marketing is you are targeting mobile users who search for service providers (such as Orthodontists) using their smartphone and/or clients of your practice.

With mobile marketing, you can target specific users of certain phones and tablets. You can target clients that use only tablets (e.g., an iPad or a Nexus). You can target iPhone or Android users. It is basically up to you.

This is one of the fastest-growing segments in the world. Smartphones are becoming less expensive and some consumers have as many as three phones with them. In this chapter, we are going to discover how we can use mobile marketing to our advantage.

Here are some basic facts: Over 20 percent of online searches are done by local consumers looking for products and services using their mobile phone. If your practice is not visible online, you just lost a high-quality lead and cash that was yours for the taking.

Demolish your competition by having a viewable, mobile-ready website for your practice. Of all of the Orthodontists' websites, 97 percent are not mobile ready, which means the site cannot be completely viewed on one's smartphone.

This is a catastrophic mistake. A large number of users search on their smartphones for local services. If you are there but they cannot view your website, you have just lost a customer for life.

To check to see if your website is mobile ready, you can use the following free tools:

- http://www.Mobiready.com
- http://validator.w3.org/mobile/
- http://www.testiphone.com/
- http://ipadpeek.com/

These free tools will let you know if your site is viewable on a customer's or client's smartphone. Sometimes they will even show you what your site looks like on a particular phone. If you have a website, it is important to now also have a mobile site ready to go so that clients can find you in mobile search. We will talk more about mobile search later in this chapter.

Take a look right now and see if your competitors' sites are mobile ready. If they are not, breathe a sigh of relief and get your site up as soon as possible. As Woody Allen says, 50 percent of success is just showing up. Make sure you show up in the mobile searches and that you are viewable on all smartphones and tablets.

Google AdWords has a very robust platform that allows you to target mobile users who are searching for you with their smartphones right now. This is also available on Bing and Yahoo!. Mobile marketing pay-per-click can deliver you highly targeted leads with less competition and a lower overall cost per lead.

The process to set up your mobile marketing campaign is

explained in your Google AdWords account. You can decide on the message and the landing pages just like you did in Chapter 7.

Get a complete, step-by-step set-up video by going to www.WealthyOrthodontist.com/Mobile-Marketing-Setup.

The setup for mobile marketing is slightly different. You have fewer words to play with in your ad than when you use Google AdWords for search on the display network.

The keyword setup and ad group categories are the same and so are the destination URL and the display URL.

The advantage you have setting up your mobile pay-per-click campaigns is you will enjoy a lot less competition. Heck, you might be the only one advertising your services in your surrounding area. However, it is important your website is mobile ready for your prospects and clients to view. (Note: Google has now implemented Enhance campaigns, which automatically adds your campaigns in mobile search.)

EXAMPLE #1:

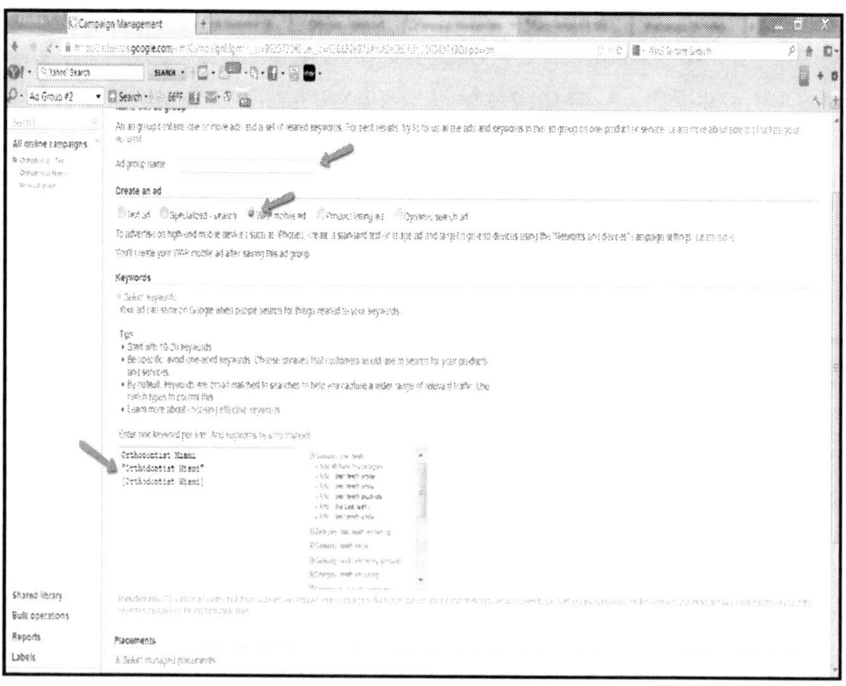

Example #2

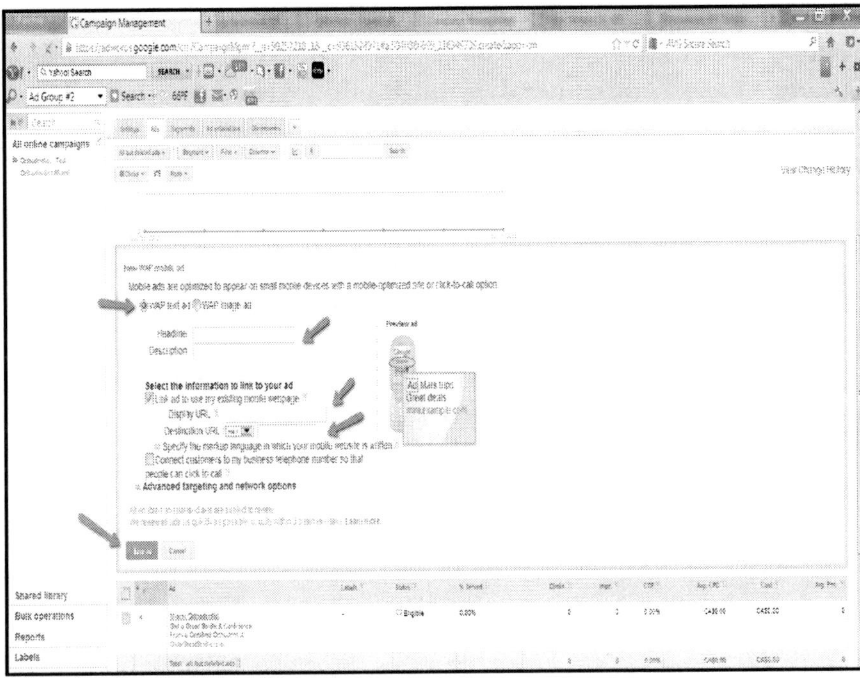

Optimizing your mobile website for the search results is the first step in getting your site ranked well in the mobile search engine. When you start off, you want to make sure you have the right description of your site so that the search engines can read your page and that you have a site map as well.

The biggest bang you are going to get for your buck is to invest in a well-thought-out link campaign for your site. A well-developed link campaign will help your site move up in rankings. This means other relevant links will link to your site, which shows your site is relevant and provides quality content for users. It is somewhat like a list of friends you have in your phone book—they all know each other and they have your number.

Another advantage of having a well-developed link campaign is your competition will not have one set up. Orthodontists in the mobile search arena rarely check their sites for the type of links and the quality of links coming into and leaving their sites.

With so many changes taking place with Google, it is hard for a business owner to keep up with the new policies and algorithm tweaks Google conducts on a monthly—and sometimes daily—basis. Consequently, you should focus on the following:

1. Have good, high-quality, unique content that is different from your competitors.
2. Develop a power link campaign.
3. Provide value on every single page on your website.

Building an effective texting campaign starts with having a series of text messages ready for your ideal prospects along with the headline to achieve a high open rate.

Once you have your ideal prospects' and clients' mobile numbers, you should start planning a text campaign. The beauty of texting is that 98 percent of all texts sent are read by whomever you send the text to. It is like FedEx; if you receive a FedEx envelope, you don't throw it away. I am sure you open it to see whom it is from and what the letter or package is all about. (Hint: use this to your advantage.)

When you set up your campaign, you should have a minimum of five texts ready to go: five texts that you are going to send your ideal prospects and five different texts you're going to send clients.

Write your texts on paper first and read them out loud to yourself. Reading them out loud allows you to fix any errors you might have. If, when reading it out loud you stop and pause at a particular sentence, you know you need to fix it.

You can have your texts set up so that they are sent on specific times and dates. Your text should have a call to action and a benefit your prospect or client will receive by taking action. Your message must connect with the client or prospect, or else it will be ineffective.

Have your five texts build upon each other, providing value and high-quality content that engages the parties to take action and pick up the phone and call you.

There are services out there that you can use to help you send your text messages to clients. Get started with this text campaign and expect a significant increase in high-quality leads and more cash in your bank account.

The following are a few text-messaging services to look at to help develop your campaign (Please note: do your due diligence with any provider.):

- http://www.message-media.com/
- http://www.mobivity.com/local/
- http://www.txtimpact.com/text-message-service.asp
- http://www.eztexting.com/business-sms-texting.html
- http://grouptexting.com/

Planning your mobile-marketing strategy is a must if you want to be successful with mobile search and texting campaigns directed toward your prospects and clients.

The first thing you want to look at is what you are trying accomplish with your campaigns. Let's take a look at the campaign for ideal prospects. This is where you want to use the ideal client profile that you developed. Hopefully, by now you have added additional information about your ideal client. This is going to help you craft your messages to encourage the ideal client to pick up the phone and call you for a consultation.

The second thing you are going to look at is the sequence and the type of messages are you going to send out.

1. Welcome message with content and value
2. Bad news (talk about clients or prospects that have made the mistake of not taking care of their problem)
3. Story about a successful client that gained the end result that they were looking for
4. Testimonials from clients endorsing your services
5. Reiterate the end results they will receive from working with

you; provide valuable information and a call to action.

6. Regarding the setup for your clients, keep in mind your goal is to get your client to buy additional products and services. It is almost the same setup as the one above.
7. Acknowledge and appreciate them for continuing to be a client and remind them why are still your client.
8. Introduce them to the product and/or service you want them to buy. Start off by providing value first.
9. Provide proof; tell a story of a client that neglected the instruction and the problem they had to go through because they neglected it.
10. Provide the stories of two to three successful clients that got what they wanted by buying your product or service.
11. Have the client (in their own words) talk about how happy they are. Provide additional, valuable content and a call to action for them to pick up the phone and call you.

Your clients like to be entertained, and they're looking to buy the experience and the end result they will get from using your services. Your text campaign must match your ideal prospects' desires, wants, fears, and concerns. Your goal for your text message is to get the result you want and to make sure your client and ideal prospect get the result they want.

The following steps outline the techniques for implementing your text messaging campaign:

1. Start by choosing a reputable service provider to send out your text messages. Many of the providers will allow you a free account that you can test for thirty days. (Please do your due diligence.)
2. Go through the provider's setup you decide to try. Many of the providers will give you a step-by-step process for the setup.
3. Craft your messages you want to send out to your list.

A successful e-mail mobile-marketing campaign allows you to target your ideal prospects' and clients' smartphones the same way you did for text messaging. The difference is that with e-mail you have more room to provide more detail in your message. Another difference is that your prospects and clients are reading their e-mail on their phone.

It is the same process, though: provide the value up front and get them to take action. You should track all results. Remember, your subject headline is going to be extremely influential when it comes to getting your e-mails read. The more engaging it is, the better the results will be. Always test and tweak all your e-mail campaigns.

Get a list of twenty-five powerful e-mail subject headlines at: www.WealthyOrthodontist.com/Email-Subject-headlines

PMET (Planning, Messages, Execution, and Tracking) is the formula you must use to build a successful e-mail mobile-marketing campaign.

The first step (PLANNING) is to decide the end goal you want to achieve with your campaign. What products and/or services would you like to promote? When do you want to promote them and to whom do you want to promote them? (Remember your ideal client profile!)

The second step (MESSAGES) is to craft your e-mail messages in a way that will get your ideal prospects and/or clients to read your messages. Here are some tips that will put you on the right track for this:

Text-only Mobile E-mail Strategies to Make More Money:

- **Capitalize your headlines – it makes them stand out**
- **Use *** (asterisks) or < (less-than symbol) at the start and end of specific words and/or phrases that you want to stand out and grab your prospects' attention. Set them in bold type.**

- Make sure to use line breaks to separate headlines from the body message and the body message from the call to action.
- Spell out your URLs to the specific pages you want your ideal clients and prospects to visit.

The third step is EXECUTING your messages to your ideal clients and prospects and setting up the campaigns to be e-mailed out through your auto-responder service. You can write out as many e-mail messages as you want, upload them, and have them delivered at a specific time and on a specific day.

The fourth step is TRACKING. You want to track the results to see which e-mail and/or campaign brought in the most money for your advertising dollars. Here is one tracking tool you should implement in your campaigns.

- I highly recommend Google Analytics.

The goal is to track the increase in the number of clicks from your ads to the final destination (i.e., the landing page of your offer and/or calls coming into your office).

Now let's look at the best e-mail design practices to follow to start putting *more money* into your pocket.

- Try to keep your e-mails to 20,000 KB or less.
- Create e-mails for the appropriate screen size for smartphones (320x480); this can vary between IOS and Android devices. Stay in the area of 372 pixels.
- Remember to keep your important information above the fold—right where your ideal prospects and clients can see it.
- The line length should be seventy characters or less to have a well-crafted message that can be read easily.
- Keep your font size at 30 for headers and 14 for the body text.

- Plan for more space (10–15 pixels for the possibility of mistyping).

Some interesting facts:

- E-mail vendor Return Path (returnpath.net) stated that the open rates for e-mail expanded by 82.4 percent from March 2011 to March 2012.
- According to exacttarget.com., more than 56 percent of US consumers have made a purchase with their smartphone after receiving a marketing message via mobile e-mail.
- According to "The Mobile Movement" published by Google in April 2011, 82% of smartphone users check and send e-mail with their device.
- According to "2013 Digital Publishing Report: Retail Apps & Buying Habits" published by Adobe, mobile purchasing decisions are most often persuaded by e-mails from companies (71%) only to be surpassed by the influence of friends (87%).

It is imperative that your e-mail campaigns are built on a strong foundation centered around the use of mobile phones. Each day, more and more IOS and Android smartphone users are checking their messages on only one device and that is their phone. Start building a successful campaign with what you have just discovered in this chapter. Implement it now and witness a dramatic increase in your bottom line.

Tweaking and tracking your results and reading the data you get from your Google conversion tracking and/or Google Analytics is a must for your mobile e-mail marketing campaign. If you don't know exactly what is working, how will you know if you are leaving money on the table?

When starting the campaign, you should focus on three things:

1. Getting new customers
2. Getting your clients to buy more often
3. Getting your clients to pay more for your product and services

The previous chapters gave you a complete plan for how to do just that. You should be tracking every campaign and every piece of marketing material you put live on your site and provide to your staff, referrals, and clients. The following are a few things you should tweak on a weekly basis:

1. Change and add new ads to beat the highest-winning ad.
2. Eliminate and tweak campaigns that provide a higher conversion; rewrite e-mail copy to get more results.
3. Test subject headlines.
4. Test new keywords.
5. Add negative keywords to your campaigns (Google AdWords).

Standards and regulations regarding your clients' and prospects' privacy are extremely important. Violating their privacy can earn you a warning from your ISP or e-mail service provider. It can also cause your ISP and e-mail provider to drop your from their service, leaving you without a list.

I won't bore you on policies and procedures, but here are a few things to remember:

1. Always give your ideal prospect and clients the opportunity to refuse to receive any further messages from you.
2. You should not send unsolicited emails; don't send e-mails for your services to those that did not request additional information from you.
3. Do not violate the CAN-SPAM Act – please visit the following website at your convenience.
4. http://www.business.ftc.gov/documents/bus61-can-spam-act-compliance-guide-business

There are advertisers who have violated these acts and have not been caught or fined for doing so. Just remember you want to develop a friendship with all your clients and prospects. You do not want to break their trust and violate their privacy.

If someone wishes for you to remove them from your list, quickly comply with their request and continue to build your list. Not everyone will want to continue to hear from you and that is fine; you don't want someone who is not interested in what you have to offer. Your goal is to obtain as many buyers as possible.

Positioning is like an engine in your car. Without the engine you can't move. If you have an engine and it does not run very well, you will have other vehicles passing right by you. It is important to have the right positioning for your practice. It makes your competition a nonfactor and sweetest of all—it delivers a truckload of cash to your business.

Many Orthodontists have said to me, "Teran, I will wait for now. My practice is doing well and I don't think this positioning is going to really bring that much more cash into my practice." Listen, don't be fooled. The longer you wait, the sooner your competition is going to pass you by, leaving you with a speechless look on your face.

The first step is to come up with a unique positioning and a USP to stand out in the marketplace. For example, we have:

- FedEx
- Domino's Pizza
- UPS
- M&M candies
- "How do you spell relief? R-O-L-A-I-D-S!"
- Listerine

All these companies and products have a unique selling proposition that positions them far ahead of their competition. Here's how you can do the same thing for your practice. Your competitors are not using this to their advantage. They are not using the mobile-marketing platform to obtain high-quality leads to position their practice as the go-to practice in the market. If you do use what I just shared with you, you will be far ahead of the game.

Engaging your prospects and clients and providing valuable content to them in all the areas where they hang out will continue to provide you more leads than you can handle. I hope you are seeing the common theme here. You want to be everywhere your clients and prospects share their thoughts and hang out. You are building your brand and positioning yourself as the only choice.

The majority of smartphone users enjoy and share their thoughts on social networking sites such as Facebook, Google+, and Instagram, as I covered in previous chapters. Google is rapidly changing based on feedback from their social network users in order to provide relevant, high-quality information to all users.

When you provide such information to your target market, Google will reward and you will rank high in the search engine. You're building trust and credibility on all levels. The more smart marketing you put into your practice, the better overall results you will see in your bank account.

Combine the two, and test, tweak, and measure your marketing messages you provide to your clientele. Enter the conversations they are having and provide the solutions they are looking for. This chapter provided you with the tools to do just that. Put your competition on notice now.

You should also be aware that two-dimensional barcodes are now available and able to be scanned into your smartphone. When they are scanned, up comes a coupon, discounts, and/or messages. There is a huge advantage to having a QR code for your practice: You can directly keep in contact with your prospects and engage them on another level than just e-mail alone.

You can create your own QR code and offer coupons for braces, Invisalign discounts, consultations, contests, or valuable reports or videos for your prospects or clients to watch.

These QR codes can be placed on books, signs, business cards, appointment cards, magazines and/or reports. Your goal is to provide valuable information that will engage the prospect to continue to keep you in mind when they need your services and even to recommend you to friends and family.

THE FOLLOWING IS A PICTURE OF A QR:

THE FOLLOWING WEBSITES ARE A FEW RESOURCES YOU CAN USE TO GENERATE YOUR OWN QR CODE:

- http://qrlicious.com/
- http://www.qrstuff.com
- http://www.pitneyworks.com/offer/qrcodes/

THE FOLLOWING IS QR CODE BEST PRACTICES AND A CHECKLIST FOR YOU:

- You must have a strong call to action to get the ideal client and clients to scan the code.
- You must have a mobile landing page to bring the ideal prospects and clients to. It should be clear and have an irresistible offer.
- Keep the URL short. Make sure to keep the QR code neat and readable.
- Always provide valuable content.

- Always test your QR code before making it live to the general public. (You want to make sure it can be scanned and read on phones, readers, and in print and in color.)
- Always track and measure the results of your QR code campaign.

The more you cover the complete digital arena for your practice, the better the results and the quality of clients and leads you will generate. Not only that, but your bank account will gladly thank you on a daily basis for adding more of his friends for him to play with.

You can also build an enormous following and provide valuable, entertaining information to your clients and prospects by developing your own mobile app for your practice. This is another extremely profitable way to keep in contact and build your reputation online by using mobile apps that can spread across social networks. Mobile apps have been all the rage for the past few years and the industry itself is just scratching the surface.

The mobile app you must create for your practice should be available on all the popular smartphone platforms. You should start with the following type that has the following elements:

1. Phone direct
2. Location with GPS mapping (goes live on activation, will pinpoint your office on GPS map)
3. "Tell a Friend" instant referrals by e-mail, Facebook, Twitter, and text
4. Home
5. Make appointments
6. Office hours
7. Services performed
8. News
9. Fan wall
10. Website

11. Photo gallery
12. FAQ
13. YouTube video of you
14. Newsletter sign up
15. Messages
16. Submit photos (Your patients can send "before" and "after" pictures directly to you from their smartphone.)

And you can text all of your customers and prospects instantly and as often as you like with tips, specials, "before" and "after" pictures, and referral incentives.

Look around you—everyone has their nose in their phones these days. There are 184 million smartphones in the United States alone. Be where their eyes are looking! Most of your customers don't know all the services you provide; put it in their hands and let them know every week or month by text and e-mail.

There are more than 3.3 billion phone subscribers in the world, and in the United States over 92 million actively participate in text messaging. If you don't get started now, your practice will fall behind. Put this chapter to use and get started.

CHAPTER 13

Pinterest

SOCIAL-NETWORKING WEBSITES continue to evolve as users continue to spend the majority of their time sharing their lives and information with their friends, family and the public-at-large. One of the fastest-growing new social-networking sites taking the industry by storm is Pinterest.

Pinterest allows users to share their photos with other users. The photos tend to be pictures of food, fashion, products, and/or services.

It is simple to set up and use a Pinterest account, and it is becoming one of the major players when it comes to grabbing the attention of Internet users worldwide. Now, you're probably saying, "Okay, Teran, what does that have to do with my practice?" That's a great question! You will find out shortly the advantages Pinterest offers, and no one in your market is using this highly targeted lead-generation site to their advantage.

Because of that, you can clean up and take as many new, high-quality leads as you want using the information I am about to share in this chapter. You are going to want to take notes on using Pinterest, and you are going to want to implement all the ideas I present to corner the area you service.

More than anything else, Pinterest is focused on the lifestyles and interests of the users of the website. The main focus of the site is pinning pictures with brief comments about the picture.

Follow these next steps to sign up for Pinterest directly at the site at www.Pinterest.com and wait a week or two to get approved to join the site. (Remember to add me as a friend: Teran Dale or Teran Dale Marketing.)

You want to research where your ideal prospect hangs out on Pinterest because knowing his or her likes and dislikes will allow you to target the right individuals to build your list and bring more cash into your practice.

Once your becomes account active, the next steps is to start following other Pinterest members that you like, those that share the same interests as you, or those about whom you would like to know more about their interests.

You are looking to build a community of friends using this platform. The more you share and the more value you provide, the better your experience will be on the board and the better the results you will achieve.

Your Pinterest board allows you to pin photos of items and subjects that you like. Start looking at areas of interest to you. Some areas may be automobiles, fashion, health, foods, restaurants, and so forth. Remember, you are looking to attract other users to your board as well. This is why you should start off by liking other members' boards and pictures and areas of interest that appeal to you.

The following pictures shows you how to set up your Pinterest account:

STEP 1

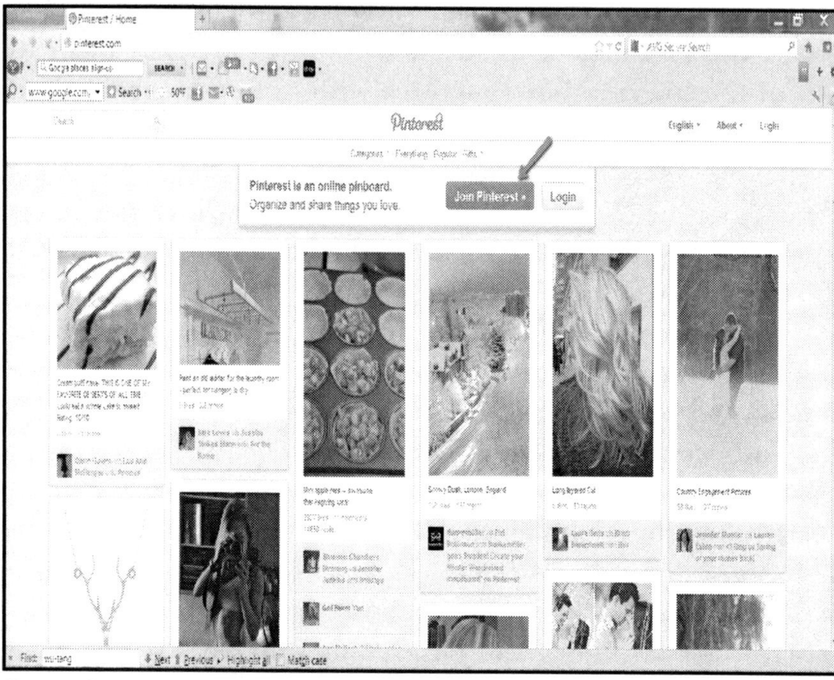
Pinterest / Home
pinterest.com
Pinterest
Pinterest is an online pinboard.
Organize and share things you love.
Join Pinterest »
Login

STEP 2

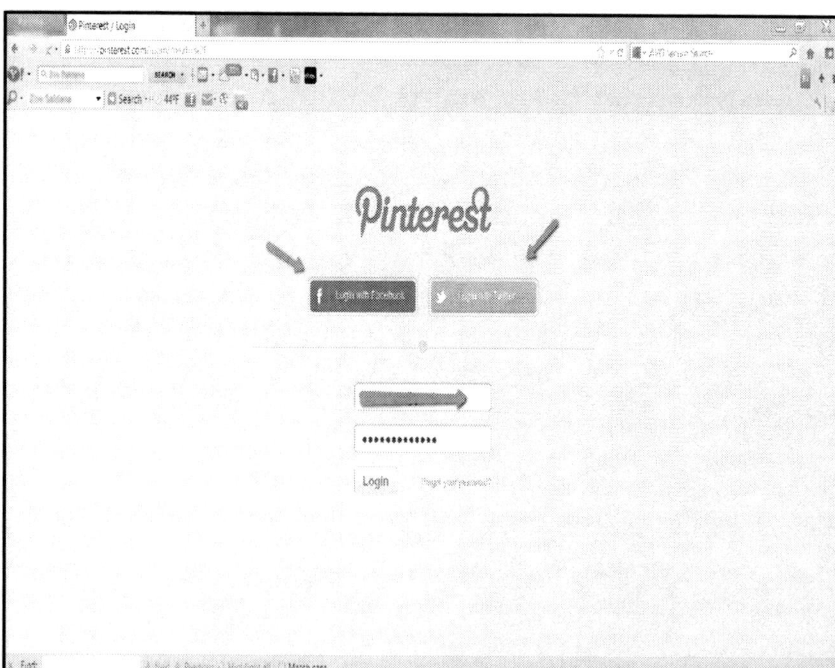
Pinterest / Login
Pinterest
Login

STEP 3

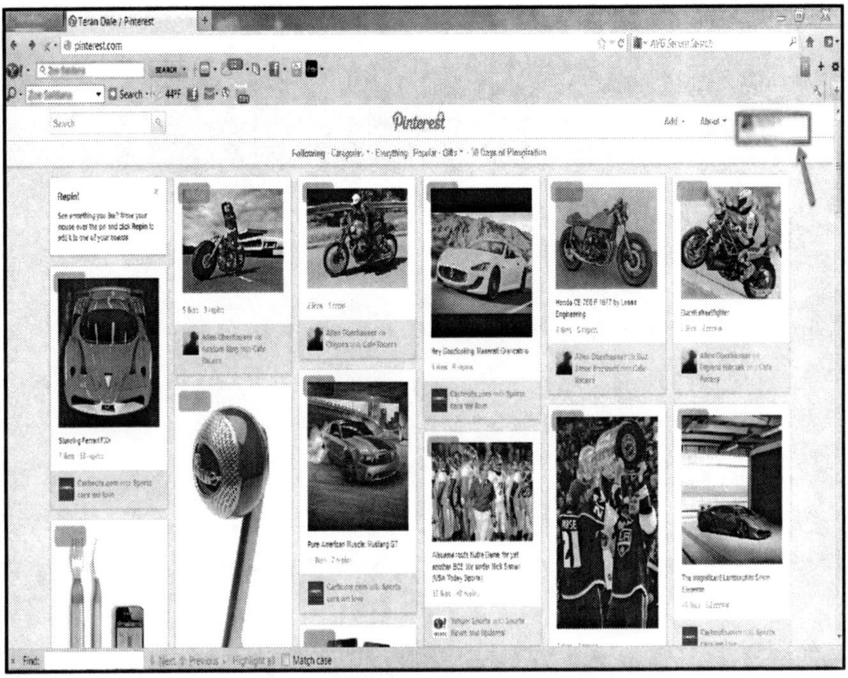
Teran Dale / Pinterest
pinterest.com
Pinterest
Repin!

STEP 4

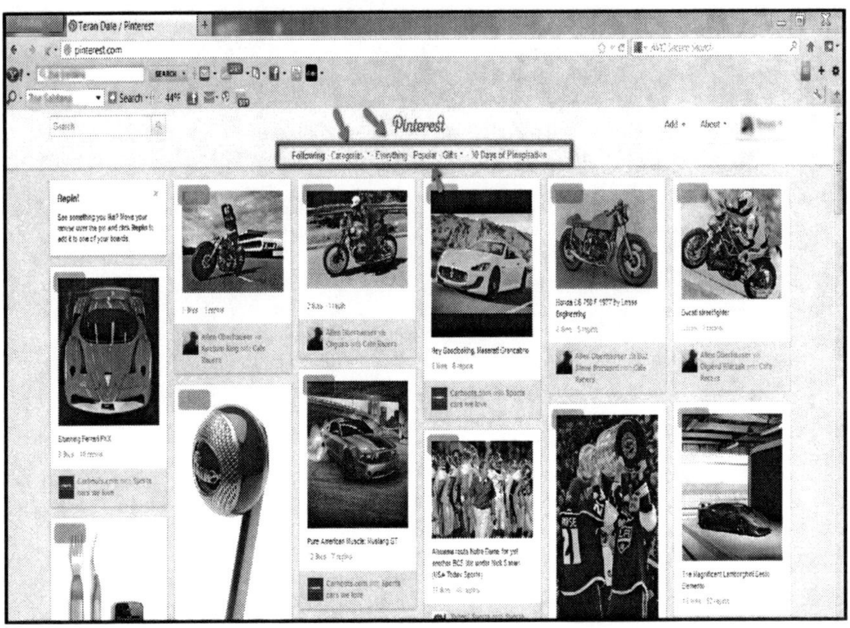
Teran Dale / Pinterest
pinterest.com
Pinterest
Repin!

STEP 5

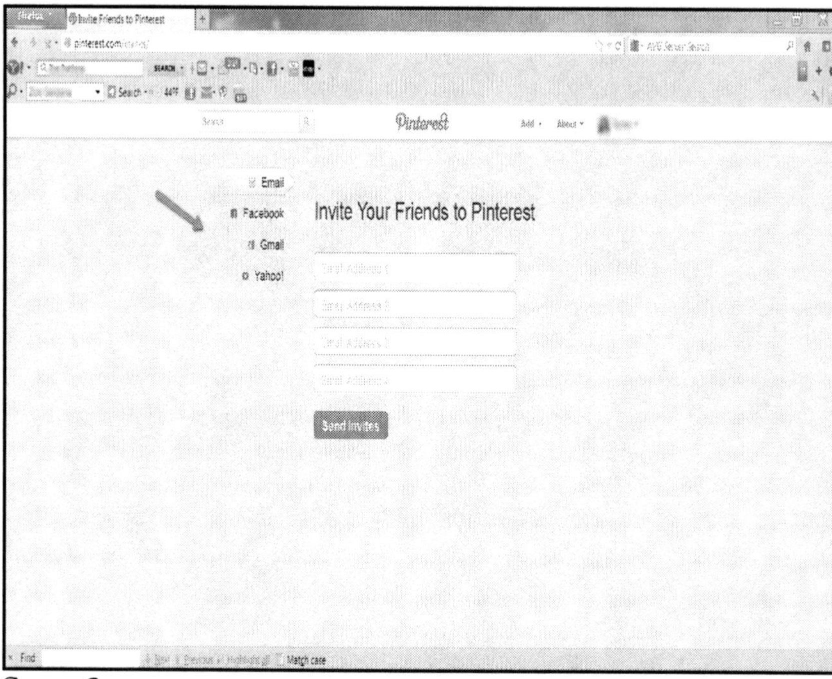
Invite Friends to Pinterest
Pinterest
Email
Facebook
Gmail
Yahoo!
Invite Your Friends to Pinterest
Send Invites
Find
Match case

STEP 6

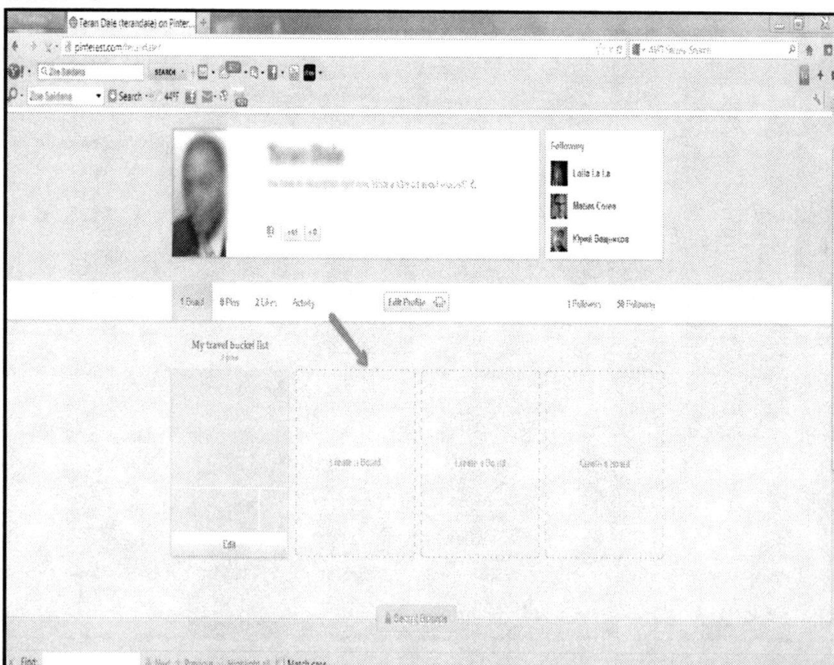
Teran Dale (terandale) on Pinter...
My travel bucket list
Edit Profile
Edit
Match case

STEP 7

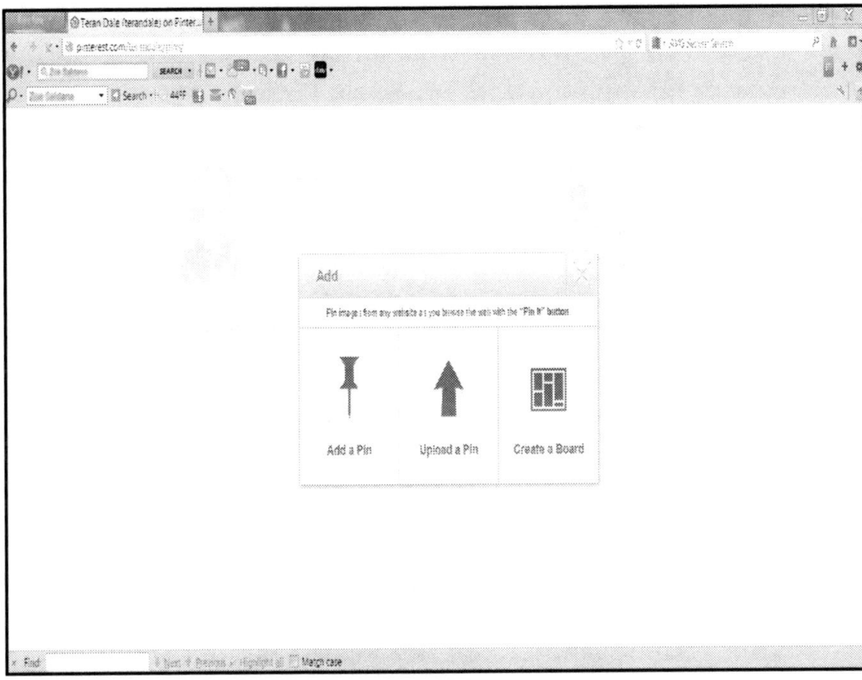

Pinning is essential to building a following with your Pinterest account. Pinning is when you go to a category and pin a photo within that topic on your board. You should always ask your followers to repin the image on their boards because this helps bring additional followers to your site.

A couple of things to remember with your Pinterest account:

1. Use high-quality images when pinning.
2. Ask your followers to repin your images and to check out the link to your site.
3. Never ever go for the straight sale and/or ask for the sale on Pinterest. Your goal is to connect first and build trust and credibility with all your relationships on Pinterest.

Use the following to build a strong base of followers to grow the quality of your leads for your practice. It won't happen overnight, but you will have a loyal following that listens to and shares your information with others on Pinterest.

You also want to remember that the message should match the market. I am going to share with you two very important techniques which will allow to you drive many new, high-quality leads to your website, which you can track and measure for your ROI.

The first technique I am going to share is called the ETL—Expanding the Lifestyle—system.

What you are going to do is use the ideal client profile you developed in Chapter 1. Please make sure you have it ready.

Now, what you will notice is that on Pinterest, you have many different types of boards of interest. You have fashion, quotes, recipes, those who like cars, health, fitness, etc. You name it—it is there on Pinterest.

What you are going to do is take a separate sheet of paper and a pen and you are going to look at your practice. Take the time to think about what you really do. You are going to look at how fixing your clients' teeth benefits any of the groups on Pinterest; you want to look at the end result your clients achieve. Here's an example:

People who fix their teeth might be interested in dating, health, fashion, smiles, confidence, and wellness. Guess what? You have just discovered other areas where you can advertise your practice.

The next step is to create a message with a high-quality image that relates to the subject.

Now, this would go under the "smiles" board and you would do the same thing for all the other boards. There are many different areas where you can expand the lifestyle of Orthodontic care because it relates to many different areas in your ideal prospect's life. Keep in mind that when you do this, your prospects and their friends will continue repin your post. This will continue to expand out to even more new prospects, so this technique will have your office flooded with new leads. Remember cater to your prospects' desires and wants.

Another system I have developed is called Pre-Sell against Objections (PSAO), which gives you a huge advantage over your competitors. What you are going to do is create six different boards. Each board is going have an image and a comment that answers and overcomes the objections of your ideal prospects and past prospects. The first five will overcome each objection your prospect has. On the last board you will sell your services with a direct link in your comments to increase the pinning and clicks on your images.

Offending your followers or those in the Pinterest community is a big no-no. Trying to automatically push your services with a hard sell is also a big NO. You should first build your credibility and trust with all your followers and community.

Posting offensive images and comments is also bad. Instead, focus on providing a message that helps those who are following you by providing value and then linking that value back to your site where you can sell to them.

Now, you will see other products for sale; however, these other companies and/or individuals have built their foundation within the community. Don't bash others or your competitors on Pinterest; let your marketing do the talking by providing value and great service, and by educating your ideal clients and prospects.

If others are bashing you, take the high road. Give facts and show testimonials and proof from your clients about how happy they are with your service. You will be astounded how your followers and your clients will back you up.

I have seen companies ruin their reputation by taking things personally and by providing more bait for their attackers. The majority of the time, your attacker or attackers are looking for a reaction from you—they want to get under your skin. Never air your practice's business in the public.

Relationship building is important not only on Pinterest, but in life in general and in your practice. Please follow the etiquette rules listed below. Your goal is to build a massive following without offending your ideal prospects and community.

1. Always provide the source of your image and/or photo. You must give the name of the photographer that owns the rights to the images you pin to your board. This is part of Pinterest's guidelines.
2. Do not create unorganized boards. The community of pinners really do not like to be fooled or tricked.
3. Do not link to irrelevant content that does not match your message and image. You will quickly be reported to Pinterest for spam and you can hurt and lose your followers.
4. Try not to pin directly from Google image search. Make sure you give credit where credit is due and provide the exact source of the image.
5. Do not pin a massive number of pictures and images all at once in a short period of time. Space your pinning out for your followers to see. Pin a small number each day or every other day. Too many pictures at once leads to your suspension as a spammer.
6. Always provide descriptions for images and photos. Your followers want to know what they are looking at. Better yet, provide a short story that sums up the picture and make the call to action perfect.
7. Do not follow everyone that follows you. There is no need to feel obligated; remember, you are looking for targeted ideal prospects and clients. If you want to include friends and family, create a separate account to do so.
8. Do not post bad-quality images or photos that are too big or small for your followers and the community of pinners to view.
9. Be respectful to everyone in the Pinterest community. Every individual has his or her own tastes and interests.

Follow these guidelines and you will be on your way to building a massive following by abiding by the rules of Pinterest.

You should start trying to gain followers with your Pinterest account by going after your ideal prospects and those that have a direct interest in what you are trying to do to grow your practice. As I said before, you want to engage and comment on other followers' boards.

The quick and easy way to gain a huge number of followers on your Pinterest account is to click the box to follow those that are on your Facebook profile page for your practice. Pinterest allows you to follow those who are following you on Facebook. This will create a massive following of new Pinterest followers for your board.

Once you have those new followers, you will be alerted by e-mail when someone follows you. This is your opportunity to introduce yourself and to thank those who follow you. Remember—just an introduction.

You want to monitor their activity and examine their interests and likes so that you can comment on them and repin their boards so that they will do the same to you. You are building your trust and credibility very quickly with this method.

The next thing you want to do is research by keyword subject the different areas of interest that are in your market. Start following those individuals as well to build your following. You repeat the same process of repinning their boards to gain more followers and trust.

Another sneaky tactic is to follow your competitors' followers; you can pin to their boards and provide a free report and/or video that will get them to visit your site. Remember to always include your USP in all your marketing material.

Engaging your followers with the right image that will get them to click and repin your post to their boards and share your information is definitely a move in the right direction. The next technique I am going to share with you will allow you to quickly generate more traffic to your website to gather more leads.

All of your messages should have value, be engaging, have a call to action, and—the secret sauce— the URL of your website or the landing page you want your ideal prospects and clients to go to. You want to have the full site in the message section of your pin, such as in the following:

HTTP://WWW.GETAGREATSMILEORTHODONTIST.COM

This technique will double and triple the click-through rate (i.e., the number of times potential clients and prospects click on your image to go to your site). Remember your goal is to move them off Pinterest and carry the conversation on to your website so that they are not distracted and you will have their full attention. Their full attention = more cash into your practice.

Branding your practice is another huge advantage for you over your competitors when you use Pinterest.

1. Make sure you use high-quality images so that your clients and prospects can see your offer and message. As you will notice, only high-quality images and photos are used on Pinterest.
2. A very successful technique you should implement right now is to provide "before" and "after" pictures of your clients with their stories. This will entice your ideal prospects to visit your site to see the images and read why your clients are so happy. You are providing social proof that they will get the same treatment and more like everyone else that chooses you as their doctor.
3. Every single message should contain a link to your website and your USP. If you do this, your clients and prospects will continually see your message. The more times they see the message, the more it is ingrained in their minds. It has been proven that a prospect must see an advertisement at least seven times before they remember what the advertisement is about. Add your USP and they will never forget.

Once you have established a Pinterest account, it is important to put your list-building campaign for prospects and clients to good use by sending them postcards and a sales letter letting them know you are now on Pinterest. Give your prospects and clients something in exchange for joining you on Pintersest—maybe a discount, a free report and/or a video, or a gift card to the movies or Starbucks.

Send each and every client and prospect an invite; this also gives you the opportunity to track and see the results of the marketing message you sent to everyone on your list. This also will allow you to see how they share the information with others that are also following them.

The more followers you have, the better results you will get. These will be an unpaid sales force singing your praises as their trusted advisor, the doctor that cares for their well-being and their family.

This will allow those that are following you as well as their followers on your list to see you constantly. When they need an Orthodontist, who do you think they are going to pick up the phone and call? That's right—YOU.

Getting your message across other popular social-networking sites (where your ideal prospects and clients hang out) is very easy to implement with Pinterest. You now have the opportunity to share your board with others on Facebook.

Please look at the example below:

Using this technique will allow you to have your message shared across your Facebook page or fan page for all your clients and prospects to see. Just click on the Facebook box in Pinterest and it will post to your Facebook page.

Success with your marketing campaign starts off with having the right target, the right message, and by providing all of that at the right time. What is often not talked about in marketing in general, and what is hardly done by Orthodontists, is to make the marketing accountable. This means it should lead to an increase in money coming into your practice and a growth of prospects and clients.

You should track all the messages in your Pinterest account. You want to know how well each message, graphic image, and post leads to an increase in your bottom line.

There are a couple of ways to do so:

1. You can add a tracking link to the message in every post. You can create the page with a URL string that notifies you each time someone clicks your link to see the results.
2. You can look at your logs to see how many people visit the page during your campaign, what browser they use to get there, and how long they stay on the page. This tells you if they are reading your message and if it is getting through. You should have Google Analytics linked to your website; remember, this is a free tool that will provide powerful data that will add HUGE amounts of cash to your bottom line.
3. You can add a tracking conversion code to your thank-you page that everyone visits after they sign up for a free report and/or video from the campaign you develop using Pinterest. Having a separate thank-you page will also tell you how well you are doing with new prospects.

These three techniques are just the foundation to get started. Once you have these down, you can continue to expand and track results. Remember you are doing this to continue to grow your practice and increase your bank account.

Getting your followers to expand your business by using contests on Pinterest is an excellent idea that can lead to a massive viral campaign, which we will talk about a little bit later. The techniques I am going to share with you will have more high-quality leads and paying clients than you can handle.

What you are going to do is set up a new landing page that will allow your prospects and ideal clients to sign up on before you start the contest.

The contest is the following:

You are going to get your followers and ideal prospects to sign up for the contest first, and then you are going to get them to do the following:

1. You are going to get them to repin your marketing message to their board and encourage others to repin and share the message on their boards as well.
2. The person with the most repins wins. They can win an iPad, a gift card, a trip, a free procedure at your practice—whatever you want it to be. I will leave that up to your imagination. Remember you want to provide a valuable gift that they want.

Now, we're taking this to the next level. This next step is not really a contest; instead offer a FREE iPad to all prospects that take on a treatment with your practice, or offer your existing clients a FREE iPad for clients they refer that purchase your service.

You are probably saying, "Teran, how am I going to pay for those iPads?" All you have to do is add the cost of the iPad to the cost of your services. This is a quick and easy way to add a substantial number of new clients and cash to your practice quickly. You can run these contests and this offer each and every month.

Throughout this chapter, I have provided various ways to attract your ideal client and to encourage them to become your followers and your champions for your services while you track all the results.

Creating your viral campaign with Pinterest starts by combining all of the techniques I have shared in this chapter and implementing them all at once.

Here are some elements to keep in mind:

1. For your contest, you want to be outrageous. You want the reward to be outrageous and believable at the same time. This will catch on like wildfire with your ideal prospects and it will spread across the Pinterest community.
2. The first step is to sit down and plan what your end result will look like. What do you want to accomplish with your campaign?
3. The second step is to develop the message for each step of your campaign.
4. The third step is to develop the sequence for implementing your marketing message to your followers and ideal prospects.
5. The fourth step is to track and measure the results of your marketing campaign. Remember your campaign should be memorable and easy to repeat to your target audience.
6. You can also pin videos to your board; just make sure that the videos are also on your site and your YouTube channel. This is a really profitable and exciting technique to get your videos and your website to go viral quickly.

Start implementing these techniques and strategies now and get results. Pinterest is an excellent way to quickly grow your practice. The beauty of using this new social network platform is there is hardly any competition. Note: Pinterest will be releasing a new advertising platform shortly which they are testing right now.

CHAPTER 14

Blogging

UNIQUE, FRESH CONTENT is what your readers are looking for on your blog. A blog is basically your perspective on a series of topics and/or posts that you want to discuss with your client. The beauty of having a blog is that Google and many of the other major search engines love blogs. They love fresh, unique content that keeps users on your page to read and contribute to what you are saying on any particular topic.

Now, it is very easy to set up and use a blog. You can write a series of posts and have them uploaded and released on specific days and/or time of your choosing. You are probably thinking, "Great, Teran, the problem is that I am not a writer and I have no idea what to write about."

The first thing I suggest you write about is your clients. Write about how happy they are for choosing you to help them get what they want. Make your clients the stars of your practice. This technique gets others raving about you and your practice in your area. In fact, this technique was used to build a yo-yo empire to over $285 million in less than two years.

So, write about your clients; feature each client. Before you do, though, you must ask them if you can write about them. Also get a video testimonial from them or conduct interviews with them about the procedure and your practice. Then from there you can start writing and commenting about new techniques, procedures, and technologies regarding the Orthodontic practice and community. Remember, your writing should be geared to what your ideal prospects' desires, and their wants, needs, and the end results they are seeking.

Engaging with your clients and ideal prospects is a must in order for your blog to be successful. This means posting content that gets your clients to express and share their feelings by responding on your blog. This makes your blog and your practice look authentic and truthful. Too many times I have seen blog authors not allow comments on the topic or their writing. You don't want to do that; you want your clients and prospects to engage with you and to share their thoughts and feelings—good or bad—because that is the only way you are going to grow your practice. (Note: you have the choice to approve each comment posted on your blog, and I recommend you do just that.)

Once your prospects and clients start engaging and sharing their feelings on your blog, you start to build trust and credibility. Your prospects and clients also tend to share their feelings with others—their friends, family, and co-workers, for example. They will tell them to go check out your blog and their comment. It makes them feel good and it will show you also care about your clients.

Your blog is basically free advertising without spending any extra money to advertise. Some things that will get your clients to engage more on your blog can include the following:

- Controversial topics
- Quizzes
- Client submissions / Client guest posts
- Contests
- Videos and/or testimonials from others
-

It is important that your blog is not boring. People avoid boring; they want an exciting, pleasurable user experience they will enjoy and share with others. Do not be dry. Write like you are talking to a friend. This is where you will build the connection with your audience.

Because Google loves WordPress, it would be highly beneficial for you to use this platform for your blogs. The WordPress platform is easy to set up and use. In a matter of five minutes, you can be posting comments to your blog for your ideal prospects and clients to read and comment on.

A few things to keep in mind regarding WordPress: You can use the platform to build out your entire site or you can have a separate site that is strictly dedicated to your blog and which can be linked to your main website. You can name the blog the following way: www.Yourdomainnameblog.com. This way you can use very powerful search engine optimizing techniques to build links to your main site.

Your blog should match the look and feel of your main site. You can get your blog custom designed, there are various themes you can purchase for your blog, and you can get your blog for free by going to www.WordPress.com and choosing from the various free themes.

One the most popular and versatile themes you can use for your blog is the "Thesis" theme. You can get your web designer to make the necessary changes to the look and feel of this template and implement the blog to go live.

Developing your writing style is important to the success of your blog. Start off by thinking of a character you would like to portray and write as if you are that character, making sure that you stay authentic at the same time. Now, that might sound weird, but it is not. Your goal is to keep your clients and ideal prospects engaged with all your marketing material.

You can do this by sharing your thoughts and feelings about your industry, new technologies and procedures, and how happy you are about your clients. This will help you develop a connection with everyone that reads your blog. You are letting them get to know you, to see who you are and that you are a person that cares about their well-being.

The advantage of using this technique is that none of your competitors are doing this with any of their clients. People care about you when you care about them, so continue to be authentic in all your writings and show that you care and have fun with your clients. Tell stories about the success of your clients and your staff and let the content direct back to their desires and wants. A big bonus would be to let your staff contribute to the blog as well. You want to create a family atmosphere that your entire market loves.

WIFM is the worldwide famous radio station everyone listens to on a daily basis. If you remember, WIFM stands for "What's in It for Me?" That is what your prospects care about and that should guide the content on your blog and your website.

Your ideal prospects and clients are looking for the right information that they can use to their advantage to make the right decision. They are looking at you as their trusted advisor and doctor who will point them in the right direction. The advantage you already have is that you are an authority figure already—you are a doctor, so they will listen to you and what you have to say. Remember, they would not come to you if they were not interested.

The second type of content you should have on your blog is interesting content focused on the industry that still circles around WIFM for your prospects and clients. This will make you stand out from your competitors without you coming out and actually saying you're the best. Your content and your clients will say it for you loud and clear.

You can start off with white papers, scientific reports, and industry news that you put in laymen terms for your audience. Simplify the information you present and they will love you for it.

Another aspect you should seriously consider is to present a controversial viewpoint on certain topics. You want to stand out from the crowd. Remember not everyone is going to like what you have to say. It is impossible for everyone to like you and for you to please everyone as well. You want only the clients that want you as their trusted advisor.

The Google Keyword tool is an excellent free tool that helps you to find the keywords that will get your blog posts ranked well in the search engines. For each topic you have decided to write about, you are going to do keyword research on the topic so that you make sure the word is in the blog post and the title.

Each and every blog post that you write should contain a main keyword you would like your post to be ranked for. This way, your ideal prospects and clients can find your blog if they are searching using Google, Yahoo!, and/or Bing. Remember, you want to make sure your keyword is in the title of your post. You also want to make sure that the keyword phrase (e.g., in body of your post) you are trying to rank for is also included in the blog post itself (as I just did here).

Keep in mind that with all of this talk about search engines, you are not writing for the search engines, you are writing for your ideal prospects and clients. The topics that you write about should flow with ease and be readable.

Another technique you can use to get a keyword to rank your post on your blog is to look at your PPC campaigns and the keywords there that converted into a successful treatment case and/or appointment. Write topics around those keywords because you know that they are generating huge amounts of cash for your practice.

The third (but not the last) way is to use your blogs on your site. Looking at the keywords your prospects and clients use to find your website will give you a good indication of what keywords you should apply to your blog posts.

Connecting with your clients and your ideal prospects is a must if you truly want to build your practice into an empire. Throughout this book, I have continued to encourage you to use your ideal client profile to bring your message to your target market so that they will buy your product and service.

As I said before, the more you connect, the better the results and the more your bank account will grow with cash. Your ideal client profile will allow you to develop stories for your blog, and you will be able to use local news as well to captivate and grow your list of prospects.

Good stories always captivate an audience; this is what you should write about on your blog. Tell stories about going through your training to become an Orthodontist. Tell stories about your clients and what's in it for them.

You can also connect and get a huge boost from the search engines by incorporating local stories as well. Adding your comments to local stories and asking for your clients' feedback builds upon the connection and rapport you are developing with them.

Remember, you want your clients and prospects to feel as if they have known you all their life. Doing it this way totally eliminates the competition. The competition will have no idea how to compete in your market.

Engaging with your clients and your ideal prospects with videos on your blog keeps you ahead of your competitors. Many Orthodontists are scared to be on camera, but don't you be. It builds credibility and authenticity with your target audience.

More consumers are watching videos every single day. Applying video to your blog also helps with your search engine rankings if you post your video to your YouTube channel because you are getting a link from an authority site that is owned by Google.

When you post your video to your blog, you give your ideal prospects and clients the opportunity to comment on your video, both on YouTube and on the blog itself. It helps build content for free, which also contributes to your blog moving up in the search engines.

Your videos can be three to six minutes in length for your blog, and sometimes even longer. However, never make boring videos. If it is boring, you will notice a huge drop off from your video when you look at your reports via YouTube Analytics. This also gives you the chance to improve your message that your video contains because you can see where your audience disconnected from your message.

Here's the thing to remember: If you look at many of your competitors' websites, you will notice just a fraction of them are using video on their blogs. If they are using it, they are doing a very poor job getting their message across and engaging with their audience.

What you have learned in this chapter will put you far ahead of everyone else. Remember being different is a huge bonus. Following everyone else just makes you like everyone else.

WordPress is set up quite well to be recognized by the search engines. As I mentioned before, Google loves WordPress and blogs in general. However, there are certain things that need to be tweaked on WordPress that will get you phenomenal results for Google, Yahoo!, and Bing.

The following site provides one of the best free plug-ins you can use to optimize your blog. It also provides a tutorial on how to set it up. http://wordpress.org/support/plugin/wordpress-seo

Each post on your blog should contain a link to popular social media sites. The following links should be on your post:

- Facebook
- Twitter
- Instagram
- Google+
- Pinterest
- RSS Feeds

You want to give your audience the opportunity to share your articles, videos, and posts with others on their contact list. This strategy allows you to spread your marketing message across all the social media platforms for free and you will not have to lift a finger. Your clients and prospects will do all the work for you because they like the content you are providing to them.

Now, make sure you track the results of how your posts, articles, and videos are being shared online. You want to see what is working and what is not working so that you can make the necessary adjustments to improve your rankings, content, and new prospects that flow into your practice.

Building credibility and a connection with your ideal prospects and clients can be a lot easier if you allow your prospects to participate on your blog by making comments and/or suggestions. Allowing your prospects to participate will show social proof that others enjoy what you have to say and it will prove you are the right doctor for their needs.

However, with that said, you don't want to let the comments get out of hand. You should control the flow of comments that are being made on your blog. You should approve every comment that hits the blog before making it live.

You might be saying, "Teran, that means I'm controlling what goes on my blog." Yes, you are right. Once you start to make noise in your market and you start taking over market share, trolls will begin appearing out of the woodwork to make trouble. Fake comments about you might appear, or your competition will try to make false rumors about you and your practice. So you must control your blog and the messages being seen by others; it is the only way to control your image and the message you send to your clients and prospects.

Getting more clients and money in your practice should be priority number one with your blog. That means offering something of value on every single blog post. Your stories, comments, and client features should lead to generating more business for your practice. To do that, you should build a list of prospects that you constantly keep contacting by providing them reports, videos, and white papers with your marketing material.

Having a constant source of leads in your practice is called lead flow, and lead flow is the lifeblood of your practice. It will keep your business alive. You constantly want and need more high-quality leads calling your practice to book appointments to see you or to be on your list where you can market to them when you want to.

Lead flow adds more cash to your bottom line, and this is why you decided to start you own practice—to make money—and there are three major ways to do that. Get new customers, increase your prices, and get your clients to spend more frequently with you. This is what this book is all about. In fact, you should be doing all three now.

Creating valuable free reports, newsletters, videos, and white papers that your prospects and clients can get for free in exchange for providing their contact information is how you start to generate leads with your blog.

On every single page you should give your prospects the opportunity to sign up for additional information by providing a section that allows them to give you their contact information. The contact information you would like to start off collecting is their e-mail address so that you can send them the report and any additional e-mails you wish to send regarding what you can do for them.

Once they are on your list, the next thing you want to collect is their mailing address. The mailing address is another opportunity to connect and provide your marketing material to them via snail mail. The reason you want to do this is that not everyone checks their e-mail on a regular basis. However, they do read their mail and you are going to send letters and marketing material that they will open and read.

To obtain their mailing addresses, offer them a small bribe to get their mailing address. The bribe can be in the form of a gift card, electronic toothbrush, or passes to the movies. The more creative you are, the better the results you will get.

One other thing you should do is provide a survey to the group as well. You want to know what is on their mind and if there are any additional services they need. Asking your prospects what is on their mind and what their needs are will expand your business once you provide what they want.

Getting referrals is also a must in your practice, and one way to flood your practice with new referrals is to hold contests on your blog. I would set up contests among your clients first. The particular contest you want to do is based on getting referrals.

Here's what you do: You contact your clients by e-mail, snail mail, and telephone and let them know you are holding a contest on your blog and that they should visit the blog for more details and to sign up. The contest will be based on a time limit—say for the next thirty days. The client that brings in the most referrals will get a FREE Fourth Generation iPad. The second place person will get an iPad mini, and third place will get dinner for two at a local family restaurant.

This technique will flood your office with quality leads because it is coming from clients that know you, respect you, and love your services.

Now, your goal with the new leads is to close them; to do that, use the techniques that I provided to you in this book. Turning one of the new leads into a client will more than cover the cost for the iPads and the dinner for two.

Other contests can center on the prospects themselves by having them sign up for a webinar. Ask specific questions around the webinar. This will tell you if they are watching the webinar in its entirety. From there, give a free procedure (that does not cost you much) to the winner who answers all the questions via e-mail within twenty-four hours. Constantly market to those who do not win because they are now on your list. Remember to provide valuable information and to go after their desires as discussed and outlined in Chapter 4.

Featuring your clients on your blog is an excellent way to take your practice to the next level and spread the news of your business across your city or town where you do business.

You want to do a short, quick exposé on a client—tell the story of the client, the problem they had and what they had to overcome. (First, you must get the permission of the client and let them know you are featuring them on your blog.)

The next thing is to tell the story of the client. Make the story engaging and completely true. Have the client provide a video testimonial reaffirming their story and the outcome.

This golden nugget is going to spread like wildfire. Here's why: Individuals like to be in the spotlight; they love to see their name in lights. When you give them this opportunity, they will not turn it down. This in return shows all your prospects that you are a caring, well-respected doctor that gets every single one of his clients great results.

The clients are singing your praises. They become a star online that other people are reading about. People love to do business with other people that they like and that are the same as them.

CHAPTER 15

SEO

OPTIMIZING YOUR WEBSITE for the search engines so that your clients and ideal prospects can find you is what is called SEO (search engine optimization).

Search engine optimization has changed significantly over the past years. In fact, it has been changing on a constant monthly basis over the last two years.

However, there are a few things that will stay the same and that are the foundation for successfully moving your website to the first page of Google, Yahoo!, and Bing. Following the procedures I outline in this chapter will reward you with the results you are looking for.

The first, most important thing is links. Having high-quality links with the right anchor text will move you up the search engine. The second key thing with SEO is fresh, unique content that is relevant and is what your ideal prospects and clients will love to read and share with others.

A little further in this chapter, we will discuss the meaning of anchor text and how to best use anchor text and linking so that Google will reward you and you can achieve success with your ideal prospects and clients.

Optimizing your website is a must if you want to be on the top three major search engines and YouTube as well. So sit back, relax, and enjoy this chapter. Remember, take action and you will witness dramatic results.

New policies put in place by Google coupled with the rapidly changing algorithms have made it harder for websites to get ranked on the first page of the three major search engines. On top of that, there has been a huge shift toward cleaning up the search engines from spam because of black hat techniques spammers have used trying to game the search engine.

Google changed the game completely in 2012 and the first half of 2013 with the penguin and panda updates. Some of the biggest companies in the world have been caught trying to game the system. In return, Google has penalized their websites and prevented them from showing up for important keywords in the search engine. One company that was hit hard because of black hat techniques, which I will talk about later in this chapter, was JC Penny. (JC Penny knew exactly what they were doing, but they tried to say that they had no clue they were violating Google's policy.)

What I am going to show you is the foundation for moving your website up quickly in the search engines for the keywords that make you money. The key thing is that you want to go after the keywords that actually make you money. This is the only thing that is important when it comes to the success of your SEO implementation.

One other thing that you need to keep on top of is the policy changes and algorithmic changes Google is constantly making to the search engines.

Remember this formula: HR + IP = $ (High Rankings + Ideal Prospects = more Cash in your pocket). It is extremely important you use SEO for your website and blog. Being on the first page is important for you to get results. Here are some facts: Being number 1 gets you 53 percent of the clicks, so these are the potential clients looking for your services. The second position gets

15 percent of the clicks, and the third gets 9 percent of the clicks. The fourth position gets 4 percent of the clicks and the fifth position gets you 1 percent of the clicks.

If you want more cash for your practice and you want to be more visible for the search engines, aim to be on the first page for the keyword that makes you money. Strive to be in the top four positions. This is where you are going to build your list of prospects you can market to continuously.

When you rank well in the search engine, it shows the prospect that you have a well-established business and it also shows Google, Yahoo!, and Bing that you are an authority site. Now, an authority site gets more traffic sent to its site. It is recognized as being important and having the right information for those who are seeking your services.

Without search engine optimization, it will be very hard for your prospects to find you. You can be the best Orthodontist in the world, but if no one can find you to buy your services, you will be out of business by the time you blink.

Yes, there are constant changes that are taking place in SEO; however, changes take place in every field of business and walk of life. It does not mean you should neglect the new information and stick with what you know. If you do, you will be eaten alive by your competitors. Build a search engine optimization plan that will get you results without using negative or black hat techniques.

You might hear "Content is King" regarding the Internet. The fact is that content is the queen and linking building is king. To get in front of your prospects and clients and to build authority with Google, you need excellent content and linking to take your blog to the next level.

The advantage that you have with blogging is the major three search engines love blogs and that gives you an advantage over your competitors. Combine your content with a high-quality link campaign, and you are set to go.

Now, SEO takes the content of your blog to the next level. You will start to see your content being syndicated on other blogs, shared with others, and commented on—especially if you have interesting topics that your ideal prospects and clients love.

Now, to get content for free so that you don't have to worry about writing something new every day or each week, get your clients to add content to your site for free. How do you do that, you ask? It's easy. You allow them to make comments on what you post, or allow your clients to post their testimonials or articles about what they want to say (with your approval).

You can also get your staff to come up with the content as well. You also have local news and industry articles and information that you can use and comment on to relate back to a point you want to make. Don't worry—you have more than enough information to put on your blog to take your SEO efforts to the next level.

Planning is the first step in developing a successful search engine optimization campaign for your website. The first thing I want you to do is take a blank sheet of paper and a pen and write down what you would like to accomplish for your website.

EXAMPLE:

- **What keywords do you want to be ranked for?**
- **What areas do you want potential clients to visit?**
- **Do you want to be ranked in Yahoo! and Bing as well as Google?**

The next step is to look at your competition. Here you are going to type in the search engine keyword phrases to see who is ranked number one. You want to see if the keyword they are ranking for matches the landing page. Do they provide enough information for prospects to make a decision to pick up the phone and call them?

For the second step, you are going to look at your PPC campaign and see what keywords are profitable for you. Which keywords are helping you build your list of prospects and what keywords are getting your phone to ring? These are the keyword phrases you want to use to start your optimization process for your website.

Search the list of keywords and see who else is ranked for these same keywords. From there you are going to look at how many links they have sent to the page.

To do this, type the following into Google Search "links: www.competitorsdomainname.com." The query above should show how many links are coming to the site and a list of the links.

TKU is the system to follow in the next phase of your search engine optimization of your website. TKU stands for Tags, Keywords, and URL. We are going to be looking at the best practices for on page SEO optimization.

The first thing, you want to look at are the tags for every single page of your website. You should look at your keyword tags, description tags, meta-tags, and H1 Tags.

Description tags will provide a sentence or two about what your page is about. This is where you want to provide WIFM information. Provide benefits and a call to action that will get your prospect to click on the link and read the entire page. Description tags show up in the search engines. Google uses this information to help users decide if they are interested in clicking your link. Yahoo! and Bing use the same format.

Please see the following picture:

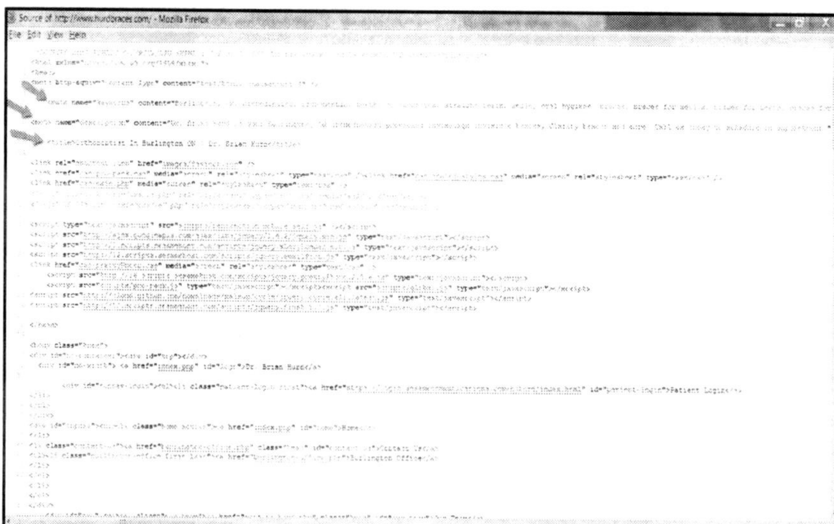

The second thing, you want to look at are keyword tags; these are keyword phrases that match the content of what is on the page. These keywords are words you want to be ranked for in the search engine.

The third set of tags, are H1 and H2 tags. These are tags that you want your headline to be ranked for on the page.

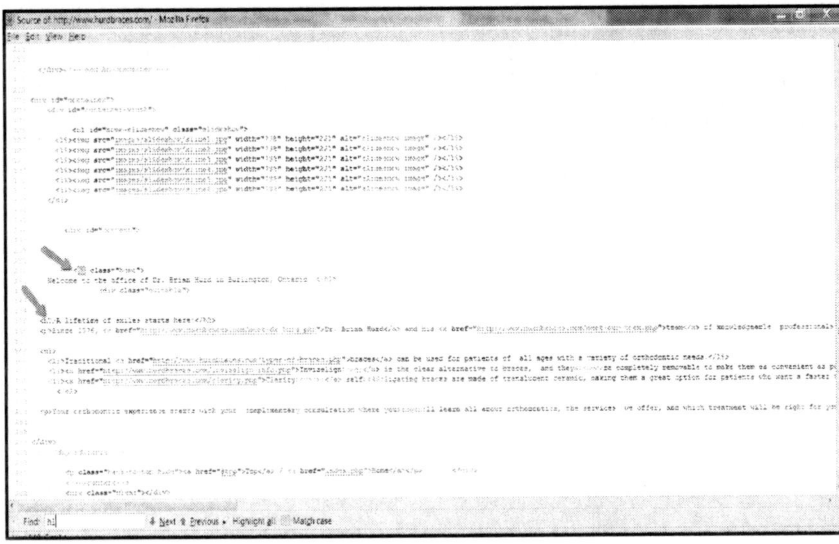

The final step is the URL of your landing page. Time and time again I see websites built incorrectly with the landing page named incorrectly. The following is an example of the wrong way to name your page to show up as a URL string:

The subject of the page is Invisalign before and after.

- **Wrong way**: www.GreatOrthodontist.com/23535.html
- **Correct Way:** www.GreatOrthodontist.com/Invisalign-Before-and-After

LAK is our next step in the process of developing a successful search engine campaign. LAK stands for Links, Anchor text, and Keywords.

To move higher in the search engines and to be on the first

page of Google and/or number one for your keyword phrase, you need to have links going to your landing page.

You need links from high PR (page rank) sites of five or more to move up in the search engine. PR is a system Google uses to identify the power of a landing page or website. The higher the page rank, the better the website and the authority of the site. Some sites that have high page rank sites include Google, CNN, eBay, Amazon; some blogs also have a PR of five or higher.

Your goal is to get links from sites and blogs that have a page rank of five or higher in order to move your site up on the first page for the keyword you want to be ranked for. This leads into anchor text.

Anchor text is a link to the keyword you want to be ranked for that is coming from another site, and in this case the site has a page rank of five or higher. Here's an example:

Say you want to rank for the keywords: Invisialign Boston.

Your anchor text would be the keyword phrase "Invisalign Boston." It would be an actual link that, if someone clicked on it, it would bring them to your page. In this case, the page would have the keywords "Invisalign Boston," and the page would talk about the services of Invisalign in the city of Boston.

The most important thing to remember for SEO is links and the anchor text of your keyword. This is important to move up in the search engine. You should start off by going after the keywords that include your profession and then the city name. For example: Orthodontist Boston, Orthodontist in Boston, the best Orthodontist in Boston, and so on. Remember, keyword research with anchor text and links is the name of the game.

Landing page selection also plays an important role in the success of a triumphant link campaign for your practice's website. The goal is to make sure you choose the landing page you want your keywords to be ranked for.

This means making sure the keyword phrases you want are on the page for your anchor text. You should aim for no more than six different keyword phrases per page that you are aiming to get rankings for in the search engine. If you go over that number, you tend to drag down your success and higher rankings will take a lot longer to achieve.

This takes careful planning: You have to make sure the group theme of keywords you want your landing page to be ranked for is mapped out beforehand. Using the example regarding Invisalign, let's take a closer look.

On your Invisalign page, you want to rank for a group of keywords themed around Invisalign like the following: Get Invisalign, Invisalign choices, Why Invisalign, Advantages of Invisalign.

You can aim these keywords to be ranked on your Invisalign page. To take it to the next level, you can have a separate page dedicated to kids and/or teens around Invisalign.

Once you have mapped out the keyword grouping of words you want to rank for each page, your next step is to get as many links as possible for quality pages that have a high PR ranking, as I stated before.

You want to keep track of the sites that are linking to you with a PR ranking of five or higher. Always aim to get links from websites or blogs that have a high PR ranking. This will get your landing pages and your website higher in the search engine.

Another advantage to using the grouped theme approach is that you will also get ranked for other words that are themed or similar to "Invisalign" as well. This is due to the fact that the page is strictly targeted to the subject matter.

A keyword phrase that you are looking to get ranked on the three major search engines that will attract ideal prospects to click the link and visit your website is called an anchor text.

Anchor text, along with links, is the lifeblood of success to your website moving up the search engines. The keyword phrase you want to rank for is the word that generated the following for your practice:

1. The keyword phrase must get you traffic to your website.
2. Your ideal clients are searching for the keyword phrase you are optimizing to get ranked for.
3. The keyword phrase must lead to you making money.
4. The keyword phase must allow you to build your list.

If the keyword phrase does not do any of these four things for your website and practice, it does not make sense to go after the keyword or keywords. You want to make sure you can track the results as well.

So, as an example, you want to rank for the keywords "Invisalign for teens" or "Straighten my crooked teeth."

You would make sure that the link is in the name of the phrase and that once a prospect or client clicks on the link, they are brought to the appropriate landing page that provides the information they are looking for.

Remember the keyword phrase must also be on the landing page. If it is not, it will be a lot harder for you to rank in the search engine for the phrase.

Relevancy and higher rankings are important for you to grow your practice and anchor links are extremely important when it comes to getting the results you want. If you do not use anchor text links, you will not be on the first page of the three major search engines for the keyword phrase you are optimizing for.

Anchor text lets Google and your prospects know that you have the relevant information that they are seeking. You are telling Google and showing Google you are an organized and well-optimized website that gives users exactly what Google and your ideal prospects and clients are looking for.

If you ignore the use of anchor text, you are telling Google the opposite. The anchor text you want to use also should be the name of your business, your name, and your office address. You want to make it extremely easy for your prospects and clients to find you whenever they search online.

Anchor text proves to prospects that you are relevant and

credible. If they can't find you when they search, it tells them you are not a real business that cares for them, nor are you willing to give them what they want.

Use anchor text to your advantage; remember you have your PPC campaigns, logs, blogs, and a lot more data to find the right keyword phrases that will move you up the search engines and put a lot more cash in your pockets.

Google, Yahoo! and Bing will de-index (i.e., remove your website entirely from the search engines) if you get caught using black hat SEO techniques. Black hat SEO goes against the policies and the foundations of the major search engines. The overall goal of black hat SEO is to trick and manipulate the search engines to gain higher rankings by providing false information.

For example, black hat SEO will show the search engine one landing page and then show their prospects something totally different. This particular technique is called cloaking. When Orthodontists hire me to do their SEO campaigns, many times I will come across black hat techniques used on their site by another vendor that they hired.

Unfortunately Google will not care if the doctor had no clue that these particular techniques were being used to move his site up the search engine. The next thing you know, their site is dropped off the first page for many of the keyword phrases that were profitable only to be found on page 60 or 100 where no one will see your site.

If this has happened to you, it is not your fault because many of these vendors will promise the moon, and you will have no idea what exactly they are doing to move you up in the first page of Google.

When you are doing your SEO, stick with white hat techniques to get your rankings higher. You don't want to kill your practice overnight.

Paid converting keywords are another huge advantage for your SEO campaign. Here's why: A paid search keyword that is delivering new clients and making you money is a confirmation that the particular keyword you are using in PPC advertising is gold.

To take your SEO campaign to the next level, you should focus on building a specific landing page around those keywords and optimize via the SEO. Now you will have two streams of income and new patients coming into your office.

PPC also confirms that you are on the right track. It takes the guesswork out of what keyword you should really go after. If it is not making you money and bringing in new prospects, you should abandon it. You have to find a way to monetize the word you want to rank for.

Pay-per-click advertising allows you to find additional keywords you can use in your search engine optimizing campaign by running a search term report. This report will bring down and provide highly relevant keywords that are not seen by you that will tell you exactly what people are searching for.

In other words, it will tell you exactly the desires and thoughts of your prospects. Your next step is to build landing pages and an SEO campaign around those keywords to dramatically increase your profits.

You want to use everything in your arsenal so that you can gain a massive competitive advantage and, I'm sorry to say, the annihilation of your competitors.

Google's Keyword tool, PPC campaign, and Google Analytics are the three free tools you can use to help you get excellent results in your SEO campaign.

To start your SEO campaigns for the right keywords to go after, you should use the free Google AdWords Keyword tool and have Microsoft Excel open it to build the list of keywords you want to go after.

First, you are going to come up with the phrases your ideal prospects and clients use to search for your practice online. For example: Orthodontists in New York; best Orthodontists in New York; affordable Orthodontists in New York; Orthodontists in White Plains, New York; Orthodontists reviews.

You want to see the local search volume for these keywords and how many searches are being conducted on a monthly basis. Then you want to see the exact match search volume and the competition level in PPC. This will give you a good indication as to whether the keyword is profitable.

In your PPC campaign, you can look at your conversions to see how many people signed up under the keyword for a free report and/or webinar. You also want to look at the click volume and the search term report I mentioned.

With Google Analytics you are going to look at the click path pattern to see how the prospects got to a specific page on your site. It will show keywords they used to find you, and you will also discover the top keywords people are searching to find out about and exactly where they go on your website.

This is valuable information you can use to increase your conversions on your landing page and provide exactly what your prospects and clients are looking for.

Google Analytics is a very powerful free tool that you should use to your complete advantage for tracking the results of your SEO efforts. There are other SEO tools for reporting, such as SEOMOZ, which tracks the results of how you are moving up in the search engine as well.

Google Analytics will give you a good indication as to what keywords are profitable and what keywords are just breaking even for your entire website. You can set up goals and paths to improve your overall conversion to an appointment and to a client accepting treatment.

To install Google Analytics on all the pages of your website, you can go to http://www.google.com/analytics/ and sign up there. You should let your web guy install the tracking codes on all the pages. From there you can develop the goals you would like to achieve.

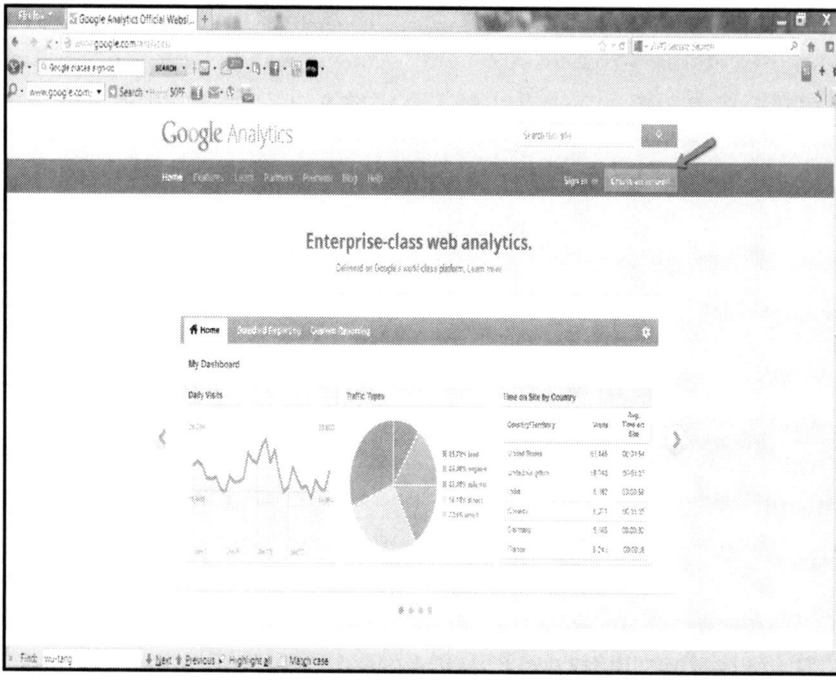

You can also run various reports in Google Analytics that will show you how people are searching and finding your services, how long they are staying on each page, and if they are reading specific pages. This allows you to see if your marketing message is grabbing their attention.

You can also track the results by a phone number. You can see what campaigns are getting calls for you by using Google pay-per-call tracking services. This way, you will know exactly what is working to lead to a phone appointment and from there to a sale. There are other expensive options available, such as the mongoose phone tracking system; however, you don't need that to get started.

Pinterest, Facebook, Google+, and all the other social media platforms must also be optimized for higher rankings in the search engines, so do not just set up your profile for each platform and forget to analyze and optimize every single page that you create for your practice.

Google is adding social media as part of the factor to move up in the search engine. The more real estate you have online where your prospects and clients can find you, the better.

One thing to remember is that you do not want to rely and depend on only one source. Things are changing every single day and new policies and procedures can affect your rankings. This is why the entire book devotes attention to other platforms to grow your practice. If one platform decides to change, you still have direct mail, PPC, social media, etc. until you develop a plan for the new changes.

This is why you must optimize for the best results and build your brand across each and every network where your clients and prospects hang out. You want to be where prospects are. It will make it a lot easier for you to keep in contact and to provide value at all times. In addition, the bonus is you make a lot more money.

CHAPTER 16

Webinars: How to Add an Easy $100K to Your Bank Account

PRESENTING SPECIFIC INFORMATION over the web in video format, whether it's broadcast to a live audience or replayed later, is an important and highly successful tool every Orthodontist should use to their advantage. Webinars are now being used in colleges, in the boardroom, and at work to teach and to show critical information to an audience. You are going to learn about using a webinar for your practice and put your competition on notice that you are the king of your market.

The main thing you are going to use your webinar for is to educate your ideal prospects and clients about new products and services and about your practice and industry. This is the biggest thing I see missing from the Orthodontic community. There is a lack of education to the target market about what an Orthodontist does and why one should choose an Orthodontist over a Dentist.

Now as I said, in a webinar you are presenting information in a live format over the web to as many people as you want. The format of the presentation can be done in PowerPoint, and it can be done live by showing your audience what is on your screen and it can also be in video format. There are many other ways to set up a webinar, but I will focus on these three that will make your practice extremely profitable.

Get ready to kick some butt and take no prisoners with what you are about to learn in this chapter. Many of you are going to have that "Aha!" moment, so please take notes because your minds are going to be overwhelmed with ideas to corner your market.

Generating cash for your practice and engaging with your ideal prospects and clients while at the same time building credibility and authority can all be accomplished by using webinars. Webinars breed money for your practice and let your clients know you care about them enough to educate them on what a specialized Orthodontist can do for them. The biggest mistake you can make is not telling your prospects and clients the difference between you and your competitors—not having a USP that makes you stand out.

Put this together so that they can listen to and watch "What's in It for Them." Hold their attention, and give them a reason to listen to you and your expertise.

Your webinars can be set up once and can be scheduled to run on certain days and at certain times. Webinars also allow you to build your list of ideal prospects. When they sign up to watch or join your live webinar, this tells you they are interested in the information you are going to provide to them.

People want to buy, and this is a fresh, new way to get them engaged and excited to listen to you and buy your services. You can use the webinar to launch new products, educate your clients, and to sell new and existing services.

Look around and see how many of your competitors are using this technology to their advantage. I guarantee you might find just one in your market—if that. This is going to put you ahead of your competitors and help you gain a big chunk of the market share in your area when you implement it successfully.

Developing the content to use for your webinar starts with the following CSP (clients, stories, proof) formula. You should use your clients, stories, and proof in every single webinar you develop for your marketing campaigns. Later in the chapter, we will discuss various types of webinars you can and should create. However, in every webinar you must use the CSP formula—clients, stories, and proof.

In your webinars you should discuss your clients. This allows you to show social proof that you are the expert, and it also provides proof to your target audience that your customers are happy with their results. In fact, it shows your audience that they will get the same type of treatment and results by using you as their doctor.

Every webinar should contain a minimum of two to three stories. These stories can be about the success of your patients, stories about a client overcoming an obstacle or making a decision, and a story about your struggle.

Stories captivate and hold your audience's attention; stories give them something to look forward to hearing and watching. They will not divert from your webinar, and they will be eager to hear and listen to what you have to say.

The content should also be educational and informational, and it should lead to your ideal prospects or clients making a decision to buy something from you or to take an action to do something you request from them. We will go into greater detail on setting up a successful webinar for educational purposes, for providing information, and for selling a service and/or product.

A professional, polished webinar is a must for your presentation to be successful. That means your webinar should be scripted. Yes, you should write out your webinar. Write the outline first, starting with the topics and sub-topics you would like to discuss, then add the stories you would like to talk about, the testimonials, and the social proof you would like to show your audience, and then finally the call to action and the offer.

Writing out your script is important because it will enable you to easily flow through your webinar. It will keep you from going off track; you will not lose your audience if you have a script.

Movies and TV shows have scripts the actors use to make the conversations flow properly. It's polished and it holds the audience's attention. Excellent movies do the exact same thing I'm telling you to do. They concentrate on the WIFM—What's in it for the moviegoer?

Start by getting a blank piece of paper and begin your outline. You should have, as I said, a minimum of two to three stories and five to eight client testimonials.

Once you have written your first draft, you want to go through it to make sure there are no hiccups in the script. Here's a trick that will get you to write the best script possible. After writing your first draft, read the draft out loud. Wherever you find yourself having a hard time going through the script is an area that needs to be worked on.

When developing scripts for Orthodontists for their webinars, I do a complete brain dump of what the doctor is looking to achieve for the webinar and then start with three to five different drafts. It is well worth the investment to get this done properly because it can literally bring in hundreds of thousands of dollars in as little as seventy-two hours. Not to worry—later on this chapter I'm going to prove it to you.

A professional, well-oiled webinar is authentic and shows your expertise. In order to take your webinar to the next level, you must practice your webinar. That means writing it and conducting a mock webinar going through your script. You should record these practice sessions so that you can look at the areas that you need work on before you do it live or record the official webinar for your target audience.

After you record your webinar, have your staff watch it. Watch their facial reactions. Don't interrupt their experience. Wait until the webinar has completed and wait for them to make their comments.

Now you may be asking, "How will I know I am ready to go

live with my webinar?" You will know because it comes naturally to you, which means you are talking like you are chatting with a friend. It does not seem hard or come off as scripted.

Not to worry, most Orthodontists following my technique get the hang of it within three to five times of going over the script. Remember, you're talking to a friend and you care about your friend. This is the way to approach practicing your webinar.

You also want to let other family members watch the script as well and listen to what they have to say. This is extremely valuable information because it lets you know if you are losing your audience.

If you do not want to present your information live, recording your webinar is the next step. The best software to use for your webinar is Camtasia. Camtasia is recording software that will allow you to record what is on your screen and then edit it and add different effects for your target audience to watch.

As of the writing of this book, Camtasia is inexpensive; it costs roughly $300 to use. It is an excellent investment considering the money you will make using the software and the results you will achieve with happy new patients. It will yield ten times (or more) for your investment.

Now it is quite easy to use Camtasia, unlike other video recording software on the market. The learning curve is easy to understand. I recommend the following:

1. For rendering, make sure you use HD format for YouTube.
2. Custom production
3. Add zoom
4. You can also add a certain call to action within the video. (Optional)
5. Save as an MP4 and Swift file (Important)
6. Use a head set with a microphone to record your webinar.

Saving the file as an MP4 allows your audience to watch the video on their computers, iPods, and any other devices that they may have in their home.

Camtasia also provides free videos and tips on how to use the software for the best results.

Setting up Camtasia is very simple. Once you have downloaded the product on your computer or laptop, take the time to go through the tutorial videos. It will be worth the investment.

This is extremely powerful software that will create a professional, studio-like presentation for the fraction of the price. Your ideal prospects and clients will be amazed and pleased with the quality of work you develop.

Remember, you can use Camtasia to record what you want and upload it onto your server for your target audience to view on a specific time and day of your choosing. You can also use MS PowerPoint to create your presentation, and it can also upload your presentation to YouTube and/or share it with your ideal prospects and clients.

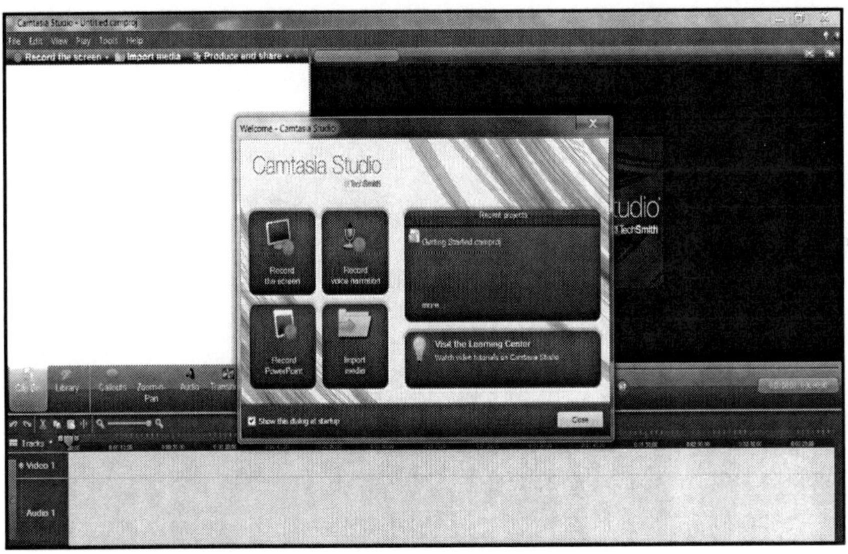

Commandment #1: You must use your clients in your webinar because it builds upon social proof, it attracts your ideal clients, and it builds trust.

Now you might be saying to yourself, "Teran, I don't have any testimonials." Well, it is time to get testimonials. Call your old clients and ask them for a written testimonial for the services that you performed for them. If you are not doing this yet, you should start immediately.

You should also ask for a video testimonial with their story. When your ideal prospects see your clients talking about their story and about you, this automatically builds trust and puts you far ahead of the competition that they are considering.

Social proof adds money to your bottom line. You don't have to come out and say you're the best; let your past and present clients come out and say it for you. It is much better to let your clients do it because, as I said before, in this day and age people trust other people's reviews more than a business tooting their own horn.

It is very important to remember to get a waiver from your clients allowing you to use their testimonial in all your marketing material.

Webinars come in three different types: information-based webinars, selling-based webinars, and pre-selling webinars. Before you start planning your webinar, you want to decide what type of webinar you want to produce.

If you are looking to educate your clients and ideal prospects about the difference between an Orthodontist and a Dentist, you would then create an information-based webinar. However, at the end of the webinar, you would ask the prospect or client to take action by picking up the phone and booking an appointment with you or to send out additional information to them by taking them to specific landing page to gather additional information from your prospects and/or clients.

The second type of webinar is produced to sell a product and/or service. The tone and the theme of the webinar are based on selling the product or service. You are providing educational information, but less education is presented. This type of webinar offers more of the benefits they will receive for purchasing your services.

The third type, the pre-selling webinar, is a combination of the selling-based and information-based webinars. In this webinar, the difference is that there will be additional informational where you will ask for the sale. This type of webinar is good to use when the item or service you're selling is a very high-ticket item.

You want to put the client through certain sequences so that you will get their money and they will have enough information to make the right decision.

Creating a powerful story with a call to action and proof to back up any claims that you make in your webinar are the most important things you must always have in your presentation. Have all three elements mapped out and ready to go.

Your story should contain a positive result the client will receive and that is focused on their ultimate desires. You can use a story about a past or present client that got the result they were looking for. You can also tell a story about your struggles and how you were able to achieve success. But remember—it has to be linked to WIFM.

Proof is extremely important. With proof, you answer many of the objections the client and/or prospect is raising in their minds. As they sit there and watch your webinar, they are asking themselves questions to justify the purchase. Your webinar is anticipating what is going through their minds and answering all the objections they have.

Third, your call to action with your offer must be irresistible. You must ask for a sale or for them to take action. You want them to do something that adds to your bottom line, that gets their money for your services. Your offer must contain benefits. In fact, it should contain the ultimate benefit they will receive when they go with you as their doctor.

Repeatable, relevant webinars that you can set up and run forever are called evergreen webinars. An evergreen webinar will not lose its luster and will be relevant years from now. These types of webinars can be set up after you have a few webinars under your belt. You can set up an evergreen webinar once and have it run on your website at a specific time and day that you want your clients and/or prospects to watch your presentation.

You can get your prospects to select a specific time of the day. I would give the prospects three different times: one in the morning, one in the afternoon, and last in the evening. I would offer either Tuesday or Thursday as the choices to view the webinar. Studies have shown on those days you will get more viewers watching the webinar.

The client will not know that the webinar is not live. When you set up the webinar, do not mention the date, the time, or the day. This technique will allow you to continuously build your list but you will have to set everything up just once. This strategy is quick, easy, and very effective. It is up to you to decide if you would like your prospects or clients to know your webinar is not live.

An engaging webinar is focused on the ideal prospects' wants and desires and will become memorable in your prospects' minds. They will then share it with others around them. Your webinar must be entertaining. Remember your prospects are looking for the ultimate benefit and a wonderful experience when they do business with you.

In your webinars, always get your prospects to participate. Get them to raise their hands and confirm what you are saying. This will keep them focused on what you are saying, and it will also tell you if you are losing your audience.

Ask if they understand what you are saying. Ask them questions that get you a YES response. For example, you can say, "By a show of hands, how many _____?" Have them respond by typing their answers into the question box; you can then read their responses to the entire audience. This keeps them engaged, and it makes them see the solution is at hand.

You want to stand out and provide valuable information that will make you and your webinar memorable. With each step you take with your prospects and clients, you want them to share their experience with everyone else they come into contact with.

Free advertising that has social proof from a third party that actually used your services goes a very long way toward building credibility and trust. Plus, your bank account will thank you for all the hard work you have put in to get your practice to the next level.

You also need to remember that boring webinars bring in no sales and create an audience that will drop off from your video or live presentation. Here are a few things to remember about live webinars and recorded webinars:

1. Your webinar should be professional and polished. You do not want to come off unprepared. You want to practice a minimum of ten times to make sure that everything is okay and set up properly.
2. You never want to rush through your webinar. You want to go through it so that everyone watching the webinar can understand and grasp what you have to offer.
3. Do not let your audience take over and interrupt the webinar if you are doing a live webinar. Let them know that you will answer questions after the webinar. If you start taking questions during your presentation, you will lose focus and momentum.

After the live webinar you can stay on for an extra ten to fifteen minutes to answer questions to reiterate how great your offer is and to emphasize the ultimate benefit your prospect will receive. This technique has proven to increase sales an extra 20 to 30 percent.

The ultimate webinar grabs your audience's attention, keeps them engaged through the entire process, provides proof they cannot dispute, and brings cash into your practice.

The following sequences are what you want to follow for your webinars:

Information seminar sequence (should be 60 minutes):

- Opportunity – Slides (what they are going to get and/or what the webinar is going to provide)
- Story positioning – Slides and pictures of the client and yourself (the story of struggle and success—the client's and yours)
- Testimonials and case studies of the success – Slides
- Busting the myths they may have – Slides
- Provide value –Tips and steps (at least three to five)
- Things they should do and not do

Selling seminar sequence (should be 90 minutes)

- Opportunity – Slides (what they are going to get and/or what the webinar is going to provide)
- Story positioning – Slides and pictures of the client and yourself (the story of struggle and success—the client's and yours)
- Testimonials and case studies of the success – Slides
- Busting the myths they may have – Slides
- Provide value – Tips and steps (at least three to five)
- Things they should do and not do
- Describing what you are selling
- The ultimate benefits they will receive from your services
- Features
- Price –You going to justify why this is a great deal compared to other prices and/or services
- Bonus – Additional value they will get for going with you as their doctor
- Provide a kick-butt guarantee
- Desire – Provide urgency to take action
- Provide one surprise bonus that will give them value

Pre-selling seminar sequence (should be 60–70 minutes)

- Opportunity - Slides (what they are going to get and/or what the webinar is going to provide)
- Story positioning - Slides and pictures of the client and yourself (the story of struggle and success—the client's and yours)
- Testimonials and case studies of the success - Slides
- Busting the myths they may have - Slides
- Provide value - Tips and steps (at least three to five)
- Things they should do and not do
- Call to action to obtain additional information (you will provide either by mail, e-mail, or another webinar)

Creating an online repeatable webinar that is set up to be viewed twice a week can allow you to generate an extra $25,000 to $100,000 per week. Yes, you read that correctly. The reason for this is people love webinars. They will attend them and they will participate. Remember to concentrate on WIFM.

What you want to do is set up the high-ticket services with the biggest margins to be on a repeatable webinar. These are the services that will bring the cash into your practice.

As I stated before, pick Tuesday and Thursday as the days and give your prospects and clients the opportunity to view the webinar three times per day: early in the morning, in the afternoon, and in the evening.

The next step is to track the results of the webinar to make sure you are making the funds you want. You want to see how many people signed up for the webinar and how many sales you have generated from the webinar.

Have your office manager track the results of the calls coming in after the webinar. You can have a specific telephone number that will allow them to call the office manager directly if you really want to track it correctly to make as much money as possible.

This system I just shared with you can easily bring $1 million into your practice just by setting up a webinar. Use this system and witness the growth of your practice. I guarantee if you do this correctly, your competition will be irrelevant.

There are four different services that you can use: GotoWebinar, ReadyTalk, WebEx, and Ilink to set up your webinars. Don't wait any longer. Get going and start putting more cash into your practice today.

CHAPTER 17

Launching Your Practice

THE DEBUT OF YOUR PRODUCT or service or the re-launch of your product or service to your clients or ideal prospects at a set date and time is a Launch Event. It allows you to launch your products and services to those you want to attract. It is a very powerful technique to tap into the existing desires and demands your clients and ideal prospects have and, in return, to be rewarded with cash for giving it to them.

The launch of products in the Orthodontic community is rarely done. In fact, I have seen it done only once and it was done quite poorly. The strategies and techniques I am going to share in this chapter will allow you to generate $100,000 or more every four to six weeks or quarterly. It is basically up to you.

However, the launch strategy can be overused and abused, leaving your prospects and clients unhappy if you do not do it properly. Being authentic and truthful in this process and set up is a must. If you come off as if you are only looking to put your hands in their pockets, they will quickly pull away and go elsewhere.

That being said, do not sleep on this technique; it is extremely powerful and profitable when done properly. Lucky for you I am going to show you how exactly to do this so that you can generate an extra $100,000 every four to six weeks.

Developing an online launch for your practice starts with a sequence of using online media properties, a plan, and strategies to capture and sell to your ideal client profile and existing clients.

This entire process starts with a set up of online properties that move your prospects and clients through a series of e-mails, videos, webinars, blog posts, and effective copywriting to get them to eagerly participate in the launch.

The entire process needs to be planned from beginning to the end. I have seen this strategy implemented in other areas of business where it has generated over $24 million in the space of forty-eight hours.

To get started, you want to tease your audience with important information regarding the particular product and/or service you are promoting. Remember, anything that you craft in the marketing message must be all about your ideal prospects and clients. The trusted radio station WIFM must be playing at all times.

You move your prospects from one video, to blog posts, to webinars. All through the entire process, you give your prospects and ideal clients the opportunity to participate by contributing and commenting on your marketing material. This strategy continues to build social proof, credibility, and trust with your target market.

You also want to use direct-mail marketing to clients via snail mail, an old-school marketing technique implemented totally offline. This is implemented by sending a series of effective marketing materials and strategies while measuring the results. Developing an offline product launch via direct mail is one of the most profitable techniques you can do for your practice. The problem is many Orthodontists say that direct mail does not work; they have tried it before with zero results.

However, looking at the following facts, you will see that this is not true. The key ingredients to making your offline product launch work is to have the right target market list (i.e., the ideal client profile) and the second most important thing is effective copy (i.e., the marketing message) that speaks to what your ideal client wants (WIFM).

The offline product launch—just like the online product launch—creates a frenzy with your ideal clients and prospects. They just cannot wait to hear from you, and they are eager to comment and participate throughout the entire sequence.

Your goal is to let them participate. Let your prospects and clients share their feelings and thoughts via mail and make sure you track every single response so that you can use them all in later marketing materials.

The MSC formula should always be implemented in your offline and online launches. This formula that I have developed guarantees more success in your launches. The formula is the following:

More Sales = Standing Out + Connection + Caring

More sales will be generated with your launches by using showmanship throughout the entire process. Showmanship through your launches makes you stand out from your competitors. One thing to remember: I did not say to brag to your prospects and clients about how great you and your services are.

What I want you to do is create a pleasing, wonderful experience for your prospects. You are looking to build that connection with your audience. Yes, they are an audience because you want their undivided attention throughout the entire process.

Showmanship is important. It is like the stars of Hollywood: There are some actors who just stand out and are genuine; very few are, but you know the type. They capture your attention and you listen to them and watch what they have to say. They build a connection with you which makes you want to watch all their movies, TV shows, etc.

This is what you want to implement with your launches. The key thing here is you must be authentic. Don't fake it. If you do, your clients and prospects will see right through you and they will know that you are trying too hard. It will turn them off and they will totally abandon what you are trying to accomplish.

More sales will be attained by adding showmanship to your launch because it allows you to stand out and you will build the connection with your ideal prospects and clients. You must care for them first. Once they see that you care for them and you bring showmanship into the mix, your sales will go through the roof—guaranteed.

When you have products and services you want to promote that benefit your ideal prospects and clients, this is when you use the product launch strategy to create a massive influx of new clients to your practice. This strategy is highly effective. You can use it for new procedures and techniques that you learn and to bring them to the public as a new, exciting, and effective way to solve a problem your client or prospect may have with their teeth and/or jaw, linking all of it to their end desire.

One thing I must say is do not abuse this technique because it can lose its effectiveness. If you are constantly doing launches that have no significant bearing on improving the quality of life for your ideal prospects and clients, it will not be effective.

The best time for your product launch is for everything to become active and live on a Tuesday. Results show that Tuesday from 12 p.m. to 4 p.m. is the best for results. This is because most people are on their lunch break during this time, so they can participate in the launch and call in and book an appointment for your new service or product. Another reason 4 p.m. is effective is because it is the end of the work day for your prospects and clients, so they can call right after work.

You want to use launches to build your list and to rapidly bring a huge surge of cash into the practice. Combining both online and offline launch sequences yields the best results. When I say "yield," I mean the most amount of cash into your practice.

In today's society most people enjoy the online aspects of reading and sharing their thoughts with their friends, family, and colleagues. On the other hand, you have others who still love to receive mail and to have and feel letters, postcards, and other materials in their hands to read.

The road to success is combining both to your advantage so that you are covering the ideal prospect that prefers online and the other that prefers to receive mail instead. You want to incorporate both into the sequence of your launch. For example:

1. You can direct your prospect via direct mail to a specific landing page to start to build the rapport and trust for your launch.
2. From there you can send a direct-mail piece outlining your product and/or service and providing quality information (WIFM) via direct mail. Ask them to call in for an appointment.
3. You can use both at the same time to keep them engaged throughout the entire launch process.

Later on in this chapter, we will look at two different launch sequences for you to generate more calls and cash into your practice—guaranteed.

When implementing your launch—both online and offline—effective copy is a must. Effective copy does one thing—it sends the right message that brings in the sale. This is the first of many things you need to consider when building out your launch. The second thing you will need is a highly effective landing page design to go with the copy to grab your ideal prospects' and clients' attention.

The third ingredient you will need is videos that get your prospects and clients engaged with your marketing material. Remember all your marketing is based on WIFM and should contain value so that they can make the right decision—which is to have you as their trusted doctor and advisor.

You will also need a series of e-mails written for each step that you want to take to bring your prospects and clients through. Each message and e-mail must make them salivate and eager to pick up the phone and call you to book an appointment. The series of e-mails should be set up as an auto-responder series with a new list created strictly for the entire launch sequence. You can use your Aweber account to do so. (Aweber is a highly effective and inexpensive way to carry out your launch sequence with huge success.) You can also use your YouTube channel page as well.

The next step is to create direct-mail pieces for the process. One thing you definitely want is a series of sales letters written and targeted toward your ideal prospects' and clients' wants. Your ideal prospect profile will help you craft the right message with the right tone and message to get your clients to buy from you.

You also want to create postcards that list the benefits as well as a call to action to move your prospects and clients to the next sequence of the launch. It looks like a lot of work at first; however, I have used this process for my clients and have brought in hundreds of thousands of dollars in as few as ten days.

When developing your launch campaign, you should not forget to create high-quality, exciting content. Let's look at excitement through the launch process.

When I say "excitement," I do not mean hype. Hype never works well because the majority of the time, it turns off the prospect and client. Most of the time, when a product is hyped (for example, a movie), it usually bombs and does not live up the audience's expectations. We don't want to create the same effect for your launch.

Excitement on the other hand is transferable from you to the client and to others participating in the launch sequence. You want to share your enthusiasm through your marketing material and by providing the proof and high-quality content. You can get your prospects excited to share the information by talking with others via your website by blog posts or by word-of-mouth to family members and colleagues. This creates a massive following without spending huge sums of money for advertising.

Quality is also important. Your message and your website must look professional. It must be easy to read and simple for your audience to participate. You don't want a cheesy-looking landing page, and you don't want to send out cheesy e-mails for this entire project. Your content must hold the audience's attention and it must provide exactly what they want while you are getting exactly what you want.

The personality you want to display with your blog is a fun, enthusiastic, and caring individual that is looking out for the best interest of his or her clients and prospects. Your marketing material, e-mails, videos, and mail should all have these qualities when presented to your prospects. If you take one away, your launch will not be successful.

People will not get excited and participate in a launch when the presenter is uncaring and does not show any excitement about his product and the launch itself.

Let the prospects participate. Use their enthusiasm and excitement to build up the launch. Keep them pumped for the big day. Use suspense to have them talking amongst themselves via the blog and/or landing page about what you are going to offer.

You will be documenting the entire process so they can witness the excitement.

Yes, this may sound weird, but Apple, a multi-billion-dollar company, uses this strategy. I can hear you saying, "Teran, I'm not Apple." I understand; you are not a multi-billion-dollar company. However, the strategies they have mastered have created a cult following for them. You can do the same thing by using what I just shared with you.

False, inaccurate information; being boring through your launch sequence; and focusing on you and your practice are all big no-nos—if you are looking to make a lot of money from your campaign.

Many times I've gone over launches only to shake my head at what was set up by the business owner. Many times the launch is focused on the business owner and their accomplishments. Remember, people care only about what you can do for them. They want to see if you care for them; then they will listen to what you have to say and from there they will care about you.

You don't want your launch to be boring. It must have the desires that your prospects and clients are badly seeking. Focusing on their desires is where you significantly differentiate yourself from your competition. You must show enthusiasm and charisma throughout the entire process.

If you are enthusiastic about what you are going to share, your prospects and clients will be too. They will participate every which way they can. They just can't wait to see what you have to say next as well as the offer you present on the day you release your new service and product.

Lastly, you want to make sure all the information you provide is true. Please do not mislead them or execute a bait-and-switch tactic with your prospects or clients. You will instantly lose credibility and trust and word will spread that you are not the doctor people should take their business.

Credibility building for your launch is a crucial element to carrying out a successful launch. One way to instantly build credibility with your launch and provide proof and trust for your services is to have your prospects and clients participate through the entire process of your launch.

This means having your prospects and clients leave comments on your blog, and then you responding to them by asking questions and creating an atmosphere of trust and credibility. My mentor once said to me, "Teran, no one wants to be pitched a sale. They want a connection."

The entire process you are launching is to build a connection with your prospects and clients. Building a connection with them will make you not only their trusted doctor, but a friend. Once you are seen as a friend, it becomes a lot easier to sell your products and/or services. They don't see their friends as salesmen; they see their friends as people who care for them and who are looking out for their best interests.

In all your marketing material, always look to build a connection. In Chapter 4 we discussed the desires of your prospects and clients and how to use words to do just that. Success breeds success. Use what works and make your practice extremely successful.

Planning your launch for success is important. There are three fundamental ingredients: (1) the goal you would like to achieve with your launch; (2) the sequence for releasing material during the launch; and (3) the planning of the launch itself.

Planning the launch is going to take time. Something you are going to look at is what type of product or service you are going to launch. Is the product or service you are presenting going after your prospects' and/or clients' desires? This is important because if you can't link your service or product to your prospects' and clients' desires, it will not be successful and it will mean you will have to go back to the drawing board.

The other things you need to look at are the type of material you will be using throughout the launch process. When will you use your blog, e-mails, video, and snail mail? When will you drip-feed valuable information throughout the sequence of the launch? What do you want to say in each and every piece of marketing material?

You will need to look at the following:

1. **E-mails** – What type of e-mail are you going to write that will get them to engage with what you have to say and present? Create powerful subject headlines so that they will open the e-mail and read what you have to say.
2. **Videos** – What type of videos will you be using? Create scripts that will get the prospect excited.
3. **Blog** – How are you going to use your blog and how are you going to create specific landing pages for the launch itself?
4. Direct mail – What direct-mail pieces will you send? What will you say and what do you want your clients and prospects to do after reading your material?
5. **Sales letter** – You need to create a sales letter selling your product or service and describing the offer.

These five steps must be planned out before you take the next step to build the sequence for releasing the material for the big day, launching what they will buy and what you are presenting to them.

Control is big part of the game when you decide to launch your product or service. Let's look at the steps— the structure of your launch—in a bit more detail:

- Build your list of new prospects and clients for the launch.
- Build a relationship with that list; have a connection with all prospects.
- Discover what your list wants, (their desires–Chapter 4) and have a conversation with them through all your marketing material.
- Create the solution your list desires and position yourself and your product and service as the solution.
- Identify potential objections and answer them throughout the pre-launch phase (building the list).
- Use testimonials from past and current clients for social proof and credibility.
- Make your launch a big even on the day of your choosing.
- Take what you learn from the first launch and apply it to your next launch.

The sequence is as follows:

1. Create the buzz. You want your prospects and clients talking about the launch amongst themselves, friends, family, and colleagues. This builds word-of-mouth across your ideal prospects and clients.
2. The landing page where the launch will take place should have a timer counting down to the day of the big event of the launch. The prospects and clients can feel the excitement.

3. Announce the launch. This is when you are going to send out messages via video, e-mail, mail, and telephone within days and hours of the big day.

   Send your message using all the different mediums directing them to the sales letter on your website with the countdown clock. Here you will be using email, videos, your blog, mail and the telephone, because everyone responds differently to a message.
4. This is where showmanship comes into play. You want to give the perception that things are hectic; there is so much excitement going on in the office. The telephone is ringing off the hook, and people are calling, trying to get through. This is where clients are calling and booking appointments and paying for the services and/or products.
5. Give an ultimate deadline when the event will be over and no more clients will be accepted. This technique creates scarcity and influences your prospect to make a decision.
6. During the last twenty-four hours of the launch, send out different messages about the excitement of the day and remind them that they have a few more hours remaining to take advantage of your offer. Let them know that the office manager is staying in late to take the calls and book the appointment.

Tracking and measuring the success of your product launch is all based on the conversions (i.e., how many successful case treatments you generated during the day of the launch). There are a few things you want to measure and track so that you can make the necessary changes for the next launch. Any successful business will track their sales and see where they can make improvements to generate more cash for their business.

You want to see how many visitors came to the landing page the day of the sale. How many came to the page and bought versus those who just came to the page and left? You want to know this percentage.

The next thing you want to track is how many prospects and clients clicked on the link through the e-mail that brought them to the page to purchase the product and how many people called in and booked the appointment for treatment.

From there you want to know the percentage of those who called versus those who came in and gave you money. You want to keep a file and track all transaction movements through the day of the launch. The more you know about the sequence of the transaction, the better the results you will get on your next launch.

Every two months or even every six weeks, you can launch a new product or service or you can relaunch with what you just learned in this chapter. The sequence and outline for how to conduct your launch will put you and your practice on the map. However, that is not only thing that you are after.

The goal of your product and service launch is to make money. Holding these launches when you are providing something of value to your clients and prospects can generate an extra \$125,000 every two months or an extra \$750,000 for the year when you implement these techniques. You choose the month, the day, and the time and watch everything fall into place when you plan your launch properly.

Remember to document and track every single launch you create. Please use all different platforms to contact your prospects and clients. You want this variety to avoid annoying your prospects and clients. You can only annoy them if what you are offering is boring and is not what they desire.

CHAPTER 18

Conclusion

GAINING SUCCESS IN YOUR PRACTICE starts by building a connection with your clients and ideal prospects. Here's the thing: No one wants to be sold. Everyone wants a connection. The more you let your prospects and ideal clients in, the easier it will be to sell your services and the more money you will add to your bank account. It is that simple.

Connecting with your clients starts with your marketing material, and extends to your staff answering the phones, to the client coming into your office, and to your consultation with the client. Your prospects and clients want to do business with you, but before they part with their money, they want to make sure you keep your promise. They start off by looking at each step of the contact: If you or your staff slips up, that will be a red flag in their mind and a possible reason not to do business with you.

My mentor once said to me, "There are masses of people just waiting to do business with you once they are inspired." Please remember this every time you speak with a new and existing client.

The information presented in this book will make you wealthy, successful Orthodontists; there is no doubt about it. It is up to you to apply the techniques and strategies you have learned to your advantage. If you don't, your competitors who have bought this book will take this and use it to put you out of business.

You purchased this book to do one thing and that is to put more money into your pocket and practice. You will be yourself doing a disservice if you decide to put this book back on the shelf and ignore what I shared with you.

Each day, more Dentists are taking your clients or stop referring clients. The referral game from Dentists is drying up fast, and the dream of becoming wealthy and having a successful practice will continue to collapse every hour until you finally decide to do something about it.

There is a Jamaican proverb my dad used to tell my brothers and I when we were kids and it went like this: Those who have raw meat seek fire. The raw meat is your practice and the fire is this book in your hands right now. It is time to cook and eat what is yours.

I wish you all the success and happiness in the world. Remember, connect first with your ideal prospects and build a rapport with them. You'll make as much money as you want if you do.

A SPECIAL OPPORTUNITY JUST FOR YOU ON THE NEXT PAGE…

GET TERAN TO WORK WITH YOU!

I HAVE A THREE-WORD PHILOSOPHY I LIVE BY WHEN WORKING WITH CLIENTS:

1 **SUPERSTAR** – The Orthodontist who wants to be a superstar amongst their peers and clients should understand that an investment of time, money, and a bit of sacrifice is required to reach their full potential when it comes to their number of patients, their overall wealth, and their success in their profession.

2. **TRUST** – In order to reach your full potential, one key ingredient you must have is trust. You'll have noticed while reading this book, one common theme I say you must have with your team is trust. If that one ingredient is missing, it could mean the downfall of your practice.

3. **RENAISSANCE** – My intention for every client I work with is for them to have a rebirth of their business. Our goal together is to rejuvenate and awaken a successful practice that allows you to have the time, wealth, and resources to work as little or as much as you want on your practice.

If this resonates with you, I welcome you to contact me and begin the voyage to monumental success.

WHEN YOU'RE READY TO GET STARTED, VISIT THIS PAGE:

www.WealthyOrthodontist.com/Ortho_Consulting

Or if it is easier, contact us at (905) 997-7021

When you arrive, fill out the partner intake form to set up an appointment with me directly.

You should know there is an investment of $800 which allows you a half hour of consulting time with me. This will include a complete and detailed look at your practice. By the end of the call, you will know exactly what to do to reach your full potential.

The longer you wait, the more money you're leaving on the table. Contact me and make a sound investment in your practice.

Contact me today and let's get STARTED.

THE MOST INCREDIBLE FREE GIFT EVER ($543.91 WORTH OF PURE MONEY-MAKING INFORMATION)

Teran Dale is offering an incredible opportunity for you to see WHY The Wealthy Orthodontist Gold Insider Newsletter is Known as The Best Info where Orthodontists seeking FAST and Dramatic Growth and Greater Control, Independence and Security read and treasure. Teran wants to give you $543.91 worth of pure Money-Making Information, which includes TWO months of the Wealthy Orthodontist Gold Insider letter. You'll receive a steady stream of Wealth Maker information for your practice.

To Claim Your Free Gift Visit:

www.WealthyOrthodontist.com/Gold_Insider

CPSIA information can be obtained at www.ICGtesting.com
Printed in the USA
LVOW10*1926190515

439068LV00010B/631/P

9 780992 143701